MAKING IN AMERICA

MAKING IN AMERICA

From Innovation to Market

Suzanne Berger

with the MIT Task Force on Production in the Innovation

Economy

The MIT Press

Cambridge, Massachusetts

London, England

MIT Press books may be purchased at special quantity discounts for business or sales promotional use. For information, please email special_sales@mitpress.mit.edu.

This book was set in Garamond and Gotham by the MIT Press. Printed and bound in the United States of America.

Library of Congress Cataloging-in-Publication Data

Berger, Suzanne.

Making in America : from innovation to market / Suzanne Berger with MIT Task Force on Production in the Innovation Economy.

pages cm

Includes bibliographical references and index.

ISBN 978-0-262-01991-0 (hardcover : alk. paper) 1. Manufacturing industries—Technological innovations—United States. 2. Technological innovations—United States. 3. Research, Industrial—United States. 4. New products—United States. I. Title.

HD9725.B47 2013

338'.0640973—dc23

2013017742

10 9 8 7 6 5 4 3 2

Contents

Production in the Innovation Economy Commission

CO-CHAIRS

Suzanne Berger
Raphael Dorman-Helen Starbuck Professor of Political Science

Phillip A. Sharp
Institute Professor and Professor of Biology

EXECUTIVE DIRECTOR

Olivier L. de Weck
Professor of Engineering Systems and Aeronautics and Astronautics

Daron Acemoglu
Elizabeth and James Killian Professor of Economics

David H. Autor
Professor and Associate Head, Department of Economics

Mary C. Boyce
Ford Professor of Engineering and Head, Department of Mechanical Engineering

Claude R. Canizares
Vice President and the Bruno Rossi Professor of Physics

Charles L. Cooney
Robert T. Haslam (1911) Professor of Chemical Engineering and Founding
Director, Deshpande Center for Technological Innovation

David E. Hardt
Ralph E. and Eloise F. Cross Professor of Mechanical Engineering

Richard K. Lester
Japan Steel Industry Professor and Head, Department of Nuclear Science &
Engineering

Richard M. Locke
Class of 1922 Professor of Political Science and Management, and Head, Political
Science Department; Deputy Dean, Sloan School of Management

Fiona Murray
David Sarnoff Professor of Management & Technology, Skolkovo Foundation
Associate Professor of Entrepreneurship, and Faculty Director, Trust Center for
MIT Entrepreneurship, Sloan School of Management

Preface

Martin A. Schmidt and Phillip A. Sharp

"To live well, a nation must produce well." So began the introduction to the 1989 *Made in America* book, which was written by the MIT Commission on Industrial Productivity. At the time, the United States was facing a crisis of productivity and quality in domestic manufacturing, leading to a loss of competitiveness to foreign firms. The MIT Commission conducted hundreds of interviews on three continents, studied in detail eight major industries, and distilled this down to a handful of key recurring weaknesses leading to the nation's loss of competitiveness. Fast forward to today, and we find the nation in yet another crisis of manufacturing. However, the nature of this crisis is different, and consequently the causes and paths forward are different. Specifically, while today U.S.-based firms do not suffer from a productivity or quality gap relative to global competition, the nation has experienced a precipitous decline in the size of the manufacturing sector and the numbers of jobs in manufacturing. In many cases, perhaps best exemplified by Apple, the model of "invent it here, make it there" is becoming more common. The central question is whether a "nation can live well" under this model. While a subject of debate, most argue that a robust manufacturing base is critical for three reasons: because it produces good jobs, because it is vital to our national security, and because it is vital to our innovation economy.

In 2010, then–MIT president Susan Hockfield charged a group of MIT faculty and colleagues to focus on innovation and its relation to production. The group was asked to determine whether a robust domestic manufacturing sector is critical to the U.S. innovation economy. Thus was born the MIT Production in the Innovation Economy (PIE) Commission. In the same data-driven, quantitative, and deep investigation style of the MIT work in the '80s, the PIE Commission launched a two-year study. Over 250 individual firms were interviewed across the country and around the world. Surveys of over 1,000 firms were conducted, along with detailed studies of companies in China and Germany to analyze the striking differences between the United States and these countries in the status and capabilities of manufacturing. Rather than focus on specific industry sectors, the PIE group studied this problem through many geographies and perspectives, including "Main Street" firms (established small, medium, and large companies), start-ups in a high-tech cluster, the manufacturing workforce, and advanced manufacturing technology trends, as well as public and private organizations that contribute to the manufacturing "ecosystem."

By carefully examining the results of these detailed studies, what unfolds is a clear picture of the changes that have occurred (particularly in large U.S.-based firms) over the past several decades that have contributed to the decline in domestic manufacturing. What equally well emerges is a clear picture of why and how local manufacturing *is*, in fact, critical to the long-term success of U.S.-based firms in converting innovative ideas to products. In other words, PIE strongly concludes that in order for the United States to continue to derive benefit from a robust innovation economy, we must maintain an equally robust domestic manufacturing base. The U.S. production ecosystem has been "hollowed out" over the past decade, and we must rebuild it in order to feed our engine of innovation. PIE also emphasizes that U.S. manufacturing is part of a world economy and must interact and be competitive on a global scale. In fact, we can learn from other countries how to organize support for manufacturing and use market demand in other countries to test and develop new products. Thus, while the focus of the PIE work has been largely targeted on the U.S. production system, the conclusions about the importance of a local production ecosystem are ones important for any nation or region that seeks economic growth through innovation.

Finally, PIE provides specific recommendations and observations of best practices that can help this nation "produce well."

Acknowledgments

Making in America started from an idea about what researchers from across MIT could contribute to national and international debates on the role of production in bringing innovation to life in the economy. Like the innovations it studies, this project could never have made it into the world without acts of faith by its initial supporters: three MIT alumni, Mark Gorenberg, Diane Greene, and Ray Stata; four foundations, Alfred P. Sloan Foundation, Carnegie Corporation of New York, Russell Sage Foundation, and the Ewing Marion Kauffman Foundation; and a generous open gift from the Lockheed Martin Corporation. The hundreds of people we interviewed in the course of the research from CEOs of large multinationals to plant managers in machine shops were unfailingly generous with time and insights, however skeptical they may have been about academic research. We will always remember emails flooding in from the Main Street manufacturers whom we had asked for interviews, agreeing, and offering appointments, plant tours, and sandwiches. We have received permission to cite some by name and have respected the wish of others to remain anonymous. We owe them all a great debt.

At MIT, the complexities of managing a project distributed across 14 departments were made into a seamless effort with the help of Maria DiMauro, Paula Kreutzer, and Kathleen Searle, in the Department of Political Science, and Ronald Hasseltine, Assistant Provost for Research Administration. Finally, the book owes far more than can ever be acknowledged to the intense discussions of the "Backbone Group," an informal weekly seminar of faculty and students that met over the course of the entire project to define key questions, research methodologies, interview populations, and to interpret the results. In the core of the

Backbone Group were six graduate students: Jesse Jenkins, Joyce Lawrence, Jonas Nahm, Hiram Samel, Andrew Weaver, and Rachel Wellhausen. They contributed not only to the specific parts of the research agenda on which their names appear in *Production in the Innovation Economy*, the companion volume to this; but they also were responsible for advancing ideas that have structured the overall argument and themes. No outcome of the PIE project is likely to have more impact in the future than the teaching and research careers of these young colleagues.

Neither the donors nor the interviewees bear any responsibility for the findings reported by the MIT Production in the Innovation Economy project or for its recommendations.

1

Introduction: How to Move Innovation into the Economy

Over the past decade, as millions of jobs disappeared in a flood of Asian imports and a severe financial and economic crisis, pessimism about the future of production in the United States swept across the country. People started to question whether U.S. manufacturing could ever compete with Asian low-wage production. The trade deficit in advanced technology products deepened—equal to 17 percent of the total U.S. trade deficit by 2011—and it seemed that even high-tech sectors of industry were doing better overseas than here. As in past times of trouble, some blamed foreign governments for damaging U.S. manufacturing by subsidizing their own companies and protecting their national currencies. But even the critics of foreign governments knew there was something wrong at home.

Everyone agreed that the United States needed a higher rate of good job creation, but no one seemed to know where jobs could come from. Could manufacturing jobs come back? The brightest corporate superstars, like Apple, were locating production abroad and still reaping the lion's share of profits within the United States. Was this going to be the American model for the future? In emerging technology sectors, like batteries and solar and wind power, even when the start-ups were created in the United States out of U.S. innovations, commercialization of the technology was taking place abroad. What could Americans do to leverage their strengths in new science and technology to rebuild a dynamic economy? Would production capabilities at home be needed to capture the flow of benefits from invention and entrepreneurship? Which capabilities? And how could they be created and sustained?

The anxieties of the public connect with many of our own deep concerns at MIT about where the American economy is heading. MIT's dual mission is educating students and creating new knowledge. What motivates the people who do this is the desire to contribute to our understanding of the great mysteries of nature and to solving the great problems of the world: disease, conflict and violence, poverty, energy, climate warming. Even for those investigating the puzzles of the natural world, the question of how their knowledge might be used is never far away. At a time of economic crisis, when it is hard to figure out who will benefit from our research, and how, or what our students will have as opportunities in career and life, the alarm bells sound loud in our halls. In one such moment, at the end of the 1980s, MIT president Paul Gray asked faculty members from across the specialized disciplines of the Institute to work together to analyze the causes of slow productivity growth and industrial stagnation in the United States and to propose new approaches for private industry, government, and universities. The book the group wrote was *Made in America*, and it became a landmark in public debates about the U.S. economy.[1]

With that legacy in mind, in 2010 MIT president Susan Hockfield launched the MIT Production in the Innovation Economy (PIE) research group. Twenty faculty members and a dozen students joined. The objective was to analyze how innovation flows from ideas through production into the economy. The point of departure was recognizing that innovation is critical for economic growth and for a vibrant and productive society. Our question was: What kinds of production do we need—and where do they need to be located—to sustain an innovative economy? We tend to use the terms *manufacturing* and *production* interchangeably. It's true, as Professor Richard Freeman, a Harvard economist, has put it, that a person knows it's manufactured when he drops it on his foot. But in most of the firms in which we carried out our research the traditional line between "manufacturing" and "services" has become so blurred that it no longer serves to distinguish separable and distinct activities or end products. Whether in a giant like Apple or in a small Ohio company that makes half-sleeves to repair pipelines and sends its technicians along with the product to stand on the oil company's platforms and shout down instructions to the divers, the activities that create most value—the ones that are most difficult for others to replicate—are bundles consisting of services and objects you could drop on your foot. We focused on those bundles, and we structured our inquiry to locate opportunities and dangers for American prosperity in the changes that have taken place over the past thirty years in the linkages between an innovation and the broad range of production processes that bring it to market.

There are many serious reasons to worry about the fate of manufacturing in the United States. And after years of relative neglect as a subject for academic inquiry, there has been an outpouring over the past four years of commentary and research on these issues. Virtually every week brings a new report diagnosing the state of manufacturing and emphasizing different aspects of its critical significance for the economy.[2] One of the key danger points identified in these reports is the declining weight of the United States in the global economy. Even though the U.S. share of world manufactured output has held fairly steady over the past decade, economists have pointed out that this reflects good results in only a few industrial sectors. And even in those sectors, what appear to be productivity gains may be the result of underestimating the value of imported components. A close look at the composition of a worsening trade deficit shows that even in high-tech sectors in the United States, the picture is deteriorating. While the output of U.S. high-tech manufacturing is still the largest in the world and accounted for $390 billion of global value added in high-tech manufacturing in 2010, U.S. share of this world market has been declining, from 34 percent in 1998 to 28 percent in 2010, as other countries made big strides into this market segment.[3] Jobs are another huge concern. The great spike in unemployment over the past five years was disproportionately due to loss of manufacturing jobs. And as the economy revived, such jobs were very slow to return. In fact, it is clear that many of them never will. Over the long postwar years of prosperity, manufacturing jobs had been especially valuable for workers and for middle-class opportunity because they paid higher wages and had better benefits than other jobs available to people with educational qualifications of a high-school education or less. New manufacturing jobs now often come with lower wages and fewer benefits attached. National security is also linked to the health of manufacturing through the procurement of new weapons and the maintenance and replacement parts for the many generations of equipment still in service. The wave of disappearance of many small and medium-sized suppliers creates worrisome and still relatively unknown degrees of dependence on foreign suppliers for U.S. military contractors.

Across the entire industrial landscape there are now gaping holes and missing pieces. It's not just that factories stand empty and crumbling; it's that critical strengths and capabilities that once served to bring new enterprises to life have disappeared. Economic progress may be preceded by waves of creative destruction, as Joseph Schumpeter claimed. But we need to know whether the resources that remain are fertile enough to seed and sustain new growth. We have found in our research that regionally based resources like training, collaborations between firms and universities, a multiplicity of suppliers, industrial consortia, and technical research centers are essential complements to the in-house capabilities of firms of all ages, sizes, and sectors. The density, diversity, and abundance of such resources distinguish a fertile industrial ecosystem from a depleted and arid regional system. Today across much of the United States, small and medium-sized companies have to operate with only the resources they can generate internally. Outside of such places as Silicon Valley, Austin, Texas, and Cambridge, Massachusetts, the industrial ecosystem cannot support the rate of innovation to market that we need for a dynamic U.S. economy.

What's at stake is not just dealing with the costs of economic change. It's a question of which capabilities, technologies, and business models will make for economic success in the future across a wide range of emerging industries. There have been some great new companies like Apple, Qualcomm, and Cisco that have virtually all of their production abroad but that still reap the majority of their profits in the United States. That kind of success has raised questions about whether we even need manufacturing domestically in order to capture the benefits of American innovation and entrepreneurship. Over the past thirty years, digital technologies and governments have opened the borders to the flow of ideas, goods, services, capital, and production. For many goods and services, it is now possible to use international manufacturing partners for bringing innovation into production and into the market. For U.S. innovators and entrepreneurs there are unprecedented new opportunities to draw on production capabilities that they do not have to create themselves. These opportunities also mean that for the first time in the history of the industrial world, innovators in developing economies can connect with partners and suppliers at home and abroad and leap to occupy niches close to the technological frontier.

But for American companies and for the country, there are also long-term risks in these relationships, and they go far beyond the loss of any particular proprietary knowledge or trade secret. The danger is that as U.S. companies shift the commercialization of their technologies abroad, their capacity for initiating future rounds of innovation will be progressively enfeebled. That's because much learning takes place as companies move their ideas beyond prototypes and demonstration and through the stages of commercialization. Learning takes place as engineers and technicians on the factory floor come back with their problems to the design engineers and struggle together with them to find better resolutions; learning takes place as tacit knowledge is converted into standardized and codified processes; as end-users come back with complaints that need to be fixed. PIE researchers observed this learning in high-tech companies like Biogen Idec as they figured out how to scale a drug for multiple sclerosis from a test tube to 15,000-liter tanks. But we also saw such learning as firms mastered the challenges of large-scale production, even of humble products like razor blades and diapers and road signs and stick-on notes. In making them, companies like Procter & Gamble and 3M find ways of innovating that allow them to reap higher profits. When production moves out, the terrain for future learning—and for profits and jobs—shrinks.

Looking even further down the food chain beneath the companies to the laboratories that generate innovations in the first place, looking at the university laboratories that are the terrain we know best, we saw reasons to fear that the loss of companies that can make things will end up in the loss of research that can invent them. None of the PIE experiences in the field were more powerful in concretizing that fear than the visit to one of our own colleagues' laboratories. When we went to the basement laboratory in MIT Building 35 of Professor Tonio Buonassisi, a leading researcher on solar cells, he walked us around pointing out all the leading-edge equipment that came from tool makers located within a few hours of Cambridge, Massachusetts. Most of the machines had been made in close collaboration between the lab and the instrument companies as they handed ideas and components and prototypes back and forth. Used for the first time in the lab, these tools were now being marketed to commercial solar companies. Buonassisi was worried. The news on the U.S. solar industry was looking worse and worse as the economy stalled, as stimulus spending on renewable energy ended, and as Chinese competitors hung in, despite losses and low margins. It looked bad for the local companies with which Buonassisi worked. And as Buonassisi thought about it, he saw that the collapse of his equipment suppliers would mean real trouble for his research, for he relied on working with them to make new tools for faster, more efficient, and cheaper cells. Even in a fragmented global economy with instant connection over the Internet to anywhere in the world, the ties that connect research in its earliest stages to production in its final phases remain vital.

On these and many other issues associated with manufacturing, we now have the benefit of major new research. The PIE team has learned much from this recent work, and we owe a special debt to a few contributions in particular that have had great impact on our own understanding: the research of Susan Helper, Susan Houseman, and Erica Fuchs; the reports of the Information Technology and Innovation Foundation (ITIF) and in particular, *"Worse Than the Great Depression: What Experts Are Missing About American Manufacturing Decline"*; Gary P. Pisano and Willy C. Shih's *Producing Prosperity* (2012); the McKinsey Global Institute *Manufacturing the Future: The Next Era of Global Growth and Innovation* (2012); the American Manufacturing Partnership Steering Committee Report on *Capturing Domestic Competitive Advantage in Advanced Manufacturing,* and most recently, the research of the National Academy of Science on innovation policies.[4] Many concerns about manufacturing have been identified and analyzed in this outpouring of work over the past four years. The policy recommendations that have grown out of this body of research are critical contributions to a new agenda for public action.

The MIT Production in the Innovation Economy study: Objectives and methods

The PIE project approach is different in two basic ways from these contributions. First, we focused on only one big question: what are the production capabilities here and abroad that are important to sustaining innovation and realizing its benefits within our own society? Though some members of the PIE team believe that maintaining manufacturing in the United States is valuable in and of itself, for the jobs it creates, and for national security, the PIE researchers as a group are ecumenical on this point. Our starting point of agreement, rather, is that innovation is critical for a vibrant and productive society. We have organized our research to discover what it takes to sustain innovation over time and what it takes to bring innovation into the economy. We have attacked these issues from multiple angles, looking at innovation in products, in processes, in combinations of products and services; at innovation in start-ups, in large multinationals, in Main Street small and medium-sized manufacturers, in European and Asian partners and competitors, in hot-spots for new technologies, like the biotech cluster of Cambridge, Massachusetts, in traditional manufacturing country, like Ohio, and in new manufacturing areas in the Southwest, in Arizona, and abroad, in China and in Germany.

Second, we tried to nail down the innovation to market links from the bottom up, that is, by tracing all the steps that a firm takes to procure the inputs of capital, labor, facilities, and expertise that are required to commercialize a new product and service. We tried in each of our research sites within the United States and abroad to trace the concrete linkages between innovation and manufacturing. Because the main focus was on identifying the pathways through which an invention or a new idea about a product or a way of improving a product or process becomes goods and services for sale in the market, we carried out much of our research in firm-level interviews. National Science Foundation statistics state that in 2006–2008, 22 percent of all U.S. manufacturing firms reported "a new or significantly improved product, service or process" but as we started our research, we really did not know what they were doing or how they were doing it.[5] We had data, too, on the high-risk venture and corporate funding of start-ups, but there was no systematic account of how these firms were finding (or not finding) the full range of inputs they would need on the road to commercializing their innovations. With the interviews and analyses we have now carried out, there is a clearer picture of what takes place within the black box of American manufacturing innovation and commercialization.

In interviews with senior managers we studied in concrete detail the trajectories along which each company moved as it attempted to make its ideas into profits. Where did the company get the skills, the capital, the suppliers, the test and demonstration facilities, the additional expertise, and reactions from early customers that it needed to move innovation into production? Did it find these inputs at home or abroad? Where did it decide to locate each of its operations, and why? Which parts of its production activities does it believe it needs to keep in close proximity to its R&D in order to bring a product to market and to maximize the gains from its own innovation? In the case of innovations growing out of existing process or product technologies, our interviews in companies allowed us to track interactions between the innovators and the manufacturers in great detail from the point at which the new idea came into play through production and into the hands of customers.

Even in the case of big, disruptive innovation, there is much we can learn from ongoing relationships in which the seeds of transformation are germinating. We often imagine radically disruptive technologies as if they were comets streaking out of nowhere across the sky of established companies and depositing whole new industries in place as old ones disappear. Some new industries, like Facebook, do seem to come out of nowhere. But even for most revolutionary technologies, whether in electronics or materials or information or medicine, the projects are long in the making. It took DuPont ten years to develop Wallace Carothers's lab discoveries in polymers in 1930 into full-scale nylon production—first for nylon stockings in 1940. DuPont's Kevlar took even longer to develop as a commercial product. Today, as we observe discoveries—in biotech, for example—moving along equally lengthy trajectories toward drugs on the market, we have the chance to learn whether in-house manufacturing or manufacturing at a nearby contractor or manufacturing anywhere in the world does better or worse in accelerating the passage from lab to customer. Does the ownership of manufacturing alter the distribution of benefits? Who learns what in the process and is in the best position to apply it to bringing the next discovery to life in the world?

In all PIE interviews (see table 1.1) teams of MIT researchers raised basically the same questions, with wording adapted to the context and circumstances of each company. The interview template prompted each researcher to ask: Tell us about two or three new ideas—new products, new processes, improvements on old products or processes—that you tried to bring to market over the past five years. What did you do to try to move it from the stage of being an idea (in a lab, in an R&D center, on the shop floor, in your head) into a product that was sold in the market? Where did you find the capital for the various stages of scale-up? Did you self-finance? Or get venture capital? Or bank loans? Or corporate partners? Where did you find engineers and workers with the right skills? Where did you find technical know-how? Where did you find suppliers? How did you decide what to do in-house and what to outsource? How did you decide where to locate production? What failed and why? What policies make a difference for a company like yours?

TABLE 1.1
PIE interviews

China	36
France	2
Germany	32
Israel	1
Japan	8
Sweden	2
Switzerland	3
United Kingdom	2
United States	178

Arizona (11)	Michigan (1)
California (16)	New Jersey (3)
Connecticut (2)	New York (12)
DC (2)	North Carolina (14)
Delaware (1)	Ohio (37)
Georgia (12)	Oregon (1)
Illinois (2)	Pennsylvania (9)
Iowa (1)	South Carolina (2)
Kentucky (1)	Washington (1)
Maryland (2)	Wisconsin (1)
Massachusetts (47)	

Total	264

An overview of the research projects

Research on large U.S. corporations (chapter 2)

The first group in our interview population was American-based multinationals that figure among the largest global investors in R&D.[6] We selected 30 with significant manufacturing operations. Ten of these rank in the top 100 of the Fortune 500 companies. Over the past thirty years these companies have changed from almost entirely U.S.-based operations to organizations carrying out R&D and production around the world. From their senior managers we sought to understand strategies for locating innovation, prototyping, pilot production, test and demonstration, early-stage manufacturing, and full-scale commercialization in the United States and abroad. In each company, we zeroed in on a few new product lines, and we probed the advantages and disadvantages of U.S. locations for carrying out each of these phases of moving innovation to market.

Research on start-ups to full-scale commercialization (chapter 3)

A second research focus was the population of new companies that grew out of patents that had been created in MIT laboratories and licensed by the MIT Technology Licensing Office over the years 1997–2008. There were 189 of them. The researchers zeroed in on the 150 companies that were engaged in some form of production.[7] These are start-ups that are especially well positioned to succeed, because they emerge from very strong research labs, they take their first steps in the world in an extremely dynamic regional hub of innovation with many complementary resources in close proximity, and they have far better access to early-stage high-risk capital than do firms in much of the rest of the country. At those points in the scale-up process where these firms, even with all their relative advantages, find serious difficulties in obtaining the inputs they need for getting their products into the hands of customers, other new American firms based on innovative technologies will likely also be having trouble, so there are important lessons to be learned from their experience. Of course, there are many reasons firms might fail to find resources to scale-up, relating to the market, or the competitive landscape, or the product, or management. But with the MIT sample we sought to stack the deck in favor of finding winners—and then through analysis of their progress at each stage of development, we tried to locate and analyze their challenges in reaching scale.

Research on "Main Street manufacturers" (chapter 4)

The third target population within the PIE company sample was small and medium-sized U.S. manufacturers. To figure out how to raise the water level of all kinds of innovations—product, process, service, incremental, radical, repurposing, business model—flowing into the economy, we knew we needed to look beyond Silicon Valley and Cambridge, Massachusetts. PIE researchers obtained a list of all U.S. manufacturing firms that had doubled their revenues and increased their headcount between 2004 and 2008.[8] Of these we retained the 3,596 manufacturing companies in the United States that had more than $5 million in annual revenues and more than 20 employees. These companies seem to be, at a minimum, *viable* companies, ones therefore able to carry forward new products into the market. In Arizona, Georgia, Massachusetts, and Ohio we carried out interviews with 53 of these firms. To this group we added 43 similar firms that we discovered through other branches of our work. In each of these companies, PIE researchers asked the same questions about new products and processes and the inputs to bring them to market.

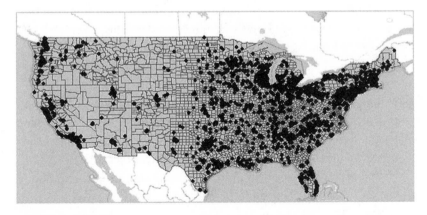

FIGURE 1.1
Company locations of the 3,596 high-impact companies with more than $5 million in annual revenues and more than 20 employees

Innovation is not all about patents. Only rarely do the novel activities of established small and medium-sized manufacturers correspond to the OECD's Frascati Manual and "Oslo" definitions of "research and development" as "creative work undertaken on a systematic basis in order to increase the stock of knowledge, including knowledge of man, culture and society, and the use of this stock of knowledge to devise new applications."[9] But a hidden wealth of innovation in process, business organization, and manufacturing exists across America in firms of all sizes. In the Main Street manufacturers' sample, there are some with leading-edge innovations (and patents). But for many, the contribution to innovation is as enablers of new ideas and new industries. As suppliers they develop and customize components and services to enable scale-up in other companies. One such company, Mass Tank in Middleboro, Massachusetts, exemplifies the pattern. A fifty-employee firm, it does its main business in fabricating tanks and selling tank inspection services for chemical, food, pharmaceutical, and water industries. But it is also working with five start-ups in the region and going back and forth with their engineers developing new materials and components that may someday be part of a blockbuster new product that Mass Tank will have helped these innovators to bring to market. Carl Horstmann, the banker-turned-manufacturing-CEO of Mass Tank, told PIE researchers that when he looked at the foundations of offshore wind towers, he suddenly saw that the tanks he makes—with the ends cut off—could be foundations. The status of the Cape Wind project off the coast of Cape Cod, Massachusetts, in which he hopes to participate is still on hold. But Mass Tank has taken one step into the wind business with a new contract to produce a wind tower for a smaller wind project in Plymouth, Massachusetts.[10] Mass Tank will be making a 225-foot tower for a wind turbine to be built by one of the biggest Chinese wind companies, Xinjiang Goldwind. Xinjiang Goldwind's advanced gearless technology derives from Vensys, a German company they bought up. Vensys technology originated in a start-up from the University of Applied Sciences of Saarland, Germany.

In other Main Street manufacturers, innovation means repurposing technologies developed in one sector for altogether different uses. A third-generation CEO of a Midwest company that makes steel components, for example, told us of developing special lighter steel he had used in construction and experimenting with bringing it into new work he was doing in defense contracting. If his ideas work out, it would help reduce the weight of aircraft carriers and lower their energy consumption. But in this company as in most of the others in this category that we interviewed in the United States, all growth depends on their internal resources. They do not find any complementary capabilities they can draw on in the industrial ecosystem as they try to develop new components: little outside funding, few connections with community colleges, weak trade associations, no research consortia (all regular fixtures, we would discover, on the landscape of German companies in the same industrial sector.) As one steel fabricator with 200 employees said in explaining why he cannot get community colleges to teach skills his workers need: "I guess we're just too small a company to have them respond." When we thought about why the contributions to innovation of the Main Street manufacturers did not lead to greater profits and faster growth, the comparison with Germany was inevitable. An Ohio machine shop is not going to take off like Microsoft or Facebook, but there is real underexploited potential for expansion, job creation, and new profitability.

Lessons from abroad: Germany and China, scale-up economies (chapter 5)

The fourth group of firms in the PIE sample were foreign: mainly German and Chinese companies. In both Germany and China we found innovative manufacturing and scale-up that challenged many of our ideas about why innovative companies in the United States so often falter before attaining the size and capacity to reach large numbers of customers. Innovation in Germany builds on legacies: in industrial specializations, longstanding relationships with customers, workforce skills, and proximity to suppliers with diverse capabilities.[11] The potential of German patterns extends well beyond defending niches against low-cost competition with incremental advances. They create new businesses, not usually through start-ups—the U.S. model—but through the transformation of old capabilities and their reapplication, repurposing, and commercialization. The companies we interviewed had moved from autos to solar modules, from semiconductors to solar cells, from machine tools to make spark plugs to machines to make medical devices like artificial knees. The Main Street manufacturers we interviewed in the United States usually had only their own material, human, and financial resources to draw on when they tried to scale up an innovation. The Germans had not only their own legacy resources, but also access to a rich and diverse set of complementary capabilities in the industrial ecosystem: suppliers, trade associations, industrial collective research consortia, industrial research centers, Fraunhofer Institutes, university-industry collaboratives, technical advisory committees. It's impossible to understand the different fates of manufacturing in the United States and Germany without comparing the density and richness of the resources available in the industrial ecosystem across much of Germany to the thin and shrinking resources available to U.S. manufacturers across much of our country.

The China interviews showed firms emerging with remarkable innovative capabilities in manufacturing. China's great initial assets were cheap factor prices—cheap land, labor, and capital, and an undervalued currency. Low-cost labor allowed Chinese companies in apparel and footwear to make huge inroads in Western markets. But today the PIE research team found Chinese firms in emerging industries like renewable energy. These are firms that excel in scale-up to mass manufacturing not because of low-cost labor, but because of their ability to move complex advanced product designs into production and commercialization. The huge China market is of course a major draw for investors of all nationalities. But even in those industries in which the main customer markets are still in the West, American and European innovators are turning to Chinese partners for capabilities in knowledge-intensive scale-up they find in China. These capabilities involve reverse engineering and re-engineering a mature product to make it more rapidly and efficiently; making designs into new-to-the-world products and processes; and indigenous product innovation.

Research on advanced manufacturing technologies (chapter 6)

Today, manufacturing is a lengthy and often inefficient process, in which the raw materials that nature provides are pushed through stages of fabrication, assembly, and warehousing and emerge as goods for sale in the market. In a future which new technologies could enable, manufacturing might become a rapid process in which human-designed and -engineered materials would be pulled by demand through continuous manufacturing and customization to meet specific and differentiated human needs. Today manufacturing remains highly centralized and concentrated in large factories, and components and finished goods are transported at great cost and with high impact on the environment through long supply chains. Trends to offshoring and outsourcing have made manufacturing plants bigger and the distances goods traverse even longer. Among future scenarios, we can imagine that one possibility is a distributed manufacturing system that would "destroy the tyranny of bulk" and make it possible to manage capacity and demand flexibly through networks of small, localized manufacturers linked by the Internet.

Research on jobs and skills (chapter 7)

In order to analyze two critical inputs to bringing innovation to market—jobs and skills and advanced manufacturing technologies—PIE researchers used surveys as well as interviews for their work. The group working on jobs and skills talked with companies, community colleges, high schools, and labor market programs across the country. They carried out the first nationally representative survey of manufacturing establishments to query employers about the skills they need in production workers. Almost a thousand firms responded. Since production workers account for over 40 percent of all those employed in manufacturing, the team focused on whether there is a shortage of skills in this population. Many people claim there is a skill shortage today in America. Economists pointing to stagnant wages and high unemployment have challenged that view. With the PIE survey and analysis, we finally have systematic evidence with which to adjudicate among these claims and make policy. The PIE analysis also drilled down into the job categories and firm types where there do seem to be problems finding candidates with the right skills, in order to identify key areas for attention.

The great transformation: The new corporate structures of the American economy and the origins of the production problem

Some fifty years ago, in January 1960, at the high water mark of American economic dominance in the world, 29 percent of U.S. workers were employed in manufacturing, wages of the manufacturing workforce had been rising for decades, and innovation and manufacturing moved together in lockstep to produce a vast new stream of products for the market. Invented in the USA meant made in the USA. As described by theorists of the "product cycle," new products were scaled up, standardized, mass produced, and brought to high levels of performance and reliability in the advanced industrial countries in which they were invented.[12] Only after the production of the good had been thoroughly mastered and standardized and after the initial premium of first mover advantages had been exhausted— when production matured and the good became a commodity—did manufacturing shift to less-developed countries with less-skilled workers.

Today we stand at a different point in history. Huge trade deficits remind us that invented in the USA no longer means made in USA. Even the first generations of iPhones and iPads were not first made in the United States and then transferred to Asia. Given the density, synergies, and capabilities that now reside in Asian supply geographies, it is most likely that the next generations of consumer electronic products designed here will still be made in Asia—even if wages continue to rise there. Research on the products and processes in emerging high-tech sectors like solar and wind energy and batteries shows that very early phases of scaling up of these new products are now taking place outside the United States. In some of these industries today, it would be very difficult to do early-stage manufacturing in the United States, because the technical expertise, the workplace skills, the equipment, and the most advanced plant lay-outs are no longer present in this country or have degraded and fallen behind state-of-the-art elsewhere.

The opening of the world economy and the rise of strong new manufacturing capabilities across the globe make it possible to find and to use production located outside our national borders. It's not only in "mature" industries like apparel that manufacturing has moved overseas. It's in newer sectors, like solar cells, wind turbines, and batteries. In the past, chip design and chip fabrication had to be carried out within the four walls of the same company; today chip designers can send files of digital specifications to semiconductor fabrication plants anywhere in the world for production. Apple can define, design, and distribute iPods, iPhones, and iPads in the United States without having any significant production facilities here at all.[13]

The possibilities for innovators and designers to draw on the manufacturing capabilities of the entire world has stimulated a huge wave of new enterprise creation in both the United States and developing economies. On the face on it, this is an enormously positive outcome. What we do not know, though, across different industries—and particularly for emerging new high-tech domains—is whether the separation of innovation from manufacturing will allow innovation to continue full-bore at its original home, or whether separation comes at the price of learning and creation of capabilities that might produce future innovation at the original home base. Separating innovation and manufacturing—in different companies, or in different locations—might make it unlikely that a firm would gain full advantage from implementing technological advances *within* manufacturing—for example, from learning how to accelerate the scale-up of a biotech drug from test tube to mass production or learning how to fabricate semiconductor chips at lower volume, higher value, and lower cost to run the medical devices that aging generations of baby boomers will need to keep them healthy and functioning at home and out of hospitals.

How did this new global economy of fragmented research, development, production, and distribution come into being? What does it mean for the future of the U.S. economy? The causes of this transformation are important to grasp, because they had their origin in changes in U.S. financial and industrial structures whose full consequences we are only now beginning to be able to weigh. What stands out in our analysis as we have tried to reconstruct what happened to manufacturing in the United States is the tectonic shift in corporate ownership and control that took place well before globalization or Asian development had come into full play.

From the 1980s the large vertically integrated corporations that had long dominated American manufacturing began to shed many of their business functions from R&D and design through detailed design to manufacturing and after-sales services.[14] These activities all once had been joined under one corporate roof. Indeed most management mantras of the time proclaimed that the tighter the integration of functions, the better the company performed. By 2013, however, very few large American companies remain with vertically integrated structures. Companies like General Electric or Procter & Gamble, with a wide range of different businesses under one corporate roof and a predominant preference for integrating research through production, are the exception. The great new American companies of the past 30 years, like Dell, Cisco, Apple, and Qualcomm, have little or no manufacturing in-house. Perhaps the single most compelling factor in the 1980s that led to shrinking the perimeter of the corporation and reorganizing it around "core competence" came from financial markets: higher stock market valuations of leaner, "asset-light" companies that had weeded out their less-profitable divisions and reduced their diversification.[15] First among the business functions that companies started moving out of their own corporate walls was manufacturing—because that produced reductions in headcount and in capital costs that stock markets immediately rewarded. Advances in digitization and modularity in the 1990s made it possible to carry out this strategy and to outsource production to manufacturing subcontractors like Flextronics and Jabil and eventually to foreign suppliers and contractors like Taiwan Semiconductor Manufacturing Company, Quanta, and Foxconn.

Today, of course, a more complete picture of the transformation of the global industrial landscape of the past thirty years would also have to include many developments that took place outside the United States. Many of them are of fairly recent origin: the radical dismantling of border-level barriers to capital and trade flows and China's entry into WTO in 2001; the development of Hong Kong and Taiwanese-led supply chains of agile, dynamic subcontractors in Asia with access to huge reservoirs of cheap semiskilled and skilled labor; new digital technologies that enabled the fragmentation of value chains; the emergence of great new Asian consumer markets requiring localization of production. All of these factors would have enormous importance for the restructuring of the world economy.

But the starting point for the analysis we have conducted of U.S. capabilities needs to be pushed back to the 1980s and to the transformation of the structures of the vertically integrated firms. Out of those changes in corporate structure have come not only great new opportunities, but also some of the most difficult hurdles we face today in trying to move U.S. innovation into the market. Here we can list only some of these challenges:

• Vertically integrated enterprises had the resources to organize and pay for educating and upgrading the skills of much of the manufacturing workforce. And long job tenure meant companies could hope to recoup their investment over the course of the employees' careers. Many of the employees who were trained in big companies or in vocational schools they supported ended up working for smaller manufacturers and suppliers.

Today, American manufacturing firms are on average smaller, and have fewer resources. They do not plan to hold on to their employees for life. They cannot afford to, or, in any event, do not, train. How do we educate the workforce we need?

• Vertically integrated enterprises like AT&T used to support long-term basic research in centers like Bell Labs and Xerox PARC and Alcoa Research Lab, each employing thousands of scientists and engineers. As corporate structures have been resized, basic research has been drastically cut, these centers have mostly disappeared, and corporate R&D is now far more tightly linked to the near-term needs of the business units. How should we fund a strong stream of basic and precompetitive research today? If much cutting-edge research no longer is taking place within companies—but rather in universities or small start-ups or in government labs—how can we propel these innovations through to commercialization? How do we diffuse new technologies into established companies?

• When innovation grew out of large firms, they had the resources to scale up to mass commercialization. In the thirties, a corporation like DuPont not only invested for a decade in the fundamental research that led to nylon, but once the lab had a promising product, DuPont had the capital and the plants to bring it into production. Today, when innovation is more likely to emerge in small spin-offs or out of university or government labs, where do the scale-up resources come from? How available is the funding needed at each of the critical stages of scale-up: prototyping, pilot production, demonstration and test, early manufacturing, full-scale commercialization? When scale-up is funded mainly through merger and acquisition of the adolescent start-ups and when the acquiring firms are foreign, how does the American economy benefit?

• Big American corporations in effect used to provide public goods through spillovers of research, training, diffusion of new technology to suppliers, and pressure on state and local governments to improve infrastructure. These spillovers constituted "complementary capabilities" that many others in the region could draw on, even if they had not contributed to creating them. As the sources of these "complementary capabilities" have dried up, large holes in the industrial ecosystem have appeared. How can these capabilities be recreated and sustained in order to maintain a terrain favorable for innovation?

As the PIE researchers looked over the interviews and surveys we carried out across the project, we saw these holes in the industrial ecosystem as the single most challenging obstacle to creating and sustaining production capabilities in the United States that enable innovation to come to market. What we have come to think of as "holes" might be less picturesquely described as "market failures" or the absence of "complementary capabilities" that companies can draw on to supplement their own resources when they seek to develop their new ideas. These holes in the industrial ecosystem are ones that have been hollowed out by the disappearance of large numbers of suppliers under pressure from global competition and by the disappearance of local capabilities once provided by large corporations as part of their own business operations. As national banks have bought up local banks, local bankers with intimate understanding of local manufacturing have become an endangered species, making it harder to get bank loans. Critical suppliers have dwindled in numbers. In small firms as well as large defense contractors, we found companies considering the costly option of internalizing some of the functions their suppliers currently perform, for fear that what's become a single-source supplier will go out of business. These are concerns even for current production. But the difficulties are far more challenging when a company seeks to develop a new or improved product or process. New inputs are needed, like different skills, financing, and components that firms cannot efficiently produce all by themselves. Even start-up companies with great novel technologies and generous venture backing cannot do it all in-house: they need to find suppliers, qualified production workers and engineers, expertise beyond their own. Established Main Street manufacturers in the regions we visited find little beyond their own internal resources to draw on when they seek to develop new projects. They're "home alone." This environment is far different from that of the German manufacturers we interviewed, who are embedded in dense networks of trade associations, suppliers, technical schools, and applied research centers all within easy reach.

What's to be done? Pathways for growth

There is much work to be done on all fronts to renew the production capabilities that the United States needs in order to gain full value from its innovation. The PIE research, however, points to one objective as most urgent: rebuilding the industrial ecosystem with new capabilities that many firms of all kinds could draw on when they try to build their new ideas into products on the market. New research suggests that it's the colocated interdependencies among complementary activities, not narrowly specialized clusters, that over time produce higher rates of growth and job creation, and they do so across a broad range of industries, not just in high-tech or advanced manufacturing.[16] The examples we have observed in the PIE research of trying to create public goods—or semipublic, or club goods—in the industrial ecosystem is the approach that may pay the greatest dividends.

The cases we have studied in detail are extremely diverse, but their efforts involve a few common principles. The key functions that such institutions perform are convening, coordination, risk-pooling and risk-reduction, and bridging. They are public goods that the market does not generate. There are initiatives in which a private company or a public institution performs a *convening function*. The initiative usually starts with the "convener" putting new resources on the table for use by others on condition that they too contribute to the pot. One well-known example is the SEMATECH Consortium that the semiconductor manufacturers and equipment makers formed in 1987 with financing both from the U.S. federal government and industry. SEMATECH today functions with funds from its members. By bringing companies together for roadmapping next generation chips, SEMATECH reduces the costs and risks of each company as it moves along the Moore's Law trajectory. New York State's investments in new fabrication facilities and new nanotechnology research in upstate New York at the College of Nanoscale Science and Engineering at the State University of New York, Albany, create common resources that the industrial partners can use.

Another example came from our Ohio interviews: the Timken Company, a manufacturer of tapered bearings and of specialty steels, initiated a partnership with the University of Akron and transferred Timken's coatings laboratory, its equipment, and several of its key researchers to the university. With resources from the company, the university, and the state, new graduate degree programs are starting; a new consortium on coatings and engineered surfaces has been created that is open to other corporate members; and a set of promising coatings technologies that had been "stranded" in a bearings company can now be developed as potential start-ups in which both the university and the corporate consortium members can invest. Potentially, companies from outside the region might join, but much of the value from participation will derive from face-to-face presence in the labs at the University of Akron, from being able to use university labs (funded at least in part with public money) instead of keeping these facilities in-house, and from the chance for local companies to hire graduates. In these cases the "conveners" hold out the lure of the use of common facilities and expensive equipment and training and proximity to cutting edge researchers. In contrast to tax breaks, which many states hand out, new resources are embedded in institutions that do not stand or fall on the participation of any one member.

Sometimes the lead in creating new *coordination* was taken by a private company. In other cases, coordination comes from a public intermediary. In Springfield, Massachusetts, the Hampden County Regional Employment Board (REB) is mandated by federal job training legislation to work with firms, localities, and educational institutions in the operation of the Workforce Investment Act. When the local machining association faced a shortage of skilled workers as the result of the closing of several large companies that had previously trained apprentices, it approached the REB. The REB brought the firms together with five vocational high schools and two community colleges. The connections between the schools and the companies had been thin and intermittent. With active intervention from the REB, the parties started to work on curriculum development; on training programs for supervisors and for unemployed workers; on organizing career fairs and firm visits to encourage high school students to consider machining jobs; and the gaps began to close.

Risk-reduction and risk-pooling are among the original functions for all forms of insurance and standard setting, and virtually all trade associations develop these functions to a greater or lesser extent for their members. For example, as we traced out the network mentioned above that connects Mass Tank to start-up companies in the New England region, we discovered that Mass Tank itself depends on a trade association, the Steel Tank Institute, for standards, testing, expertise, and insurance. The dangers of leaky tanks create enormous potential hazards—and lawsuits—and no small company on its own could afford adequate insurance from the regular insurance market. By working with the Environmental Protection

Agency to develop safety standards, the Steel Tank Institute has been able to offer its members technology, testing, and insurance that covers them.

These very old uses of association for risk-pooling today are being put to new purposes as policymakers harness them to innovation and to commercializing innovation in the United States. The first of the National Manufacturing Innovation Institutes, the National Additive Manufacturing Innovation Institute (NAMII) in Youngstown, Ohio, offers companies, universities, and government agencies a way to distribute the risks of investing in new technologies while still deriving many of the potential benefits. As one industrial partner from a metal-working company expressed his perception of the risks: "We don't make plastic toys, so we couldn't justify investing in-house in a technology like this that may just be a flash in the pan. But just suppose it does work out and we're not close enough to it to have a voice in shaping its development ... what then?" For those firms that do already have proprietary stakes in additive manufacturing there are yet other risks, and some forms of association with NAMII can help protect against them. For a region like Northeast Ohio and Southwest Pennsylvania, there's the enormous promise of technologies that could revitalize many of the small and medium-sized manufacturers but no way of finding a single industrial champion that would have an interest in carrying the project. The gains from 3-D printing, if it ever succeeds in overcoming its many current limitations, would be harvested by a multiplicity of users across diverse industrial sectors. When gains from innovation are significant but distributed thinly across many firms, it's unlikely that any single one of them will invest enough to bring it to life. NAMII offers potential ways to induce collaboration and spread risks that could bring a new technology to life and inject new vitality into the regional economy.

The cases we have described as exemplifying new approaches to rebuilding the industrial landscape are so new that we cannot know if any one of them will ultimately work or not. If we believe, nonetheless, that they have a real chance, it's because what's held manufacturing in the United States in the last resort—even as so much turned against it—was the advantage firms gain from proximity to innovation and proximity to users. Even in a world linked by big data and instant messaging, the gains from colocation have not disappeared. If we can learn from these ongoing experiments in linking innovation to production, new streams of growth can flow out of industrial America.

2

What Happened to Manufacturing?

Does manufacturing have to take place on our own shores for us to have an innovative and competitive economy? The debates over manufacturing in the United States go back to the founding of the Republic, to a time when Americans questioned whether we should remain a country of yeoman farmers or become a great nation by industrializing and overtaking Great Britain's lead. Today's advocates of encouraging industry still draw on lines of reasoning that trace back to Alexander Hamilton's 1791 *Report on Manufactures*. Now, however, industry's supporters are making a case for manufacturing, not against agriculture, but against the claim that a nation can thrive if its economy is based on services alone. When the issues are the broad ones of how to create a dynamic economy and a diverse and prosperous society, or even more specific points, like how to encourage innovation by protecting intellectual property, or whether to encourage immigration of skilled workers—Alexander Hamilton had already anticipated many of our modern dilemmas. What Hamilton could not have foreseen, though, was a world in which the tremendous productivity of industry would allow us to satisfy so many human needs and desires with so much less labor, or a world in which goods, capital, and many services would flow freely and cheaply around the globe. That unforeseeable future is our situation today.

A theory of economic evolution

In today's advanced economies, many people reason that the decline of manufacturing is just a natural and inevitable outcome of economic progress. From that perspective, any public or private efforts to support production look suspiciously like protection for inefficiency or politics for electoral gain. But the idea of natural decline is only one theory among others that claim to account for the current state of manufacturing in the United States. Globalization is another strong contending explanation, which highlights two key processes: the import of foreign products that compete with domestic goods, and the export of jobs and companies that once were located (or new ones that once would have been located) in the United States. The "natural decline" theory and the globalization theories about the role of manufacturing in an advanced economy have very different accounts of what happened to manufacturing, when it happened, and of what the future trajectory will be. But the two theories are alike in pointing to the conclusion that public policies aimed at sustaining manufacturing would be deadweights on the economy. Some of those who see the decline of manufacturing in this light still believe it would be worth supporting manufacturing because of the good jobs it creates—even if this "artificial support" has a cost to the economy in inefficiency and higher prices. But this is a conclusion that concedes what ought to be questions: Does manufacturing today contribute to innovation and growth? Which manufacturing contributes? Where does it need to be located?

The PIE research traces out an evolutionary path for production in advanced economies different from simple "natural" disappearance or decline from loss of comparative advantage. From ground-level research in 264 interviews and analysis of the pathways from discoveries to market, we find that manufacturing firms have a critical role both as sites of innovation and as enablers of scaling up to commercialization the strong flow of innovations from America's research laboratories, universities, public laboratories, and industrial R&D facilities. Along these pathways to economic growth, it is not only manufacturing that develops and commercializes great patentable ideas that matters; it is also manufacturing that brings less radical improvements in product and process onto the market that sustains economic vitality. It follows that we see a strong rationale for manufacturing in innovative economies—even when and where services are the predominant activity and employer. The grounds for arriving at this conclusion form the main part of this book. But first we need to consider why the disappearance of manufacturing as a significant part of the economy has come to seem so obvious and inevitable an outcome.

The origin of this view is an idea about how economies evolve over time. Rather than deduction from a theory, it was inspection of a large set of employment and output statistics from many developed and underdeveloped countries that led Colin Clark, an Australian economist writing in the 1930s and 1940s, to claim he had discovered that economies progress over time from being predominantly agricultural to industrial to service based. In his book *The Conditions of Economic Progress* (first published in 1940), Clark divided the economy into agricultural (in which he included mining), manufacturing, and services sectors. He defined manufacturing as "producing on a large scale and by a continuous process, transportable goods."[1] The concept of "transportable goods" is basically the same as what we today call "tradable goods," since they are ones that do not need to be consumed in the same locale in which they are produced. They can be sold and transported to ever larger and (with the fall in the cost of transportation) ever more distant markets. Some services, like apps for smart phones, are transportable and tradable, but many services, like nursing care for the elderly, are not. The nursing aide has to come along with her service and she cannot sell it in China unless she immigrates there (and gets a work visa as well).

One insight from Clark's definition might be that in advanced industrial economies, as new technologies drive down the cost of transportation and communication, ever-larger fractions of the goods and services produced are transportable and tradable. Some societies may come to excel at turning out more of their production as tradable and transportable goods and services and other countries may get stuck in making mainly those goods and services that can only be sold in close proximity to the producer. Those societies that excel in producing "transportable goods and services" within open global economies would have major competitive advantages, because they can sell to larger markets than just those in close proximity.[2] The cost of making one microprocessor, for example, is enormous, but once the knowledge and equipment are in place, millions of additional chips can be made for very little more per chip. The larger the markets in which they can be sold, the greater the profits. These economies of scale do not apply to services like the home aide's nursing care, though they do to software like apps. Nor do they apply to highly customized manufactured goods—unless, of course, these goods serve as essential inputs to products that can be sold in large numbers: the highly specialized capital equipment that German machine makers sell to Chinese mass-goods manufacturers is an example. How to identify the most valuable parts of modern manufacturing related to producing "tradable and transportable goods" is a question to which we return later in PIE's analysis of manufacturing. This approach was not, however, the one that Clark himself, or other economists following in his footsteps, would pursue.

Clark instead emphasized "a wide, simple, and far-reaching generalization ... that as time goes on and communities become more economically advanced, the numbers engaged in agriculture tend to decline relative to the numbers in manufacture, which in their turn decline relative to the numbers engaged in services."[3] Clark pointed out that Sir William Petty had formulated the same "law" four centuries earlier. Writing in 1691, Petty calculated that per capita income was higher in the Netherlands than in France or Britain because the Dutch had moved on from farming and mechanical activities into commerce. Clark claimed that "Petty's Law" had now been generally confirmed for all nations. To back this up, Clark expanded his investigations of output and income to cover virtually every corner of the earth from which he could find statistics, and included both developing and developed nations.

Productivity growth and the agricultural analogy

Today, the way Clark's point is usually made is that just as rising productivity in agriculture has made it possible to feed the American population with about 2 percent of the workforce employed in agriculture—whereas in 1900 it took about 40 percent of the workforce—so too in manufacturing the extraordinary productivity increases in industry have made it possible to produce ever greater quantities of goods with many fewer people. In 1980, 22.1 percent of the workforce was employed in manufacturing; by the end of 2011, only 10.2 percent.[4] But manufacturing value added over the same period grew from $803.5 billion to $1,831.6 billion in constant 2005 dollars.[5] In fact, by 2011 the United States still produced almost the same share of world manufacturing output (19.4 percent) as it had in 1990 (21 percent) with millions fewer workers employed in manufacturing.[6] Nobel laureate economist Gary Becker started from exactly this point in criticizing the Obama administration's emphasis on manufacturing:

> Commentators have always lamented a sizable fall in jobs in any large sector of an economy. A prominent example is the huge decline in farm employment during the twentieth century in all developed countries. With about 2 percent of the labor force currently on farms, the United States not only manages to provide the vast majority of food consumed by 300 million Americans, but American farmers have enough production left over to export large quantities to the rest of the world. Big productivity gains in manufacturing are also a major cause behind the decrease in manufacturing employment in the United States. Higher productivity lowered prices of manufactured goods relative to prices of services. Yet employment in manufacturing fell because the lower manufacturing prices did not stimulate a large enough increase in the demand for manufactured goods to offset the productivity increases of the manufacturing workforce.[7]

Becker's fellow blogger Richard Posner agreed that this "agricultural analogy" was just the right one. Agricultural subsidies are "pure social waste and the same would be true of subsidizing manufacturing." He concluded: "Like manufacturing, American agriculture is thriving with its historically small labor force."[8]

In this explanation of the trajectory of advanced economies, the main factor at work in driving down the numbers of those employed in manufacturing is productivity growth. To understand why manufacturing is shrinking, there's no need to bring in globalization or outsourcing, or to point an accusing finger at China's undervalued currency or exploitative labor practices. Productivity-increasing capital investment, new skills, and innovation within our own domestic economy are sufficient to account for most of the change. Analysts who focus on productivity gains in industry may acknowledge that imports from low-cost labor countries contribute to the troubles of manufacturing in the United States, but they do not see globalization as the key issue. In fact, it's almost the rule that in such accounts the author points out that the numbers employed in manufacturing are declining even in China. As Lawrence Summers, the first director of President Obama's National Economic Council and former Harvard University president, expressed it in December 2010: "Technology is accelerating productivity in mass production to the point where even China has seen manufacturing employment decline by more than ten million jobs over the most recent decade for which data is available."[9]

There have been enormous productivity gains in manufacturing over the past hundred years, and they can certainly explain some part of the decline of the manufacturing workforce in the United States. But it does not follow from this that manufacturing like agriculture is destined to shrink to a small fraction of the economy. There are at least three reasons to doubt that agriculture's role in the American economy is the right guide to thinking about the future of manufacturing. First, the agricultural analogy does not exactly fit our situation as a nation of consumers. In agriculture, the United States grows all we can eat and more. Aside even from consideration of the effects that increased agricultural production would have on the land and on the environment, there's the question of what we would do—within the United States—with more food. While we could make potatoes into higher-value-added products like potato chips and corn into corn chips or maybe biofuels, most of us seem to have reached some kind of saturation of our appetites and our waistlines. But with manufactured goods our appetites as consumers vastly exceed our production, and we import far more than we export, hence our huge trade deficits. In 2011, the United States had a deficit in traded goods of $738.4 billion.[10]

Trade deficits—and negative savings in the United States—lie at the origin of global imbalances and high levels of U.S. debt. These imbalances were powerful contributing factors to the financial crisis that broke out in 2007. Making more of what we consume in manufactured goods would certainly help in solving our nation's major economic problems in a way that producing more food would not—and so in this respect at least, the agricultural analogy does not fit. Of course, making more of the goods we buy might not be the best way of tackling the trade deficits, particularly if the measures adopted to achieve that outcome involved some measure of trade protection that induced retaliation by other countries and U.S. exports suffered. Without adding layers of trade protection, we might try to export more. It would be extremely difficult to reduce the trade deficit by increasing exports of services alone; indeed, most economists consider it would be impossible. But we might export more services and goods and food. Or we could tackle these problems by consuming less and saving more. Each of these options, however, requires us to think of the output of U.S. manufacturing not only as fixed by the productivity of its workforce but as determined by the terms of trade within the international economy and by the fiscal and monetary decisions of government. Each of these possibilities moves away from any simple transposition of the "agricultural analogy."

Second, and equally important, recent research challenges the conclusion that the decline in manufacturing jobs over the past decade can be largely attributed to productivity growth in manufacturing. If it were really the case, as official statistics suggest, that the output of U.S. manufacturing had grown significantly over the past decade and even that it still amounts to about the same share of global manufactured products as a decade earlier—despite the loss of millions of manufacturing jobs over the same decade—then there would be a clear case of greater productivity killing jobs. But economist Susan Houseman and colleagues have called these output figures into serious doubt.[11] Their work shows the multiple biases that have been introduced into national statistics on manufacturing output because of major measurement errors when suppliers of intermediate goods shift from domestic to foreign origin. Overwhelmingly the impact of these measurement errors is to overstate U.S. productivity gains. U.S. manufacturers have been using more and more imported components, and the value of these foreign inputs is not accurately captured in U.S. statistics. When a U.S. manufacturer starts buying foreign-made components that are cheaper than the U.S.-made components that used to go into the final product, and when there's a drop in final cost, it may look in statistics like a gain in output and productivity. But in fact, the U.S. producer may not be any more productive than before. He may just be using cheaper foreign inputs. Houseman and Ryder estimate that in the ten years before the financial crisis, these measurement errors resulting from failure to identify shifts from domestic to foreign suppliers and to correctly price the foreign components may have overstated the growth in real value added in manufacturing (excluding computers and related electronic equipment) by one-fifth to one-half.[12] It's doubtful if there were any productivity gains in manufacturing overall in the last decade. The actual productivity gains in that period—once the numbers have been adjusted to fix the measurement errors—can be almost entirely attributed to one industry within it: computers and electronic products.

It's not only the estimates of the magnitude of productivity gains that have been called into question by recent research. Economists Susan Helper, Timothy Krueger, and Howard Wial have challenged the assumption that there's any automatic connection between periods of productivity gains and periods of job losses. They refer to the work by William Nordhaus on manufacturing over the period 1948–2003. Surprisingly, Nordhaus found that the industrial sectors with productivity increases were also ones with job growth (or decreases in rates of job losses). Helper and colleagues then used Nordhaus's methodology to look at changes in manufacturing output between 2001 and 2009 and their impact on employment. They found that though productivity growth had less effect on job growth than in the earlier periods that Nordhaus had studied, there was no significant association of job loss and productivity increases.[13] In short, the latest research[14] casts great doubt on the size, even the existence, of productivity increases in manufacturing sectors over the past 10 years. And to the extent that we can track productivity growth and changes in manufacturing employment, the connections are not the clear pattern of productivity gain and job loss that we might have expected.[15]

Finally, the idea that in successful advanced economies manufacturing will come to employ only a small fraction of the workforce does not hold up well when we look abroad to other major exporting countries. In 2011 in the United States, after the big job losses following the financial crisis, only about 10 percent of the labor force worked in manufacturing; in Germany, close to 20 percent of the workforce is still employed in manufacturing. Germany has a large trade surplus, mainly with the European Union member countries, but also even with China. Japan has close to 17 percent of its workforce in manufacturing; and Italy—another major world exporter nation—has 19 percent of its workforce in manufacturing.[16] The factor explaining the strength of manufacturing employment in these global economic powers can hardly be lower wages. On the contrary: in 2010, total compensation costs per hour in U.S. manufacturing were $34.74; in Germany, $43.76.[17] Japan and Korea are not low-cost countries either. Chapter 5 will consider what we might learn from the ways in which other high-wage economies have retained strong manufacturing sectors in the face of intense global competition from developing economies. But with respect to evaluating the fate of manufacturing in advanced economies, the point here is that these foreign examples challenge conventional views of decline as natural and inevitable because of productivity gains. Over time, manufacturing has come to employ a smaller share of the workforce across all major exporting nations, advanced and developing. In the future, it may be smaller yet, but there is no predestined or natural endpoint.

To account for the level we have reached and the availability of choices for the future, productivity growth is at best part of a larger story. The periods of the greatest job losses do not match up with the periods of greatest productivity gains; productivity levels do not explain why countries like Germany have manufacturing sectors that are so much stronger than the American or why manufacturing employment fell so much more in the United States than in other high-wage economies subject to much the same competitive pressures from emerging economies.

Globalization

No question about the economy is more hotly contested by ordinary citizens and by famous economists than whether globalization is good for the country and good or bad for particular groups of citizens. This debate is intense both in advanced economies and in developing economies like India and Brazil. Do free trade and the free flow of capital across borders contribute to economic growth? Do they increase economic opportunities across all groups in society or do they widen economic and social inequalities? Who benefits? Who loses? Underlying these debates about the costs and gains of globalization are some shaky assumptions about whether we actually are "in globalization," how far globalization has proceeded, and how many of the changes in the economy over the past forty years can be accounted for by globalization. For understanding what has happened to manufacturing over those forty years, the starting question then should be: how much of the change in manufacturing in the United States can be explained by globalization? Then we might ask: are these changes good or bad and good or bad for whom? For the country as a whole? For manufacturing workers or for companies or both? For supporting an economic ecosystem in which innovations can scale up into new commercial products, processes, and services?

Let's begin with a simple common definition. An economic view of globalization shows the emergence of a single world market for labor, capital, goods, and services.[18] Globalization can then be defined as the processes and competitive pressures that operate toward integrating distinct national economies into this single world market. If there were to be one global market, then wages, interest rates, and the prices for the same goods and services would all converge and tend to be the same wherever on earth we found them.[19]

The world's economies are far from this endpoint—and probably will never reach it—but the factors of convergence that work toward such an outcome do exert extraordinary force within domestic economies today. This book will often return to these drivers of globalization in tracing out firm practices and strategies, for these factors play a major role in determining how and where innovations are brought into the market. Here, however, as a preview, the multiple and complex changes driving convergence are briefly sketched out under technological, financial, and political headings. On the technology side of the ledger are radical innovations in transportation and communication that have revolutionized the cost of moving goods and services and information over long distances. Firms from around the world now compete in markets that used to be just too costly to reach. Access to larger markets has increased the potential gains for those who can sell outside their own country; it has also increased the premium for those capable of producing outside their own home base in order to be close to new customers.

New digitization technologies have made it possible to separate many functions that once had to be carried out within the four walls of the same company and to organize these functions in separate firms, each with a specific competence, all linked in supply chains through the exchange of digital files over the Internet.[20] Silicon chip design and chip fabrication, for example, once had to be done in the same company by engineers and technicians working in close proximity in order to get the degree of conformance that guaranteed high quality. Today, the engineer who draws the circuits for a mask can save them in a digital file and send them over the Internet to an automated cutting machine anywhere in the world. Design and manufacturing functions, then, can take place in different companies in different locales—chip design perhaps in Silicon Valley in a company like Qualcomm, fabrication of the chips most often in a Taiwanese company like Taiwan Semiconductor Manufacturing Company (TSMC).

These technological changes have enabled a radical restructuring of the corporation, a point we return to later in this chapter. New companies can focus on their own specialization—their "core competence"—and obtain the critical components and services they need to build their products via subcontracting and outsourcing, rather than building them from scratch up within the company. These technological opportunities—and the changes in financial markets that reward companies that are "asset light"—have accelerated a fragmentation of corporate structures. In a world in which a company does not need to have all vital functions within its own four walls, it's a lot faster to grow. New firms can enter the market rapidly. The same forces produce more competition, since rivals can be born and catch up more quickly.

Changes in financial markets are a second set of factors driving toward convergence. During the first globalization (1870–1914), the fastest new communication technologies available to investors were the telephone, telegraph, and cable. Before the transatlantic cable was laid in the 1860s, it took three weeks for bond and stock prices to circulate between New York and London. After the transatlantic cable, data were almost instantaneously available in the major financial markets around the world, much as it is by Internet today, though Internet can handle far larger amounts of information even faster. By using the new communication technologies to unlock the potential of the new financial institutions of the nineteenth century, like limited joint stock companies, vast new funds were raised from small as well as big investors, and poured into floods of portfolio and foreign direct investment across borders. The result a hundred and fifty years ago, as today, was to integrate world markets and greatly reduce price differentials across markets in different national economies.[21] Since the 1980s, new financial market innovations together with new information and communication technologies have worked to the same effect. Derivative instruments, credit default swaps, foreign exchange hedging, and myriad other new financial products have redistributed the risks of trading and manufacturing outside one's own country, and driven ever-higher levels of investment abroad.

Finally, at the head of the list of globalization's drivers are the transformative political developments of the past three decades. The opening of China from 1979 on, the fall of the Iron Curtain and emergence of independent states in East Europe, liberalization in once-closed countries like Vietnam or once-pariah regimes like South Africa and recently Burma have wholly altered the terrain of the international economy. As the political barriers to contact and exchange fall, new consumer markets slowly emerge. Workers at all levels of education and skill become potential participants in the global economy. Above all, the major economic powers of the world have agreed over the past fifty years to dismantle most of the border-level barriers to the free flow of goods and capital. Progress has been made, too, on reducing beyond-the-border obstacles to trade, like food and safety regulations that discriminate against foreign products. Through the years between the two world wars and over the Great Depression, most of the tariffs and quotas that protected national economies stood firm, often reinforced by governments pressured by special interests and desperate to shield themselves from the conflicts raging outside their boundaries. The rollback of protection began to take effect from the 1980s on with international agreements in the GATT (General Agreement on Tariffs and Trade) and then its successor organization, the WTO (World Trade Organization). With trade liberalization, firms have increasingly had to adopt new strategies and structures and respond as if they were all competing in the same world market.

The opening of national borders to unimpeded flows of goods, services, capital, and labor is still very far from complete. As governments try to ward off the economic repercussions of the financial crisis and the recession that followed, there has even been a slight swing back toward protectionist measures. In any event, the current Doha Round of WTO liberalization negotiations is stalled, and unlikely to be relaunched in the near future. For one critical factor of production—labor—the frontiers are still mostly closed to legal entry. Strong and rising anti-immigration sentiments in the United States and in Europe seem likely to ensure they remain that way for a long time. To obtain the economic benefits of employing foreign workers, a company has only a very restricted chance of bringing them into the United States on H-1B and L-1 visas. Instead, to gain the services, talents, and lower wages of foreigners, companies usually need to resort to moving work abroad and then importing the products and services they make overseas back into the United States.

Even for capital—the factor of production that is most mobile and that can be shifted across national borders by a simple stroke on a laptop keyboard—there is a lot of stickiness at national borders. Financial markets still have strong national characteristics. There was much evidence of this in the wake of the financial crisis, when some national governments intervened effectively in order to save banks headquartered within their own territories, as for example in the United States and Britain, while others, like Iceland, could only stand by helplessly. But even though the single world market is far from a reality, the competitive pressures that push toward that outcome are potent forces in the economy.

Who gains from globalization?

When Americans are asked in surveys whether these changes in the international economy that have opened the door to more economic exchanges with foreign societies are good for the country and good for their own individual welfare, their answers vary widely. In part, it depends on the wording of the question and the year in which it was posed. Before the financial crisis, in 2006, when asked whether free trade was a "good thing" or a "bad thing" for the country, 44 percent of those polled by the Pew Research Center for the People & the Press were positive; 35 percent negative; and 21 percent did not know. But in the same poll, respondents divided about equally over whether their own finances were helped (35 percent) or not (36 percent) by free trade; only 28 percent thought trade led to growth and 34 percent believed it "slows the economy"; only 12 percent saw trade as a factor that created jobs, while 48 percent said it mainly led to job losses. Four years later, Americans were even more negative, with only 35 percent thinking free trade was good for the country and 44 percent responding it was bad.[22]

The uncertainties about globalization's impact have far deeper causes than the vagaries of response to surveys. It is not surprising that people's views about the consequences of globalization should be so mixed and volatile. Each person is at the same time a consumer and a producer, and depending on which interests come into focus in particular situations, globalization may seem either beneficial or menacing. As a consumer, a person is likely to realize that the prices of the TVs, computers, shoes, and toys she buys in Walmart or on Amazon are cheap because they are made in Asia. As an employee, though, she wonders whether her own job is safe from outsourcing. Even if she's not doing assembly-line work in manufacturing, but has a job in insurance, or a law firm, or an architect's office, she sees many jobs similar to her own being transferred overseas. It's troubling, too, to citizens to recognize that whatever leverage they once had on the economy through the election of their representatives in Congress and the presidency is reduced as the national markets are integrated, however partially, into world markets. Out in the global economy, there's no one to hold accountable.

Mainstream economists have not on the whole suffered the doubts of the general public about whether the free flow of goods, services, and capital across borders contributes to the betterment of all countries in international exchange.[23] Economists generally start from theories of comparative advantage that were first laid out by the early-nineteenth-century economist David Ricardo and then expanded by twentieth-century economists in the Heckscher–Ohlin and Stolper–Samuelson trade models. These theories describe the benefits for productivity and incomes on all sides that result from trade in open international markets in which countries export those goods in which they have a relative "comparative advantage" and import those in which they have no or relatively less comparative advantage. Comparative advantage derives from having a relatively more abundant (hence relatively less expensive) supply of one or another factor of production—labor or capital or land—than one's trading partner. In a simplified example, the theory would predict that since China has a more abundant supply of low-wage, semiskilled labor than the United States and uses it in making products for export, Chinese goods for sale in the United States will be cheaper than those made in the United States with higher-wage workers. As the U.S. and Chinese firms making these products compete in the market, the U.S. firms are likely to go out of business (or at least, out of that line of business).

For all groups in society to benefit from trade, those who derive their incomes from making goods that are no longer domestically produced but imported will have to be re-employed in new jobs, once they lose their old jobs in uncompetitive sectors. To get new jobs, workers may need retraining—more feasible for the better educated and the younger ones than for the older workers. They may need to move to other parts of the country. For some, there may be no good solution in the labor market, and other forms of compensation will have to be provided, for example, through unemployment insurance or trade adjustment funds or disability payments. As many economists acknowledge, these processes of transition and adjustment may take some time, and inflict more painful losses on some groups in the population than others. But in the long run we should be better off, the theories predict.

Is globalization to blame for manufacturing decline?

Even if one accepts these general propositions, however, through much of the period since 1979 in which manufacturing jobs have been disappearing in the United States, it has been difficult to figure out whether globalization is really to blame for manufacturing's situation, or whether some other processes are at work. The striking fact is that the proportion of imports entering the United States from low-wage countries relative to imports from higher-wage countries has been until recently very small.[24] Until this past decade it was so small that it was hard to hold it responsible for manufacturing job losses. The ratio of imports from low-cost economies relative to imports from other prosperous high-wage countries was even lower in West European countries. Since the "globalization effect" is imagined to work mainly through trade among countries with very different factor prices, it was hard to conceive how trade among countries where the cost of labor was quite similar could produce large changes in the numbers employed in manufacturing in any one of these high-wage countries.[25]

Even taking into account job losses resulting from outsourcing as well as import competition, it was difficult as recently as a decade ago to find clear evidence of a heavy impact of open borders on manufacturing employment.[26] The Department of Labor's surveys on big layoffs caused by outsourcing jobs overseas showed very small numbers, but an upward trend from 1999 to 2004. In 2003, they involved less than one percent of all layoffs; in 2004 they went up to two percent.[27] These surveys did not capture the total volume of jobs being transferred abroad, but even the larger numbers that other accounts came up with were only a small fraction of the total annual job turnover in the U.S. labor market. Research carried out in other advanced industrial countries in the same period also failed to turn up solid evidence that trade with low-wage countries hurt low-skilled workers.[28] Absent substantial evidence of the effects of trade, a decade ago most economists still concluded that job losses in manufacturing were mainly the result of productivity gains (as discussed above)—which might reduce the total numbers of those needed to produce a finite quantity of goods.

Researchers also considered the possibility that job loss was due to skill-biased technical change. The idea here was that the composition of jobs involved in manufacturing was changing, with more demand for people with higher education and advanced skills and less demand for the semi-skilled. Automation was making it possible to reduce routine activities to standard operations that could be programmed into machines. It was the workers with high school diplomas or less and fewer of the skills required in sophisticated, automated production who were losing their jobs.[29] Jobs requiring face-to-face interactions, like those of the nursing aide, and ad-hoc judgment calls, like those of a traffic cop at a busy intersection, were not likely to disappear. The nursing aide and the policeman might not have or need advanced education and degrees, but many or most of the jobs in the new labor market are predicted to take more education and different kinds of reasoning capabilities than the old manufacturing jobs. From this perspective, the downward pressure on manufacturing employment would come from technologies requiring people with the skills to deal with sophisticated software and equipment as well as aptitude for dealing with people, thus reducing the demand for semiskilled routine jobs by automating them or possibly transferring them (using digitization and Internet connections) to low-wage workers overseas. The fall in manufacturing employment resulting from skill-biased technical change, like that from productivity gains, basically involves the internal working through of technological change within the American economy. To understand how this plays out, we do not need to assume any major changes in capabilities in the rest of the world, nor to bring into the explanation any theory of comparative advantage. Chapter 7 of this book contributes to this debate with an analysis of skill requirements for U.S. jobs in manufacturing on the basis of a nationally representative sample of manufacturing establishments.

Globalization on steroids

Any doubts about the impact of trade on U.S. manufacturing vanished as Chinese imports began to flood into U.S. markets after 2000. On the supply side, this reflected enormous increases in the capabilities of Chinese manufacturing. The new factories that Taiwanese, Hong Kong, and some Western manufacturers started building in the southern coastal regions of China that had been declared reform zones were able to recruit workers from a vast labor pool from all over China. This new production came on line in the 1990s. Once tariff and quota barriers came down, these goods could flow into Western markets. Chinese membership in the World Trade Organization in 2001 and the final days of the Multi-Fiber Agreement proved potent accelerators. For example, after the Multi-Fiber Agreement's restrictive quotas on textiles and clothing trade ended in January 2005, imports of those items from China into the United States soared over the course of one year from $8.93 billion to $15.4 billion.[30]

In "The China Syndrome: Local Labor Market Effects of Import Competition in the United States," David Autor, David Dorn, and Gordon Hanson chart the overall rapid expansion of imports from low-income economies, from 2.9 percent of U.S. manufacturing imports in 1991, to 5.9 percent in 2000, and to 11.7 percent in 2007.[31] Most of the new growth came from China. From 2000 on, the effects that globalization theories had predicted that were premised on change through trade based on comparative advantage could be clearly identified in the devastating impact of Chinese imports on manufacturing jobs in the U.S. local labor markets most heavily exposed to import competition. These were regions with labor-intensive industries like apparel and furniture in which China had a comparative advantage because of low labor costs. Even in an earlier period (1977–1997) with far lower levels of imports from low-wage countries, researchers had already found that manufacturing companies whose products competed with low-wage-country imports were the more vulnerable and slower-growing ones.[32] Now the evidence pointed not only to impact on firm-level growth, but also to massive job loss.

Autor, Dorn, and Hanson provide a compelling analysis of the effects of trade from low-wage economies over the period 1990–2007 on U.S. manufacturing workers. Their research focused on identifying the impact of imports from low-wage countries—China in particular—on U.S. local labor markets that are more heavily specialized in labor-intensive production as contrasted with U.S. local labor markets with manufacturing establishments that are less exposed to low-wage competition. The geographic units they studied were 722 commuting zones, built from county groupings that have strong commuting ties. They found substantial impact in local labor markets of rising import competition, resulting in rising levels of unemployment, declining labor force participation, and rising levels of public benefits receipt transferred through unemployment insurance, trade adjustment assistance, Social Security Disability Insurance payments, and Medicare and Medicaid. The researchers calculated that a $1,000 increase in Chinese import exposure at the commuting zone level increased the number of unemployed workers by 4.9 percent and the numbers of those out of the labor force by 2.1 percent.[33] Simultaneously, government transfer payments rose by $58 per capita, reflecting the increased demands that displaced workers and dependent family members made on social welfare programs.[34]

Contrary to what one might have expected, manufacturing wages did not fall significantly in the zones that had experienced heavy job losses. Possible explanations are that the preponderance of job losses occurred among less productive, lower-wage manufacturing workers, or alternatively, that manufacturing firms in those zones may have altered their operations to become less labor intensive.[35] But wages in nonmanufacturing employment in those zones did go down significantly, perhaps because people who could no longer find work in manufacturing looked for local service sector jobs. Surprisingly, there was little migration out of heavily exposed commuting zones—perhaps because moving is expensive and chancy.

Depending on the industrial composition of any particular commuting zone and whether or not its output competes with Chinese imports, the impact of the increases in China supply varies considerably. Imports into local labor markets that ranked in the 75th percentile of import exposure had two times as much impact per worker as on workers situated in the labor markets that ranked in the 25th percentile by import exposure.[36] Autor and colleagues introduced controls into their analysis to verify that the effects they were picking up were caused by increased imports, and not by some other factor(s) causing a decline in U.S. manufacturing, like automation or offshoring. The results were still clear. The bottom line was that Chinese imports accounted for about 33 percent of manufacturing job decline between 1990 and 2000 and 55 percent between 2000 and 2007. The estimated impacts are lower when the authors focused exclusively on the subset of increased import exposure that they could confidently attribute to exogenous developments affecting import supplies, including rising Chinese productivity and falling China-facing trade barriers. Using only this supply-driven variation, the research conservatively estimates that 16 percent of the manufacturing job losses between 1990 and 2000 and 26 percent between 2000 and 2007 were attributable to rising import competition from China.[37]

Another consequence of the surge of imports from low-wage economies was the drastic downsizing of large manufacturing plants in the United States. A study by economist Thomas J. Holmes found that the number of manufacturing plants in the United States employing more than 5,000 workers had dropped from 192 in 1977 to only 49 in 2007.[38] The number of plants with more than 1,000 workers fell by half over the same period. Many of these firms downsized and could be identified in smaller-size categories in more recent years. Some disappeared entirely. Import competition was not the only factor at work in this decline; as we will discuss below, the change in corporate structures of the past twenty-five years has had great impact on plant size. But as Holmes dug deeper into the changes in the seven-state Piedmont area, a region that once had a larger than average share of the U.S. large manufacturing plants, he found that the surge in imports from China had had an enormous effect. Many of Piedmont's larger employers had specialized in furniture and clothing and other labor-intensive industries that now were being inundated by Chinese products. Of twenty-one big plants in these sectors in the Piedmont in 1997, only one remained in 2007, and it was making quite a different line of furniture products than it had in the past.[39]

Finally, globalization in the form of new waves of imports from low-wage economies seems to have had at least one strongly positive impact on production. Research on the impact of Chinese imports within twelve European economies between 1996 and 2007 found that those firms that survived the onslaught of competition became more innovative: they spent more on R&D, registered more patents, introduced more information technology, and improved their management.[40] Bloom, Draca, and Van Reenen estimate that pressure from Chinese imports raised patenting and productivity by close to 15 percent between 2000 and 2007 in the European countries they studied. The mechanism through which competition induced technology upgrading, they suggest, was by inducing firms with sunk investments ("trapped factors") in worker skills and equipment to innovate in order to extract any benefit at all out of their legacy assets. Basically, lowering the return on low-tech products stimulated firms to innovate toward higher-value-added products.

These pioneering studies of the local consequences of free trade joined to powerful new production capabilities in low-wage economies provide evidence of the heavy costs of globalization for some groups in the American population and its positive effects for others. They still leave open, though, many questions about manufacturing and globalization and, most important, whether globalization overall is good for the U.S. economy. Nor does this research provide insight into the effects of the collapse of manufacturing jobs in labor-intensive sectors on manufacturing in general. It could be the case that even as jobs making shoes, for example, disappear in the United States, U.S. exports of sophisticated automated shoe making robots might rise and lead to increases in manufacturing jobs in robotics. Changes along this line allowed Germany to abandon much of its low-end manufacturing while simultaneously retaining and even expanding employment in higher-value-added segments. Finally, there remains the open question of whether we have the right capabilities for doing the kinds of manufacturing that would make it possible for the United States to exploit its greatest strengths in innovation and technology in world markets. Before moving on to chapters that present the PIE research that explores these issues, however, we need to consider briefly the transformation of American corporate structures, the third set of changes of the past thirty years that have had a major downward impact on manufacturing.

Downsizing the corporate giants

From the middle of the nineteenth century on, the great new American companies were ones organized to exploit the potential of producing and selling to the huge national market that railroads, the telegraph, steamships, and canals had unified. Companies like DuPont, G.F. Swift, Singer Sewing Machine, and Ford Motor grew into multidivisional, manager-run enterprises that basically flattened the competition.[41] Virtually all of these companies followed a common path of development by extending the range of functions they carried out within their own four walls to encompass everything from inventing and defining a product to delivering it into the hands of the customer. When new industries, like transistors, and then semiconductors, came on line after World War Two, those companies also built up as vertically integrated enterprises. Companies like IBM, Motorola, Texas Instruments, and Hewlett-Packard kept research, design, development, fabricating, packaging, testing, and sales in-house and also developed many of the products, like computers and printers, in which the components were used.

As mass consumer markets greatly expanded after World War Two, the vertically integrated companies were able to profit from high and stable demand, long production runs, and long product cycles. They largely relied on retained earnings, not bank loans or equity markets, to fund new operations. These companies had become the most powerful actors on the economic landscape of American society. They dwarfed even the power of financial institutions. Peter Drucker, an influential thinker on American management, writing in 1949, described this dominance in terms hardly believable today:

> The mass-production revolution has … dethroned the ruling groups of bourgeois society: the merchant, the banker, the capitalist. Symbolic of this change is the slow but steady decay of the great merchant oligarchies: the "City" in London, "Wall Street" in New York, "State Street" in Boston. Where only twenty years ago the bright graduate of the Harvard Business School aimed at a job with a New York Stock Exchange house, he now seeks employment with a steel, oil, or automobile company. It is not only that money has become less important than industrial capacity to produce; the old financial powers have also lost control over money and credit itself, as witness the shift of the financial headquarters from Wall Street to the government agencies in Washington and from the City to the British Treasury.[42]

The ownership of upstream and downstream functions allowed firms to reduce the risks of dealing with suppliers. When they did subcontract production to suppliers, they tended to dominate the relationship and often could drive competition among suppliers to push down costs. Ownership of all the stages of production gave the vertically integrated firm control over the quality of production. And pushing out the periphery of the corporation allowed them to preempt the advance of rivals into their competitive space. When, for example, DuPont considered whether or not to carry out basic research within the company, one of the factors in the decision to do so was that by extending the boundaries of the firm, they would be able to ward off competitors at their edges.

The simple list of Ford Motor Company's activities in the 1949 *Encyclopaedia Britannica* entry gives some idea of what vertical integration could involve. Ford was founded in 1903. By 1949, according to the encyclopedia entry, Ford had "its own lighting heat and power plant; its fire department; paper mill; its foundries, hot and cold sheet mill; hot roll bar mill; tire plant; sintering plant; coke ovens; tool and die shop; press shop; cement plant; body plant; open hearth furnaces; box factory; blast furnaces; telephone and telegraphy exchanges; machine shop; paint factory; artificial leather plant; freight and express offices; hospitals; laboratories; and a trade school for boys."[43] Ford owned railroads, iron and coal mines, and forest lands in Michigan, West Virginia, and Kentucky; a 2.3-million-acre Brazilian rubber plantation; and its own ships to transport car parts to be assembled in Ford factories abroad. Even among vertically integrated companies, this scope of control may have been unusual. But the notion of keeping in-house all the operations needed to bring a product or process from start through to commercialization was common.

Even at the height of mass consumer markets and large-scale integrated production facilities, there were other forms of industrial organization in advanced economies that also turned out excellent performance. In Japan, giants like Toyota, Toray, Mitsubishi, and Matsushita in some respects resembled the U.S. vertically integrated corporation. The large-company Japanese corporate structures, however, linked not only functions within firms, but also companies in business groups, through tight vertical and horizontal links to banks, suppliers, and affiliated businesses (*keiretsu*). Japanese companies like Toyota, Matsushita, and Toray differed from their American counterparts not only in their relationship to capital markets and suppliers, but also in their internal functioning. The hierarchies of authority were flatter in Japan; labor relations depended more on trust and loyalty than on collective contracts. These companies excelled at building relationships among employees at all levels to promote continuous improvement and learning and to eliminate inventories and waste. Alongside large companies in Europe and Japan, there were also high-performing industrial districts or clusters of small and medium-size companies, with each firm specializing in one or only a few stages of production. Coordination in these districts grew out of long-standing collaborations, a fairly high level of trust, proximity to customers and markets, and local institutions like trade schools, unions, and employer associations. However much American vertically integrated corporations, Japanese companies, the industrial district firms of the Italian Veneto, and the German Mittelstand family businesses differed, they were alike in one key respect: manufacturing was an integral part of their basic business model.

All of these models would be deeply affected by the changes in world markets and in technology over the last thirty years, but perhaps none as radically and rapidly as the American vertically integrated companies. The key point is that in the course of transformation, most of them shed manufacturing. By 2012, very few large American companies remained with vertically integrated structures. Companies like General Electric or Procter & Gamble with a wide range of different businesses under one corporate roof and a predominant preference for integrating operations in-house from research through production (including manufacturing) are the exceptions. Far more typical are the new boundaries of companies like Hewlett-Packard (or IBM or Levi Strauss or Apple or Boeing or Nike) that have restructured to focus on a narrower set of activities considered as "core competence" and have spun off or sold off or closed all those activities not in the "core."

Financial market forces continue today to press for the break-up of companies that investors see as still too integrated. At a May 2013 shareholders' meeting of Timken, a hundred-year-old Ohio company specializing in bearings, steel, and power transmission, a large pension fund together with an activist asset management fund passed a nonbinding resolution to spin off the steel company in order to raise the stock prices. Ralph Whitworth, the head of the activist shareholder Relational Investors declared: "Shareholders have made it clear that they want the true investment value of Timken's businesses to be properly realized, and that the Company's conglomerate structure, which has proven to be an ongoing impediment, must be eliminated."[44]

Manufacturing tops the list of the functions that have been moved out from within the four walls of the corporation's ownership and control and are now carried out in foreign or domestic plants owned by subcontractors. And the great new companies of the past thirty years, like Dell, Cisco, and Qualcomm, have never had any large manufacturing capabilities in-house. Given the great strength of American manufacturing in the postwar years, the massive break-up and restructuring of American vertically integrated companies from the 1980s on is a puzzle. Why did it happen? What were the pressures at work to force through such changes? Why was this shift to "asset-light" companies so much greater in the United States than most other places in the world? Next, what made it possible? How could companies coordinate the functions needed to bring new products to market without any longer owning these resources? How could they break apart activities that once were carried out in close proximity to each other? How could they disperse these into the hands of different independent suppliers around the world and still get products of the right quality at the right time? How could they get them to work together seamlessly? Finally, what were the consequences for manufacturing of the great fragmentation of corporate structures?

The most convincing explanations of the transformation of American corporate structures point to deep changes in financial markets and in government regulation from the 1980s on. Here we draw on the analysis of Gerald F. Davis, professor of management at the University of Michigan, in his book *Managed by the Markets: How Finance Re-Shaped America*.[45] Davis describes how the reform of antitrust regulations by President Ronald Reagan's Justice Department removed the incentive for companies to grow by diversification into multiple unrelated businesses. Since markets already undervalued companies with underperforming divisions, the relaxation of antitrust constraints provided a spur to breaking up conglomerates and reorganizing the pieces into firms centered on similar activities. This produced a vast wave of takeovers and mergers resulting in the disappearance of about a third of America's large companies. By 1995, Davis calculates the median large manufacturer operated in one broad industry category, whereas two decades earlier it would have been three.

Over the same period, the idea that companies exist to create value for their shareholders came to dominate all other conceptions of how companies should be organized and how their various stakeholders should be rewarded. Davis traces out the triumph of the notion that the company's composition and boundaries should be defined in order to maximize shareholder value (and executive compensation) through legal debates and academic literatures in economics and management. As creating shareholder value came to be the dominant management mantra, companies kept selling off pieces of their operations in order to raise the stock market valuation of the parts that remained in the "core." This process led

to a massive reduction in the composition and size of the major corporations. Davis concluded:

> The new consensus around shareholder value made clear what the
> purpose of the corporation was, and this consensus had a decisive
> hand in shaping the transition of the American manufacturing econ-
> omy. Financial considerations—market valuation—would drive
> choices about the boundaries and strategy of the firm. Firms should
> focus on doing one thing well, and that one thing was often deter-
> mined by the stock market.[46]

The companies that emerged from this restructuring process in which
financial markets played so large a role had fewer employees, a narrower
scope of functions, a more concentrated focus on "core" specializations, and,
most important, an asset-light structure in which manufacturing facilities
were seen as drags on the stock market's evaluation of the company's worth.

What made it possible for companies to shed their in-house manufacturing were new options: first, digital technologies that allowed firms to
outsource production to subcontractors but still have a high degree of
control over product and quality; and, second, newly available pools of
semiskilled and skilled workers in low-wage countries like Hungary,
Poland, Mexico, and China. In the first stages, in the mid-1990s, digitization allowed engineers to start sending more or less complete files of
instructions to their subcontractors' CAD-CAM machines. Of course,
outsourcing and offshoring had been going on well before the Internet
made it possible to transmit large digital files, but moving work out of the
United States had then required frequent, time-consuming, and expensive
travel by U.S. managers to oversee the work abroad.

Digitization made it far easier to separate product creation from
manufacturing. And technological advance continues at a rapid pace in
this domain. Angel Mendez, Cisco senior vice president for Cisco Transformation, told us recently:[47]

> The separation of R&D and manufacturing has today become possi-
> ble at a level not even conceivable five years ago. Progress in technol-
> ogy allows us to have people working anywhere collaborating. We no
> longer need to have them located in clusters or centers of excellence.
> We now have the ability to sense and monitor what's going on in our

suppliers at any place and any time. Most of this is based on sensors deployed locally, distributed control systems, and new middleware and encryption schemes that allow this to be done securely over the open Internet. ... In other words, not only do we monitor and control what's happening inside a factory, but we're also deeply into the supply chain feeding in and feeding out of the factory.

The possibilities of separating early stage R&D, design, and prototyping phases of production from manufacturing were augmented by the explosive growth of giant manufacturing contractors, companies like Flextronics and Jabil, and Taiwanese firms like Quanta, Foxconn, Pou Chen, and TSMC, who specialize in manufacturing. These manufacturing contractors are suppliers to the brand-name product design companies which continue to be called OEMs—original equipment manufacturers, even when they no longer are manufacturers at all.

As manufacturing moved out of the once vertically integrated companies to the contractors' plants, some of it stayed in the United States, but increasingly, it shifted to suppliers located in low-wage countries. The technologies that made fragmentation and modularity possible also made it possible to shift production just about anywhere in the world where there was a supply of workers and shop floor engineers with standard skills. The lure of cheap labor had enormous attractive power. With more experience, companies would begin to realize that labor was not as cheap as a simple reading of wage rates might suggest. Productivity was far lower in developing economies. What counts for the bottom line are unit labor costs—how many hours of labor it takes to make a product times the wage rate. Where productivity is low, even cheap labor can be very expensive. Shipping became a big item, even with low energy prices; delivery delays were costly. Exchange rate risk could be hedged—at a price. Even after great efforts, quality was variable. And protecting intellectual property was an enormous concern. Where intellectual property could not be "black-boxed," that is, made invisible to those who worked with it, companies locating in developing countries usually had to resign themselves to losing it. The weakness of legal enforcement together with the spread of information via high turnover of workers jumping from one employer to the next made it virtually impossible to keep trade secrets or even patents. "All ye who enter China, abandon all hope of intellectual property," one of our interviewees quipped, in a parody of Dante, but an accurate reprise of the common experience of firms that outsourced and offshored. Despite these problems, it has been only recently that companies are coming to have a more balanced view of labor costs and to recognize that they represent a relatively small fraction of the total cost equation for most operations. By now, however, the overseas contractors that are supplying manufacturing services have matured a wide range of capabilities that allow them to offer much beyond low-wage labor.

As the vertically integrated corporations reorganized themselves to focus on core competences, manufacturing facilities were among the activities that disappeared from within the four walls of the company, but production was not the only function that was radically transformed. Other shifts that accompanied the restructuring of corporations would also have major implications for American manufacturing: changes in where R&D was carried out; changes in who funded the scale-up of new products and processes from prototypes to market, and changes in who provided skills and training. Companies like DuPont, AT&T, GE, and Xerox had in the post-war years become major engines of research. There had always been tense debates within corporations about allocating resources between longer-term versus more applied, shorter-term research and between organizing research in central research laboratories versus locating it in product divisions. But for a time during the heyday of the vertically integrated corporation, it came to seem as if basic research was a strategy that would pay off.

DuPont, for example, until the 1920s, tended to acquire new technologies by buying other companies.[48] But as it became concerned about maintaining a competitive edge in its established lines of business and developing new products, DuPont started hiring researchers with more open-ended missions to explore the fundamental science underpinning DuPont's businesses. A 1927 Executive Committee approval of the chemical department director's proposal for hiring people for "pure science or fundamental research work" marked a new departure.[49] The number of research chemists and managers DuPont employed increased from 133 in 1922 to close to 1,300 in 1940 and 1,500 in 1942.[50] An exceptional series of discoveries in neoprene synthetic rubber and polymer research followed, with products like nylon, Orlon, Dacron, and Kevlar that became hugely profitable businesses for DuPont. Changes in the external environment also reinforced the wisdom of support for basic research within the company. The increase in antitrust investigations and prosecution under the Roosevelt administrations ruled out DuPont's old strategy of acquisition of technology through buying up companies in closely related fields and made it more than ever important to grow new businesses in-house.[51] And the war itself with its extraordinary demonstration of the power of science and technology gave support to the idea that investments in the lab could pay off rather rapidly in practical applications.

Research labs like DuPont's were created in a number of other major American corporations. The number of industrial research labs in U.S. corporations grew from four in 1890 to 1,030 in 1930.[52] One of those that would have great impact on the American economy, Bell Labs, was created by AT&T in 1925, shortly before the DuPont initiative,[53] and grew rapidly from the original core of about two thousand scientists and technicians. In contrast to DuPont, AT&T did not have competitive pressures to face or antitrust indictments to fear, at least in the short term, since the 1921 Willis–Graham Act had exempted the telephone business from antitrust regulation. But in many other respects, the underlying inspiration for setting up Bell Labs seemed to be the same as that motivating DuPont's 1927 initiative: the belief that fundamental open-ended research would eventually produce valuable commercial products. In the early years, Bell Labs did revolutionary work on vacuum-tube technology. In 1948 a set of fundamental discoveries in the amplification of current applied to germanium gave birth to the transistor. Other major innovations followed, in optical fibers, lasers, advances in information technology, communication satellites, cellular technology, innovations that like transistors were general-purpose technology platforms, innovations that would ripple through and transform multiple industries. Eleven Nobel Prizes would be granted for work carried out at Bell Labs; virtually all domains in modern information and communication technology depend in significant measure on discovery and invention from Bell Labs.

This extraordinary succession of scientific and engineering triumphs had enormous importance for the American economy, for many of the great new companies of the past thirty years have been built more or less directly out of Bell Labs' innovations. How much of this value AT&T and the local phone companies it owned were able to capture is quite another question. In the middle 1950s, however, it seemed as if basic research and commercial interest converged. As William H. Whyte, author of *The*

Organization Man, a widely read analysis of American companies in their glory days, commented: "If ever there were proof of the virtues of free research, General Electric and Bell Labs provide it. Consider three facts about them: (1) of all corporation research groups these two have been the two outstandingly profitable ones; (2) of all corporation research groups these two have consistently attracted the most brilliant men. Why? The third fact explains the other two. *Of all corporation research groups these two are precisely the two that believe in 'idle curiosity.'* "[54]

The R&D labs of American vertically integrated companies obviously differed along many dimensions—and perhaps most critically, with respect to the company's ability to appropriate the value of its scientific breakthroughs by developing them as products or processes that could be sold to customers. But there were broad-brush similarities that characterized the ways different vertically integrated companies scaled up their discoveries from R&D. These companies could fund development, demonstration, and full-scale manufacturing stages of a project from lab and prototype all the way to large-scale commercialization without having to seek outside finance. In the case of Bell Labs, AT&T's monopoly and the steady flow of revenue from the local phone companies made it possible to carry on work for years without having any returns.

In DuPont's case, even without a monopoly, ample corporate reserves permitted development work to take place over a long period before commercialization. It took DuPont ten years to develop Wallace H. Carothers's lab discoveries on long-chain molecules in 1930 into full-scale nylon production—first for nylon stockings in 1940. Orlon and Dacron were even longer and more costly to develop, because about a million pounds of each had to be produced to be tested by the company's customers before they could be put on the market.[55] More than fifteen years were required to work out how to incorporate the new fibers into tire cord. Despite the exceptional properties of Kevlar—described in 1980 by *Fortune* magazine as "a miracle in search of a market"—it took almost fifteen years to develop products and customers for it.[56] Amazingly, the company was willing to push forward with research and development of these new fibers—even though they killed off DuPont's old rayon and acetate businesses. Contrary to what we might expect for an established and entrenched market leader, it was the large corporation itself that introduced radically disruptive innovation, even at the cost of its prior investments. Finally, when the lengthy development processes had been completed, the corporation's funds, both its own cash reserves and what it raised in equity markets, financed the building of manufacturing plants from which the new products poured out into the market. The dilemma for today's start-up innovator of finding the funds and facilities to scale a product up to commercialization was basically a minor matter for the vertically integrated corporation.

It's hard to place a single date on the end of the great corporate R&D labs or to identify exactly the point at which companies decided to pare back their longer-term research. Some, like RCA Laboratories, which was responsible for color TV, the electron microscope, liquid crystal displays, and many of the other basic building blocks of modern consumer electronics, have disappeared. Others, like Xerox PARC, continue, but no longer carry out wide-ranging open-ended research, rather projects focused on specific commercial objectives. As in Tolstoy's unhappy families, each of these organizations seems to have entered into decline for quite different and specific reasons. But while there were particular triggering events in each company, viewed in retrospect, the common underlying causes were the changes in regulation and in corporate structures of the 1980s. Bell Labs faced far more active federal antitrust enforcement in the 1970s as the legitimacy of AT&T's monopoly eroded, and aggressive new telecommunication companies pressed the government to let them into the telephone market. The turning point was the 1982 settlement of the antitrust proceedings in which AT&T agreed to divest the local phone companies. The cash cows were now free to graze on their own turf.

Bell Labs continued quite successfully for a time, but as AT&T, now shorn of its monopoly and of its reliable customers and competing with sharp new rivals, began to stumble, funding for the labs dried up. Some of the researchers were attached to labs at the phone companies; others began to head out to more exciting places like Silicon Valley. By 2008 only four scientists working in basic physics were left. Most recently, in May 2012, Alcatel-Lucent, which had acquired Bell Labs along with other former AT&T assets, finally received local zoning permission to scrap the historic Bell Labs Holmdel facility and to build houses on the land there as a real estate development.[57] For DuPont, the turning point came earlier, in the seventies, when several of the new fiber programs failed to realize their promise and when the oil crisis triggered major cutbacks in funding. Today, DuPont still has a strong research program—but organized in ways radically different from the labs in the days of nylon.

What has become of the vertically integrated U.S. company today?

Today, many of the largest U.S. corporations have outsourced much of their manufacturing and moved operations abroad to reduce costs and to serve customers in large new markets. As the CEO of one of the Fortune 500 companies we interviewed told us: "Vertical integration is a trap. We started in the late 1990s by de-capitalizing ourselves and distinguishing among proprietary activities—those which are truly valuable; activities which might be valuable if at scale, but otherwise should be transferred to suppliers; and commodity products which should be shifted to suppliers. We've had no reason to reconsider these decisions. We can spend more on R&D and less on fixed capital." At the same time, this company, along with other global corporations, continues to rely heavily on American early-stage research to initiate the stream of innovations that flows into its new products and services. Some of that research is still carried out in-house, though far less than in the past. The fragmentation of functions as American vertically integrated enterprises restructured also involved greatly reducing in-house research capabilities.

Looking back at even the greatest of the research centers of the 1950s and 1960s, like Bell Labs or Xerox PARC, many of the corporate leaders we interviewed think that those engines of research did not actually contribute enough to the company's bottom line, so today's managers express few regrets about the shrinking of central research labs. At present, in a world with myriad opportunities for identifying and acquiring promising start-up companies, many of the corporate giants reckon that a strategy that mixes in-house research capabilities with acquisition of young innovative firms and licensed technology is the most productive approach. They see such a strategy as reducing risk and transferring a fraction of the upfront expenditures onto someone else's ledgers.[58]

A Booz & Company study of innovation by global companies found that the top 80 U.S. corporate R&D spenders were using slightly more than half their R&D funds in the United States.[59] But these figures do not include outlays on acquiring young innovative firms as part of R&D expenditures, although such acquisitions have today become a major vector for advancing new research within big companies. Research by Robert Hall and Susan Woodward on 22,000 VC-backed companies from 1987 to 2008 found that 26 percent of them were later acquired.[60]

The MIT PIE research on scaling up start-ups reported in chapter 3 also found large companies building their research portfolios through acquisitions. Such acquisitions cannot be chalked up entirely to R&D, since they often have multiple objectives: to get new technologies, but also to capture new market channels, to eliminate potential rivals, to recruit people with special expertise. Another gray area is the division of resources between R and D. There is no reliable way of figuring out what proportion of the R&D funds spent at home (in-house or for acquisitions) or abroad are used for generating early-stage, potentially game-changing, "R" as contrasted with possibly more pedestrian, localization "D." Looking at the numbers of patent applications filed in different countries cannot resolve the issue, since rates of patenting and the value of patents filed in different localities vary significantly.[61] American-based "R"—both that carried out in large companies and that carried out in innovative start-ups that may eventually be acquired by large companies—plays a far more significant role in catalyzing the disruptive emergence of new products and services in big companies than the overall figures on corporate R&D spending at home suggest.

We see investment in early-stage research in the United States by large corporations—either in-house or via their acquisitions of start-ups—as still strong, even after the massive corporate restructuring of the past three decades, but we know little about changes in how and where early-stage innovation is scaled up and commercialized. As we asked senior corporate managers to trace out the trajectory of some of their important new products from lab to market, we zeroed in from many angles on the key issues of the PIE research agenda: Do companies that are counting on U.S.-based innovation for their future streams of revenues need or use U.S.-based manufacturing to bring new products to market? What kinds of production do they use to bring ideas from new concepts in labs to prototypes to the stages of testing, demonstrations, pilot production, production for some early customers, and then to full-scale commercialization? Does proximity between researchers and manufacturing matter to whether or not the idea can actually be developed into a product on the market? Does it accelerate development? When large firms acquire start-up companies, how well do they integrate them? Does the innovative thrust of the small firm survive acquisition? What are the advantages and disadvantages of using overseas production capabilities for scale-up?

Finally, and critically, does having manufacturing nearby contribute in any way to sustaining innovative capabilities?

What we learned from the PIE research about these issues is the subject matter of chapters 3, 4, and 5 of this book, as we analyze the findings from the study of innovative start-ups, of Main Street manufacturers, and of U.S. firms contrasted with German and Chinese companies. But within the American economy, the great investors in R&D are still large companies. After thirty years of restructuring and massive shifts in the global economy, the once vertically integrated behemoths of the 1960s have become much leaner creatures. Large companies like Cisco that were newly created from the 1980s on were from their founding far more concentrated on "core competence" and less likely to use in-house manufacturing than the old vertically integrated firms had been. Today the pared-down vertically integrated firms that dominated the field in the 1960s as well as newcomers like Cisco and Qualcomm buy from suppliers much of what used to be produced in-house—from early-stage research to screws. Their decisions about commercializing innovation through production in the United States or offshoring that production are still prime drivers of the fate of the manufacturing economy.

To understand how those decisions are made, the PIE team carried out interviews in thirty large U.S.-based companies, ten of them figuring among the Fortune 100. We selected only companies that have significant manufacturing capabilities (in the United States and/or elsewhere). While in no way a random sample, they represented quite diverse industrial sectors: electronics, power generation equipment, consumer goods, pharmaceuticals and biotech, chemicals, autos and auto parts, metal fabricating, materials, aerospace, and defense. In many of them, it was an MIT connection—often an MIT alum—who paved the way to talking with top management about the sensitive issue of how decisions are made about which operations would be located in the United States and which would be moved or even initiated abroad. In these interviews, as in all the others reported in this book, we promised that we would publish nothing from the interviews that would identify the speaker or the company unless we had explicit authorization of the text.

There was general consensus across the senior executives that bringing new ideas through early stages of prototyping, testing, demonstration, and pilot production works most efficiently when it's kept close to key scientists and engineers within the company. As one manager expressed it: "It's in the transitions between stages that we crash and burn." These are operations that companies want to control closely, and control functions best within the four walls of the company or in partnerships with old and trusted suppliers and customers. Proximity is important not only for control and to avert disaster, but to accelerate time to market and to explore and develop multiple variants (and price points) of a new product.

Michael Idelchik is General Electric vice president for advanced technologies at GE Global Research, in Niskayuna, New York, the oldest central corporate R&D laboratory in the United States. General Electric remains one of the most diversified of the large American-based multinationals and one that retains significant manufacturing in-house, even as it has built production facilities and R&D labs outside the United States. While General Electric has retained far more of its integrated corporate structure than many of the other U.S. leading firms, it, too, has initiated profound changes in its structuring of connections between innovation and research. Idelchik explained to the PIE Commission that in the past, industrial R&D proceeded through distinct sequences moving from design innovation to materials selection to manufacturing and supply chain planning.[62] Today, he sees advanced industrial R&D as involving the management of concurrent, nonsequential interactions with multiple exchanges between scientists and engineers and manufacturing specialists and with the product passing back and forth between the hands of experts with fundamentally different competencies. Innovation in materials now can be the catalyst for new designs for manufacturing. He cited the example of GE's intermetallic turbine blades for the new GEnx engine. The new alloy was patented in 1989, but the complexities of working with this material meant it took until 1992 to be cast. The casting involved continuous interactions between manufacturing and R&D. There are patents on the blades, but most of the casting and the materials depend on trade secrets—yet another reason for keeping these exchanges in-house. The first engine test was in 1993—and this took collaboration between designers, R&D, and manufacturing. Finally in 2009 GEnx entered into service.

All of the thirty companies we interviewed have overseas operations and, within them, facilities identified by some kind of R&D designation. But the implicit division of labor between their R&D centers in advanced economies and those located in emerging economies often seems to follow a "defend-extend-create new-to-world" pattern articulated by Amir Aghdaei, the CEO of Tektronix, a test and measurement instruments company.[63] Tektronix is a $1 billion company in Beaverton, Oregon, with more than 4,000 employees. It has weathered a tough transition from being a 24,000-employee company—with the same annual revenues as in the 1980s. Today it's an operating company within Danaher Corporation.

As Aghdaei sees it, for the long tail of legacy product lines—some like the traditional oscilloscopes over a decade old—the key issue is defending the company's existing models by improving them and bringing down cost. The competitors are Asian; the new customers for these products are mainly in Asia; and more than half of the value of the components going into this oscilloscope (and other existing products like it) was coming from Asian suppliers, so Tektronix was paying to ship the components from Asia to Oregon and then to ship the finished goods back to Asia. Tektronix has now moved production and a portion of R&D for these "defend and maintain" product lines to Pudong, in Shanghai. But products where Tektronix seeks to "extend" the platform and repurpose its rich legacy capabilities in ASICS and applications for new products are ones that require being in the United States, close to its big civilian and military customers. A product like Tektronix's high-end sampling scope, used for test validation in design and manufacturing, has a limited list of key customers, themselves at the cutting edge of new technologies. Some of these customers like IBM are codevelopment partners. The R&D for entirely "new-to-world" products is done in Beaverton. The RF products will be manufactured in the United States because of proprietary components from U.S. suppliers. Products with complex manufacturing that's hard to stabilize are also made in Beaverton. But a new product like the mixed-domain oscilloscope that marshaled more than fifty Beaverton R&D engineers to develop will probably end up being manufactured in Pudong.

Like Tektronix's new oscilloscope, many of the new products from large companies will end up being manufactured far from the place where they were first created. The reasons for moving volume production to distant often foreign sites are multiple. Sometimes it is lower costs—cheap wages or low land prices or subsidies or tax credits in one or another form from foreign governments. Even among advanced industrial countries, costs vary significantly. Over the past decade, corporate taxes have been lowered in many of the OECD countries, while in the United States they have not come down.[64] In interviews carried out at the MIT Industrial Performance Center at the end of the 1990s, taxes virtually never came up as a factor determining industrial location. But in the PIE interviews of the past three years, U.S. corporate tax rates were frequently mentioned by senior executives of major American-headquartered multinationals as a reason for manufacturing outside the United States—in Europe as well as Asia. A senior executive at one multinational commented: "Labor and labor costs used to matter a lot, but they're less relevant now. Taxes matter more now."

Alexander Cutler, the CEO of Eaton, a power transmission equipment and solutions company with 103,000 employees, told us:

> For the United States to be competitive, the U.S. must embrace competitive corporate tax reform. One of the current problems remains uncertainty: you just don't know where it's going to end up. If you put a job in Canada, you know what their regulations and taxes will be. In the United States, there are competing philosophies in Washington, and rules can flip overnight. Global tax regimes have changed markedly from the 1990s, when U.S. corporate tax rates were competitive. Today the U.S. 35 percent statutory rate sticks out. We're now the highest since Germany and Japan have recently moved to reduce their statutory rates. Along with several small countries, we're the only large country trying to compete in a global economy with a territorial tax regime. We need to move to a 25 percent statutory rate (the OECD average) and adopt a territorial tax regime so that U.S.-headquartered companies can compete globally.[65]

PIE researchers interviewed Mr. Cutler on January 17, 2012, at Eaton Corporation's Cleveland, Ohio, headquarters. At the end of November 2012, Eaton Corporation acquired Cooper Industries, a power equipment company, in the biggest U.S. merger of 2012. The merger created a company called Eaton, with headquarters location in Dublin, Ireland. The corporate tax rate in Ireland is 12.5 percent.

As wages rise in low-cost Asian countries and with some form of corporate tax reform on the agenda in the United States, the cost advantages of foreign manufacturing environments may shrink. But those changes are unlikely to affect the weightiest of factors that our respondents cited in explaining why they carry manufacturing abroad: to gain access to large new customer markets. Sometimes access means simply physical access.

The transportation costs of heavy products like Procter & Gamble diapers or the ceramic beads (proppants) that Saint-Gobain makes for hydraulic fracturing operations virtually require that they be made close to the customers. For many of these products there is little or no localization of features for specific markets, and the manufacturing plant is constructed along the same principle as Intel's for its new plants: "copy exactly" the lay-out of the plants already in operation at the most advanced site. The availability (and transport costs) of raw materials also matters in separating manufacturing from the point of origin of the product.

But the role of large new customer markets in determining manufacturing location goes far beyond any cost calculation. It's explosive demand that compels companies to be present in countries like India, Brazil, and China. When China invests 46 percent of GDP a year in infrastructure, many multinationals need to be there to grow with longtime customers and suppliers—as well as with new Chinese customers. When suppliers and customers are increasingly concentrated in Asia, the round trip to bring Asian components to the United States, to assemble products here, and then to ship them back to Asia is just too lengthy and too expensive. Moreover, the new customers demand localization of production—sometimes, because they or their governments want technology transfer; sometimes because there are local conditions requiring special features.

Finally, and equally important, as we analyze in detail in chapter 5, companies are scaling up manufacturing and commercializing their production abroad because they are discovering capabilities in the foreign partners that are not available in the United States—or are no longer available in the U.S. industrial ecosystem. On the basis of extensive PIE interviewing in China and the United States of companies that are partnering in scaling up innovative products in China, we found that these capabilities are not simply production at low cost, but novel design, talented engineers, and the ability to marshal the efforts of multiple producers in a rich and dense local ecosystem in order to accelerate product introductions.

That large American corporations are transferring some of their production abroad to lower costs and reach new customers are topics now so much debated in the press as well as in the research on globalization that there were few surprises on that score in what we heard in PIE interviews. What was new for us, though, were some of the reasons that companies value keeping production in-house in the United States. We had of course foreseen some of the factors that the managers cited as determining domestic manufacturing. Defense contractors are required to manufacture in the United States, and export controls on advanced technology constrain offshoring even for some businesses with customers that are not primarily Department of Defense. We had also anticipated that companies might keep activities involving precious proprietary knowledge—both patent-protected and trade secrets—in-house within the United States, and this point came up often in the interviews as managers detailed which operations they had kept in-country and which they had moved offshore. Manufacturing of heavy, bulky items and manufacturing of products made in smaller batches to customer specifications—these all tend to remain domestic.

But the surprise that revised preconceptions that a number of us on the PIE team shared was learning how much innovation resides in the manufacturing process itself and makes it a source of value from which companies draw profit. A powerful example came from the biotech industry. John G. Cox, executive vice-president of pharmaceutical operations and technology at Biogen Idec, explained to the PIE researchers why Biogen Idec sees innovation in manufacturing as one of their core competences, along with cell culture, protein purification, and analytics (metabolomics).[66] Replicating laboratory results on a large scale in biotechnology involves extreme complexity in manufacturing. When production involves living organisms, in a sense each batch is unique. Improving titer ability, increasing yields, and raising output; moving a product from 2,000 liter tanks to 15,000 liter tanks, are all critical to profitability. Biogen Idec has commercial-scale production in three sites: Cambridge, Massachusetts; Research Triangle Park, Raleigh-Durham, North Carolina; and in Denmark. Tysabri is a drug for treating multiple sclerosis, and for some patients, the only one that averts serious relapses. Even to start new production facilities for making Tysabri in Denmark when Biogen Idec was already making it in North Carolina was challenging, and Biogen Idec stocked two years of inventory in case anything went wrong. Biotech is a highly regulated industry, and changes in manufacturing processes need approval by the Federal Drug Administration. When Tysabri was removed from the market because of dangerous and fatal complications in a subset of patients, Biogen Idec was able to work with the FDA on reintroducing the drug for those MS patients who need Tys-abri and on ways to monitor their health. Control over difficult-to-stabi-lize manufacturing processes and responsiveness to regulators and demand fluctuations are powerful factors working to keep production in-house even as some platform technologies emerge that enable the use of contract manufacturing in pharmaceuticals.

It was above all what we learned talking with senior managers about key decisions to keep some commodity production in-house that chal-lenges conventional thinking about manufacturing. Procter & Gamble is a global company that actively seeks to connect with resources outside its own four walls to grow its capabilities and expand its innovation opportu-nities. For example, in order to expand in biotech, green chemistry, and health care, they invested, along with other venture capital funds, in sev-eral start-ups. They also entered a joint venture with Teva Pharmaceuti-cals to market generic and over-the-counter drugs. But in making some of P&G's best-known products, like Gillette razor blades and Pampers dia-pers, P&G keeps much that might be considered commodity production in-house. The company recognizes there is valuable proprietary knowl-edge in the manufacturing processes that they do not want to lose.

Bruce Brown, P&G's chief technology officer, describes a key com-ponent of P&G's overall innovation capability as the ability to make something at low cost, high speed, and high quality. Diapers, for example, are made in thirteen to fifteen unit operations or modules connected in series. It's essential to maximize efficiency in each one of these modules as the efficiency of the system is the multiplicative effect of efficiency in each of the unit operations. R&D on diapers starts from simulation and mod-eling using a database from babies around the world. P&G partnered with Los Alamos National Laboratory on process development tools. Once the simulation works, they move to pilot production and usually do that in the R&D labs. Full-scale production testing takes place in their main U.S. production plants with testing in each of the fifteen modules involved in making a diaper. About 10 percent of a production plant's time is dedi-cated to new product development.

At companies like 3M, P&G, and others we visited, there are mixed strategies of locating manufacturing of new products in close proximity to the R&D product development centers still (in our sample, at least) pre-dominantly in the United States, together with locating new manufacturing facilities across the globe close to big new markets. The variants of integration and outsourcing and offshoring we observed in firms also extended back in the chain to their capital equipment. Few of these companies still build their own dedicated equipment; most end up buying machinery from the same suppliers and tweaking and customizing it. A senior executive at one of P&G's European competitors told us: "We get value out of controlling the whole span of production. You need to know the product in order to evolve it, and for this you need to be in manufacturing. For competitiveness, you need scale, and know-how." People in his company still long for the days when "real men made their own machines." But this has just become too costly. The problem is that when everyone buys equipment from the same suppliers, it can be handicapping if a supplier provides a new machine first to a competitor. So two years ago, this European firm entered a partnership with a machinery supplier, and hopes to be in on new machines earlier and thus gain market advantage. The old vertically integrated manufacturing firm may be an organization of the past, but the advantages of tight integration of functions along the path from innovation to the market still can play a critical role. What we found is much experimentation. No one best way.

3

Scaling Up Start-Ups to Market[1]

When new products and processes poured out of industrial research centers like those at DuPont and Bell Labs into the American economy, the challenges of finding the skills, capital, and facilities to scale these innovations up to mass production were met within the four walls of big companies.[2] Companies mostly used their own cash to finance scale-up. They drew on their own large employee pool for the necessary skills, and added training when new technologies required new capabilities. Careers in these companies were usually long, even lifetimes, and so over the years of an employee's tenure, a firm could recoup its outlays for upgrading an employee's skills. As for suppliers, in industrial communities with dense populations of small and medium-sized manufacturers, large companies usually did not have trouble locating contractors capable of making components for new products and processes.

When U.S. vertically integrated companies did have problems in scaling-up innovation, they stemmed not from lack of internal resources, but rather from failure to integrate these resources and to mobilize them efficiently for product introductions and mass markets.[3] In comparisons drawn between U.S. and Japanese corporations at the end of the 1980s, the inferior performance of U.S. companies often seemed to derive from poor communication and coordination between their R&D and design engineers, on one side of the company, and the manufacturing engineers responsible for making products, on the other. People described the R&D staff simply "tossing the designs over the transom" and then expecting the production engineers to be able to manufacture the products rapidly and at low cost. The remedies proposed at the time for the production failures and delays in bringing innovation to market were "re-engineering" and streamlining the corporation and building "cross-functional" teams to design for "manufacturability." So, for example, instead of designing a printer like Epson's with 120 parts, IBM engineers were encouraged to design a printer for manufacturability—with 60 parts.[4]

Today's scale-up challenges are in many ways very different from those of the 1980s, since they start from the scale and scope of the innovator's firm. New goods and services for sale at home and abroad now often have their origins in innovation coming from small companies, ones that lack the internal resources to bring their ideas to commercialization by themselves. Three big changes in the economy have been driving this shift in the origin of innovations in the United States from big company central research labs toward much smaller companies.

The first factor, as chapter 2 described, was a massive transformation of corporate structures over the past quarter century that resulted in narrowing and focusing big companies' range of activities and reducing expenditures regarded as peripheral to the firm's core competence. Resizing the corporation shrank early-stage research work and recentered American companies on core activities defined as ones in areas of current specialization and with prospects of near-term commercial success. Fred Block and Matthew Keller have identified one measure of the declining role of large corporations in producing significant innovations in the number of awards received in the *R&D 100* competition by new products and processes coming out of Fortune 500 companies over the years 1971 to 2006.[5] In the 1970s, the big company entries dominated the competition. By the end of the 1990s, the majority of the awards were won by much smaller companies that came out of university or federal research labs.

Next, as the internal sources of innovation dried up, large companies searched to find innovation outside their corporate walls and to buy it through licensing, mergers, and acquisitions.[6] When they looked around for external innovation, companies found a much richer array of possibilities than they had been able to access in the past. Changes in federal government research support and patenting policies now provided strong encouragement for university researchers to work on projects with potential commercial applications. The passage of the Bayh–Dole Patent and Trademarks Amendment Act of 1980 gave a big push in that direction, since it allowed universities and individual researchers to gain from patents filed on work carried out with federal research funds.

Over more or less the same period, venture capital became a significant source of funding for new enterprises, so research coming out of laboratories could find early high-risk capital funding for launching start-up companies. (See figure 3.1.) From very small numbers in the 1970s, venture capital funding surged to close to 100 billion dollars in 2000 invested in 6,420 companies. As Josh Lerner, a Harvard Business School professor and expert on venture capital, has pointed out, though, venture capital over the years became strongly concentrated in sectors like information technology, computers, and telecommunications, where the scale-up of firms typically took place over a relatively short period—three to five years.[7] In areas like materials and energy—where firms take much longer to develop commercializable products and processes—VC investment has not done so well, and venture capitalists have pulled back recently in these areas.

The blossoming of new populations of innovative start-ups gave large companies the opportunity to identify promising candidates, buy them, and scale them up in-house. DuPont's early work on cellulosic ethanol incorporated some technology from the National Renewable Energy Lab in Colorado and, starting around 2003, benefited from a four-year grant totaling $20 million from the Department of Energy's Integrated Corn Biorefinery project. DuPont coinvested a "much larger amount" alongside the grant. In 2010, DuPont began operating a demonstration-scale plant in Louden, Tennessee, with financial support from the state of Tennessee, and with technical collaboration with Genera Energy, a start-up spun out of the University of Tennessee. In December 2012 DuPont broke ground on the first commercial-scale plant in Nevada, Iowa.[8]

In organic light-emitting diodes, DuPont in 2000 acquired Uniax, a start-up spun out of Professor Alan Heeger's laboratory at the University of California Santa Barbara.[9] DuPont continued to develop the technology in Santa Barbara and Delaware. In late 2011, DuPont announced the first commercialization project, under license to a major display manufacturer. DuPont also purchased Innovalight, a Silicon Valley start-up with a silicon ink process for printing solar cells that had received $6.4 million in U.S. Department of Energy funding and had figured in *R&D Magazine*'s top 100 innovations list in 2011.[10] When purchased by DuPont, Innovalight already had major Chinese customers like JA Solar and Yingli Green,

Venture capital investment in the United States 1970–2010

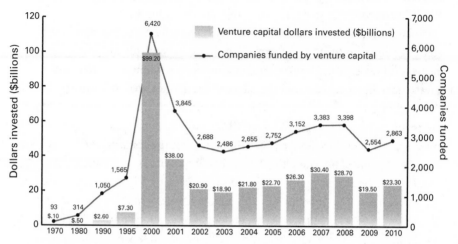

Venture capital investment by region 1970–2010

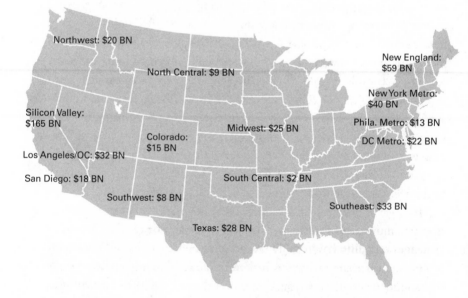

FIGURE 3.1

Venture capital investment in the United States, 1970–2010

Source: The Money Tree Report by PWC and NVCA based on data from Thomson
Reuters, National Venture Capital Association and IHS Global Insight, "Venture Impact:
The Economic Importance of Venture-Backed Companies to the U.S. Economy" (2011).

and these firms had made significant contributions to developing Innova-light's products.[11]

Over the past ten years, companies have also been experimenting with "open innovation" and crowd-sourcing as ways of accessing new technologies that need not be grown from start in-house.[12] There are a few frequently cited cases of big success like Linux and Wikipedia, in which online communities of individual innovators as well as well-established companies contributed knowledge that was freely shared. Just how productive these channels will be for developing proprietary goods and services is still an open question. As of 2009, most research funding (81 percent) in manufacturing still comes from companies' own funding; for outside funding, the principal source is the federal government.[13]

Third, the new digital technologies that transformed industrial possibilities from the 1990s on have also played a major role in shifting the origin of innovation from large companies to very small ones. These firms often grow out of university and government research laboratories or are founded by entrepreneurs who first work in and subsequently leave large established firms. These digital technologies enable small companies without a full panoply of their own production capabilities to draw on subcontractors and suppliers anywhere in the world for building products that the small company conceives and designs, even when the new company has none of the infrastructure or capital or skills to develop them for commercialization in the market. Viewed overall, this pattern has led to an enormous expansion of the possibilities for innovation—not only in advanced industrial countries, but in emerging economies as well, since these technological possibilities can be exploited by small newcomers, as well as by large established firms.

The little companies that have become drivers of innovation in emerging industries over the past twenty-five years face, however, a set of challenges very different from the ones that an AT&T or a DuPont or any other large vertically integrated corporation confronted in the past when these large firms were bringing their innovations to market. For the large corporation in the past, finding the capital and the skills and brick-and-mortar factories to scale-up production was a problem that could be solved within the four walls of the company and largely with internal resources.[14] For the small start-up today, finding these essential complements is an enormous and daunting task. The explosive growth of software and IT companies over the past quarter century has proved that for some industries at least the new model of venture capital funding of innovative start-ups that after a few years go public with sales of shares in the company in the stock market works well. The companies receive the high-risk capital they need in early years; the sums the investors need to raise are not enormous, because companies selling digital technologies can thrive without heavy investment in physical infrastructure; and the investors can exit after a few years with (potentially) high returns. The key question, though, is whether this model can work across the economy. Can it work for start-ups that take longer to develop their products, or require far larger sums of capital to fund building large production facilities, or have products like clean energy that will be purchased not by individual consumers and businesses, as software is, but by large entrenched entities like utilities?

Whether and when a start-up can acquire these resources, the price it has to pay for them, and where, geographically, it needs to go to get them—near home? Silicon Valley? China?—all these factors have a huge impact on the future of the company. In the PIE research, we have observed that for many of the companies where and how resources needed for scale-up were acquired determined the future trajectory of production at the company, with implications for future innovation. The course of an innovation in a company that grows through an IPO seems to vary from the course of an innovation in a company that is acquired or merged and varies also from the path of an innovation that is scaled up to mass commercialization by finding an Asian partner for production. These divergent trajectories produce new companies, new jobs and new streams of revenue in different localities. Depending on the path that is taken to bring an idea into full-scale production, we are likely to find quite different short- and long-term winners. That is why understanding and mastering scale-up is so important for the future of economic growth in the United States.

This is a complex issue to study. At any particular moment, we can calculate, approximately at least, what share of the profits, what share of the jobs, and what share of the wages accrue to each of the actors joined in long supply chains through analysis of the kind that Linden, Kraemer, and Dedrick have conducted for Apple's iPods, iPhone, and iPads.[15] But there is no exact way of calculating how the learning and mastery of technology of each of the partners in the chain will position them for strength in future rounds of innovation and execution. By strength we mean developing capabilities and products that others have difficulty in replicating and that therefore command higher returns in profits and wages. We need to understand better the multiple pathways that innovative companies follow to scale production if we are interested in better outcomes for firms and society in terms of jobs, investment and innovation.

The MIT PIE study of scaling up innovative companies

In order to examine more systematically how and where start-ups find the inputs they need to bring new products and processes to market, a team of PIE researchers focused on a population of companies close to home, ones that had licensed technologies from MIT over the years 1997 to 2008. The MIT Technology Licensing Office (TLO) mission is to license inventions from MIT laboratories to companies that will translate them into products and services, and in this activity, it has been among the most successful of bridging agents in American academia for moving research into private industry. In 2011, for example, the TLO registered 694 invention disclosures, filed 305 patents, had 199 U.S. patents issued, and facilitated the start-up of 16 companies (with a minimum of $500,000 in initial capital) out of MIT patents or licenses. The numbers launched out of the TLO vary of course from year to year, so the PIE team studied a population of firms initiated over a ten-year-plus period including both boom and bust times for high-tech companies.

During this period, 189 companies started with technology licensed from MIT patents.[16] The researchers set aside the pure software start-ups and zeroed in on companies that were engaged in some form of production, leaving 150 firms.[17] These firms seemed to provide a more challenging test of the possibilities for scaling an idea from a small firm, since scaling a product takes more time and is more capital-intensive than building a software company. This focus on innovative production-oriented companies was chosen in order to examine in close detail the process through which innovations demanding complex production capabilities are scaled and to identify the critical inputs needed to grow these companies.

Why this case matters

The sample set of MIT consists of start-ups that are exceptionally well positioned to succeed, because they emerge from very strong research laboratories, because they take their first steps in the world in an extremely dynamic regional hub of innovation with many complementary resources in close proximity, and because they have far better access to venture capital than do firms in much of the rest of the country. This is, then, a critical case in the sense that the deck is stacked in favor of finding winners. At those points in the scale-up process where these firms, even with all their relative advantages, find serious difficulties in obtaining the inputs they need for getting their products into the hands of customers, we can certainly anticipate that the "average" American new firm based on innovative technologies will also be having trouble. Of course, there are many reasons firms might have trouble finding the resources for scale-up, which could relate to the market or competitive landscape in which they are entering, or indeed to the company's product or internal operations or strategy. The point is only that the firms in this MIT sample are likely to have the wind at their backs as they start out.

The greater Boston area is widely recognized as one of the most robust economic regions in the United States. Based in Cambridge, Massachusetts, MIT has a long history of successful technology commercialization. In a recent study using a direct extrapolation of survey data, Edward Roberts and Charles Eesley estimated that active firms founded by MIT alumni employ 3.3 million people and have global annual revenue of $2 trillion, equivalent to the GDP of the eleventh largest economy in the world.[18] Given the historic role of MIT and Boston in successfully commercializing new ideas (Boston is continually ranked among the top innovation hubs in the country[19]), if any firms can successfully scale novel technology, firms within our sample set should be among those most likely to do so. Likewise, if firms in this sample set, with all these resources available, encounter significant challenges in reaching scale, we could predict that those start-ups not located in a robust region nor affiliated with an elite university might face even greater challenges.

The time frame of 1997–2008 allows us to look at companies formed roughly five to fifteen years ago. While in some industries like social media, innovation cycles are extremely short and firms can grow from lab to market place in a matter of five years or even less, firms scaling novel technology in which production plays a critical role may take ten years or more to bring a product to market. The biopharmaceutical industry falls into this category, as do semiconductors. A five to fifteen-year time period in the life cycle of a new company covers the stages after a company has taken an innovation from lab to start-up and focuses on the stage in which the company builds a prototype and in some cases a pilot facility and tries to find "early adopters" for the technology. For the older companies, many will have entered into a mass production stage in which a product is commercially produced and brought to market.

The MIT sample covers a range of industries, technologies, and stages in development of the companies. It thus offers a broad angle of vision onto the dynamics of growth in innovative companies. In particular, following the growth patterns of these start-up companies allows us to track closely the relationship between innovation and production, a relationship often presumed to exist but usually not documented. The case studies explore the role of process innovation in the development of new products and the connections between innovation in production and product introductions. These cases reveal significant diversity in the pathways along which companies advance in later stages of scale-up—ranging from going public, to being acquired, to engaging strategic partners. Finally, our analysis of this sample sheds light on the strengths and weaknesses of the industrial ecosystem both regional and national for nurturing innovative firms that make products.

Sample characteristics

As seen in table 3.1, of the 150 production companies, 59 percent are still active as independent firms while another 21 percent were acquired and 20 percent were closed. This survival rate is 1.5 times higher than Robert Hall and Susan Woodward find in a recent national study of venture backed start-up firms.[20] Firms in the biopharmaceutical and medical device industries make up 60 percent of the sample while semiconductor and electronics firms make up an additional 17 percent. Thirty-seven percent of the firms received Small Business Innovation Research (SBIR) funding in their early stage of growth, while 55 percent have reported

TABLE 3.1
MIT TLO licensed start-ups 1997–2008*

Industry	# of firms started	Percent of total	Percent receiving SBIR	Percent receiving venture capital*	Percent operating^	Percent closed	Percent merged
Advanced materials and energy	15	10	40	33	73	27	0
Biopharma	58	39	36	59	55	26	19
Medical devices	31	21	39	52	65	3	32
Robotics	5	3	60	0	60	20	20
Semiconductors and electronics	26	17	31	85	62	19	19
Other	15	10	33	33	47	27	27
All production companies	150	100	37	55	59	20	21

*Reported by VentureXpert

^As of June 2012

receiving venture capital funds.[21] Geographically, 63 percent of the sample firms are headquartered in Massachusetts, 15 percent in California, and the balance spread across the country. Only 3 percent are based overseas.

As the firms matured, however, we observed increasingly their funding and activities took place overseas. As of 2012, only 13 of the 52 firms that remained independent have generated more than $10 million in revenue after ten years from founding.[22] The lack of revenue at this stage of firm growth should not be surprising, particularly in industries with long development cycles.

Financing the scale-up of innovative firms

Because of the absence of significant revenue for the majority of firms and the importance of early-stage financing to the success of these firms, we analyzed available financing data to better understand how firms finance their technology development and commercialization efforts. Using the VentureXpert database, we identified 82 (of the 150 production) start-ups in our sample as having received high-risk capital (venture or corporate). These 82 firms had raised a total of $4.7 billion, of which 71 percent came from venture capital and 12 percent from corporate investors. Some firms have raised significant capital. Of the 82 firms for which we have data, 33 firms raised over $50 million and of these, 18 firms raised over $100 million in investments, which suggests a strong market belief in the technology they are developing.

Fifty-seven percent of the firms in our sample were still raising capital beyond the fifth year from founding. Of these firms, 39 percent were still raising funds after the seventh year, and 15 firms or 17 percent of the sample were able to raise high-risk capital ten years after founding. Notwithstanding this long-term capital horizon, we still found few firms that had reached commercial production. The ability of this group of firms to raise significant risk capital over an extended period—even without significant revenue—may demonstrate the potential of these elite university start-ups. It also suggests that the conventional wisdom on the need of venture investors to exit within five to seven years may need qualification.

Consistent with recent trends, almost half of the venture-backed firms received a financial investment from at least one corporate investor in addition to venture capital. While strategic corporate investors represented only 8 percent of total funds raised by biopharmaceutical firms (of $1.7 billion), they represented triple the amount or 21 percent of total investment ($1.1 billion) in semiconductor firms. While bringing in strategic investors is one pathway to raising significant funds for scale-up, another is to sell shares to the public through an initial public offering. Only nine firms or 11 percent of the 82 followed this path. Of these nine, eight were in the biopharma or medical device industries (the exception was a battery manufacturer), which might explain the smaller percentage of funding from strategic investments. As is evident, these firms have had little trouble raising significant amounts of capital.

Selecting firms for interviews

To better understand how firms choose strategies in scaling novel technology, we interviewed senior managers at seventeen firms. Given that firms must signal continued progress to potential investors even before they have the possibility of generating significant revenue, we looked for firms that had received in excess of $50 million in high-risk capital as a proxy for continued market potential. Interviews typically lasted between one and three hours in length. Not surprisingly, these highly innovative firms are predominantly located in high-skill, technology-leading regions in the United States. Of the seventeen firms in which we conducted were headquartered interviews, sixteen firms were headquartered in either Boston (seven) or the San Francisco/Silicon Valley region (nine); one firm was in Berlin, Germany.

These cases reveal significant diversity in the pathways along which firms advance in later stages of scale-up—ranging from going public, to engaging strategic partners, to potentially being acquired. Finally, our analysis of this sample sheds light on the strengths and weaknesses of the industrial ecosystem both regional and national for nurturing innovative firms that make products.

Findings: The innovation ecosystem

The following outlines our key findings in two primary areas: what firms need from the ecosystem in which they are located and how they finance their growth in their first years of scale-up.

1. Talent and skills

Rapid access to diverse talent is the critical input for all of these firms, particularly in the early stages of growth. It is at this point when iterations between lab and production are taking place that roadblocks in developing the technology might appear, and new strategic directions might evolve based on what can and cannot be done with the technology. "High-intellect" talent, as described by one semiconductor executive, is essential at this stage—representing 70 percent of the budget in one firm's estimation. Firms locate where they can find a diverse and specialized set of skills that often crosses disciplines, overlapping, for example, material science, mechanical engineering, and biology. The ability for rapid hiring is important. One firm hired 25 people almost overnight as equipment engineers, process engineers, device engineers, and a MEMS (microelectromechanical systems) device team.

This need to draw from a diverse set of skills—primarily from engineering—and to hire a workforce in a relatively short period of time drives these firms to locate near educational institutions with strong track records for graduating well-trained engineers, and in regions with reservoirs of engineering talent from previous rounds of industrial creation. This was apparent with all of the semiconductor companies we interviewed on both the east and west coasts; so too with the biopharma firms we interviewed, where the hiring crosses disciplines such as chemical engineering, biology, and chemistry and benefits from a thirty year industrial history of generating new capabilities.

A significant number of the companies we interviewed believed that finding the right talent and capabilities is more of an issue in later stage scale-up, as these firms begin to think about and engage in commercial production. Even when these firms could find the skills they required during the initial phases of scale-up, they could not locate people with these skills in the numbers they need when the firm expands rapidly: "In certain industries, a whole generation of engineers is missing," the CEO of one nanotechnology firm told us. The American workers employed in his firm, both in its own small fabrication shops and in the workplaces of its strategic partners, are on average 50 years old. There is a concern about where the next generation of workers will come from.

2. Network nodes

The importance of connecting start-up firms to networks of capital, human resources, potential strategic partners, and early adopters and customers has been well documented. In the small, innovative firms we studied, we usually found that there was at least one individual playing a critical role in the initial formation of the firm as well as in "networking" the firm to resources, talent, and partners. Such individuals, who have deep industry knowledge and experience, as well as strong local networks, are especially important at three stages in the firm's development;

In the formation of the firm   In several cases, a venture capitalist or "technologist" sees the potential for a certain technology and pools the IP from across different universities. He then brings together the initial team to launch a business around a particular technology;

Once the firm is formed   The key node might be a person who is intimately connected to a particular industry (semiconductors, biotech) and can make important introductions to potential funders or partners;

In the early stages of scale-up   As the firm decides how to integrate its technology into incumbent systems, the key node is represented by seasoned industry executives who have deep knowledge of the prevailing industry production architecture, how new technology can be incorporated into it, and what facilities are better suited for introducing such technology.

In the first case, the individual acts as a "visionary" who understands the potential of a type of technology and assembles the right intellectual property and team to help build a firm. In one medical device company case, this involved assembling IP from five different universities and funding a team that would ultimately build a billion-dollar firm. Once a firm is formed, within each industry there are several "go to" people who have worked in an industry for years, participated in building several firms, and achieved great respect in both the national industry network and a regional innovation network (for example, Silicon Valley). These individuals guide firms as they test the market viability of their technology and help to identify the most appropriate capital providers. In one case, this key person arranged to have a major potential customer from Asia come to MIT to see the prototype.

Based on the potential customer's enthusiasm for the product, the team went forward, created the firm, and began hiring a team and raising money. At this stage, key individuals were retired production executives of large integrated petrochemical firms who understood which plants had the managerial and technical ability to successfully integrate a new technology. They also could bring in experienced production engineers on an as-needed basis to ensure that the technology could be inserted into existing larger production lines, without the sort of disruptions that have scuttled other previous projects.

Our sample firms' ability to access networks through these individuals appear integral to their success. While not limited by geography, these networks are often geographically mediated and encourage firms to locate in places where there are dense networks within their specific industry.

3. Depth and breadth of suppliers

While these firms draw on a wide talent pool, they are also drawing on a range of suppliers for certain products, services, and skills. The complexity of the engineering and manufacturing that these firms are engaged in is high. One medical device firm that has successfully scaled production has a product with 10,000 components and 300 suppliers of custom pieces, 65 percent of which are provided by local suppliers in its area. As the firms start out, they are more concerned with speed and quality over cost. As such, being located near a strong supplier base that can turn around product very quickly is a priority.

Initial prototypes often come out of the university lab in rough form and need iteration, either within a lab setting, or in partnership with suppliers. This process can be time-consuming and labor-intensive but must emphasize speed and quality. Thus, companies like to have their suppliers near at hand. In the case of one east coast semiconductor company, the loss of control and time that came with working with a third-party fabricator in the United States pushed them to build their own fabrication shop. They did not consider going offshore because of the expense both in time and money of transferring people and technology—as long as 18 months to transfer the process offshore and to set up a new line of production. It took a full two years to get their prototype to be a fully functioning product, but they benefited from the proximity of talent and suppliers nearby.

In the case of another semiconductor equipment firm on the west coast, they built a prototype in four months and then iterated on it every six months for three years before they were ready to ship product to a potential customer. This is consistent with other semiconductor firms located in the Silicon Valley area. These firms could find a relatively strong supply chain in semiconductors. One firm described how they kept eight machine shops busy for two weeks at full capacity getting a "system" ready to ship to a potential customer.

But not all the needs of the new firm can be satisfied by the capabilities of the nearby suppliers. One Silicon Valley firm in advanced materials found a supplier in Ohio with a long legacy of coating film with whom it could develop its prototype and scale pilot production. The firm was very responsive but not qualified to build the product at scale. They now manufacture their product at scale in South Korea.

When the PIE Commission met with entrepreneurs who had started companies in Massachusetts, those leaders also emphasized how important finding the right suppliers had been to their success. The importance to the innovator of locating a supplier with the right specialized skills came up again and again in the interviews. In a number of cases, founders relocated companies in order to be close to the suppliers they needed. Kiva Systems, for example, makes systems combining hardware and software for automated materials handling in order fulfillment warehouses. It uses inventory storage pods, mobile-robotic drive units, control software, and operators in pack stations. As Mick Mountz, the founder of the company, described it, the innovation effectively turned material handling in a fulfillment center into a software and algorithms problem assisted by mobile robots carrying out the physical inventory movements.[23] By automating many of the steps involved in "pick, pack, and ship" operations, and moving goods around to workers instead of having workers walk through warehouses to find objects, Kiva speeds up order processing and cuts down unit labor costs. Founded in 2003, Kiva grew rapidly. In March 2012, the company was acquired by Amazon for $775 million.

As Mountz described the early days of the company, the first challenge was to get a proof of concept system up and running in twelve months with $1.6 million in angel funding. In order to get the engineering talent he needed, Mountz moved the company from San Francisco to Boston in 2004. The East Coast venture capitalists were more open to supporting hardware development than the West Coast venture capitalists had been. And—equally important—Mountz found a full range of manufacturers in New England that could supply the gearboxes, motors, plastics, castings, wire harnesses, and machine parts needed to build the robots. He hunted for a machine shop that could make a complex lifter screw for the robotic drive unit. This consists of an inner and outer pair with a precision-machined ball race that accepts a set of nylon ball bearings. The screw was the key to how Kiva would swivel-lift the shelving pods off the ground. The Kiva hardware team found Demusz Manufacturing, a 40-year-old family-owned precision machining shop in East Hartford, Connecticut, as uniquely qualified to create those parts.

As in many of the contract manufacturers that we studied, the state-of-the-art equipment and capabilities of Demusz have been honed over years of learning how to fill orders requiring the machining of complex precision components for the aerospace, aviation, and defense industries.

4. Financing and capabilities in later-stage development

As outlined above, the sample of MIT start-ups was able to raise significant amounts of risk capital over extended periods of time. However, as they moved into pilot and demonstration phases of their technology, they needed a new influx of significant capital to finish codifying their technology processes and bring products to commercial scale. Traditional venture capitalists, having invested in the earlier stages of the company, are not typically funding at this stage and at these levels (anywhere from $15 to $40 million) so these companies must look elsewhere for funding. We found that at this "inflection band," often the money comes from corporate investors (multinationals) or national investment funds of emerging or developing countries. We refer to this as an inflection band rather than a point because this period of time, when companies are iterating as they learn how to scale their technology for commercial production, can take several years. Both the need for additional financing as well as production capabilities at scale lead companies to seek partnerships to help them at this critical stage of scale-up.

Several examples highlight the challenges companies face at this stage. In one case, an advanced materials firm that had withdrawn an earlier IPO received a $30 million investment from an Asian multinational firm twelve years after founding. At this stage, "venture investors [in the firm] look for certainty; they are willing to trade upside for certainty. The investors understood the possibility of acquisition by a foreign firm when they took the money [from the Asian multinational firm] in the last round."[24]

In another case, the CEO of an advanced materials company said, "The VC model does not work for manufacturing companies. VCs cannot make any money on something that costs $100 million and takes at least 10 years to build. The technological risk is high and there is a high burn rate. They are much more comfortable with a software deal that will cost them $20 million. They have to pull away at what is a critical time for the company—just as [the company] is trying to finalize the product and get it ready for commercial production ... eventually people won't start companies like this because they can't get financing." Ultimately, the company raised $40 million from an emerging economy government investment fund with a quid pro quo that some R&D and manufacturing would be set up in that country.

One alternative path was taken by those firms that went public. A senior manager at one firm, an integrated surgical device manufacturer, stated that having the money from an IPO allowed them to get through an extended stretch to develop their technology for the market, after they had consumed most of the $125 million they had raised in venture funds. The tendency of the board was to sell the firm. One of our respondents said: "98 percent of the conversations in Silicon Valley are around an M & A exit, not an IPO."[25] The surgical device firm remained independent, however, which may be the result of a product that fell "in a crack" between the diagnostics and interventional equipment industries as well as the determination of management to resist the board of directors' desire to sell.

Life sciences as an industry seems to offer public exits. Eight out of the nine firms in the TLO sample that went public were in the life sciences sector. These companies benefited from an IPO, raising capital that has helped fund their long development cycles. For these firms, the complexity of the early stage scale-up of their products and the close interface with R&D teams leads them to develop capabilities in-house, even while they might work with a contract manufacturer on clinical production.

Case studies

The following brief case studies focus on several examples of highly advanced manufacturing and the pathways companies have followed to scale their production. All of these companies have several factors in common—complex technologies, longer development cycles (over five years), and significant capital requirements. The cases provide a window into the strengths and limitations of the U.S. innovation ecosystem for scaling production companies.

Company A

Company A is a semiconductor equipment company founded in 2007. The company moved to Silicon Valley to be close to the large semiconductor cluster located there. The company has benefited from its proximity both to strong universities as well as a good supplier network of machine shops that can quickly ramp up and turn around new prototypes.

The company has scaled quickly, raising over $75 million in five years. The company understood early on that the complexity of their product would require raising capital in this range and would take at least five to seven years. As a result, they sought out investors who would understand this and stick with the company over time. Strategic partners have not played such an important role on the financing side, but more on the technology development and evaluation side, providing knowledge and expertise in helping to scale the technology.

There are only ten customers in the world for the kind of product Company A makes and five of them (the most important) are all in Asia. Volume is low for these high-margin systems and commercial production would represent approximately 100 units a year. Because of the significant scale and cost of taking the product from prototype to pilot (approximately $30 million to build the pilot plant, $150 million to build a commercial production facility) and the benefits of iterating during scale-up in proximity to the customer, Company A is partnering with potential customers who are paying to be "early adopters" and help develop and evaluate the technology during a demonstration phase. While the first machines will be made in California to perfect the process and keep some production close to R&D, they expect to build a pilot plant closer to the customer because of the lower costs. A commercial plant would also most likely be in Asia where customers might insist they locate production. Subcomponents can be made anywhere and contract manufacturers are everywhere, so the location of the commercial production is not dependent on proximity to any particular skill. They could potentially keep production in California and do the final assembly and testing closer to customers, but this seemed unlikely.

Company A would like to stay independent and potentially go public, as they see a very profitable market for their product.

Company B

Company B is an advanced materials company working in nanotechnology. Put together by a "visionary" who sought out a network of researchers in this field and pooled their research through license agreements, the company was founded in 2000 in Boston and moved soon after to Silicon Valley. The company has 100 patents. It currently has 100 employees, a third of whom have graduate degrees.

Unlike the life sciences, nanotechnology does not have a "big win." Markets are smaller and more specific and there have not been any big "home runs." For many years, the company survived on research funding from the Department of Defense and private companies as it searched for profitable applications of its technology. The company has developed multiple products and continues to develop new ones in conjunction with one of their strategic partners. For their primary products, they develop the prototype and do pilot production in rented space in a machine shop in the Midwest. Once they had the product to scale, they moved production to South Korea where there is established expertise in production at scale. All of the customers for their primary product are in Asia.

In terms of financing and future directions for the company, relatively early in its growth (within four years), the company attempted to go public, but the offering was withdrawn because of a lack of confidence in the application of the technology. The company went on to raise over $100 million in the past 12 years, approximately a third from strategic partners based both in the United States and in Asia. The company expects it will most likely be acquired, by either its U.S. or Asian strategic partner, which they believe is the most appropriate strategy. In recent years, IPOs have not been particularly successful for nanotech companies (most of them trading down) and an acquisition provides certainty to investors. Scale issues would also disappear by their being acquired by a large multinational. "There are very few benefits to staying independent," said one of the senior executives.

Company C

Company C is a biopharmaceuticals company founded in 2001 in Boston that is working to develop drugs for the generics, biosimilar, and novel biotech drug markets. Unlike many biotech start-ups, this company had a successful product early on that has helped fuel its growth. This allowed the company to go public within several years of founding, again helping to fund their drug pipeline development.

Like many small biotech companies, they have overseen the production of their successful drug during the early stages of lab-scale production at the pilot phase, pre-GMP (Good Manufacturing Processes) when the process needs FDA approval. The company designs and controls the biomanufacturing process, but outsources the actual production to a contract manufacturing organization (CMO). Using the supply chain of one of their multinational partners, with whom they partnered to take advantage of their marketing and distribution channels, they source the raw material from China, purify the product in Europe, manufacture it in the Northeast in the United States at a CMO, and "package" it for distribution at a fill/finish facility in Chicago. They have built up a substantial manufacturing team in-house from nothing, and now 80 of the 170 people in the firm are working on the early-stage production of their other drug candidates. This emphasis on having in-house manufacturing expertise, even while they are contracting out some production, is indicative of the complexity of the product.

The biomanufacturing process is integral to the development of a new drug, particularly in the early stages of scaling the drug for pilot and clinical production and often necessitates close proximity between the R&D team and the bioprocessing team. Because of the complexity and critical nature of the product, biopharma companies prefer to have control over the most important aspects of the process, overseeing the design and quality assurance and quality control in the early stages. Most small biopharma companies will use CMOs to develop their drug during the clinical trial stages because of the costs for a small start-up of setting up a GMP facility. If a drug is successful, the company may consider developing capacity internally to bring the drug in-house to maintain control and reduce the timelines and costs associated with contracting out. In the case of a very successful drug—a blockbuster—companies often move much of the commercial production offshore to tax-advantaged locations.

In Company C's case, the CEO believes advances in biomanufacturing technology, with the development of more flexible, lower-cost processes in the form of disposable technologies, will make the biomanufacturing process more accessible to more companies and encourage more companies to keep control of their manufacturing in-house. Interviews conducted with other biopharma start-ups confirmed this possible direction. Company C intends at this point to build manufacturing capability internally.

Company D

Company D is a biopharmaceutical equipment company based on technology from advanced materials and biology. The company was founded in 1999, is based in San Francisco, and employs close to 200 people. The product is a consumable, and thus needs to be produced at high volume and low cost.

Company D developed a platform technology used in biotech and medical research. The company had a challenging time scaling the technology and spent several years demonstrating what it could do and finding the right application for it. Four years into development, their prototypes were not working because they could not manufacture them within tolerance. Early on, the company focused on figuring out how to scale and manufacture the product because they saw this as part of their core competency and their desire to build a stand-alone company. "If you want a stand-alone company, you need to think about scale," said the CEO. "If you are building a company to sell it, manufacturing can be the acquirer's problem."

While the company had a lab in San Francisco, they needed to develop expertise to scale the production, which led the company to Asia where they found the skills they needed (drawing from those trained in the semiconductor industry) as well as significant government incentives to locate the production there, including tens of millions of dollars to build a plant. The company would have liked to manufacture in the Bay area but they couldn't do so at an affordable level. For example, a plastic part they need that involved high-end molding cost $30–$40 in the United States and had a yield rate of 10 percent. In Asia, the same part was made for $3 and their yield was 75 percent. Manufacturing skills in the United States were either highly specialized or it was too expensive to hire those with diverse skills. In their fields, there is a 30 percent difference between the cost of highly skilled workers in the United States compared to Asia and wage costs differ by a factor of two or three for technicians.

Financing began with important angel and venture capital investors. The company did not attract strategic partners, who found the technology too risky to invest in, with an unclear application. Large companies tried to acquire the company several times but management declined, instead focusing on building the company. The company tried to go public in the fall of 2008 but the financial crisis made them withdraw until a few years later. The desire from the outset was to build a stand-alone company. The company continues to grow. Like many U.S. companies, its R&D team is based in the United States (San Francisco), while its production is in Asia.

While only five of the companies we interviewed had made the leap into commercial production, all of them talked about their plans to scale and, with a few exceptions, many of them anticipate doing this outside of the United States. The companies that were most likely to keep their production in the United States as they scaled up were mainly in the life sciences (biotech and medical devices). For this sector, the complexity, regulatory concerns, changes on the horizon in technology, and the rise of more personalized medicine and niche markets, make it more desirable, even necessary, to be conducting commercial production within the United States.

These case studies show a variety of innovative start-ups that are engaged in highly advanced production processes. Because of the complexity, it takes years and significant capital (always longer and more expensive than the CEO originally believed) to bring a product to market, in most cases, before the company has seen any revenue. And while these companies have all developed the initial technology in the United States at the prototype and even pilot stage, in almost all cases, the costs and skills required for later-stage scale-up tend to lead companies abroad, whether it is through strategic investors who are also potential customers, grants and investments from other countries, or the skills and supply chains that exist in manufacturing abroad.

Conclusion

The findings discussed above paint a picture of a very robust regional innovation ecosystem for new firms that are in their early stages of development. These firms find advanced skills across a wide range of disciplines, suppliers that can help them iterate prototypes, networks that can provide contacts with both funders and potential customers, and, most important, early-stage capital to support the firm's growth. This ecosystem helps incubate the early development of the technology and allow the firms to focus on quality and speed to market.

However, these small firms are rarely able to scale without partners. Except for one company that went public and has been highly successful, all of the companies we interviewed had multinational partners for a number of reasons, such as financing, scaling capabilities, lead customers, and major suppliers. Whereas large, vertically integrated firms of the past kept all firm activities within their boundaries, the emergence of the high-tech entrepreneurial firm has created a new model for innovation in which these firms, trying to both scale novel technologies and enter the global marketplace, must seek out partners.

The nature of the U.S. innovation ecosystem for this type of firm, in terms of venture financing, demand from growing markets and customers overseas, and the lack of capabilities for scaling production in the United States creates momentum for these companies to continue their development offshore at a critical point in their scale-up process. The aggressive pull of emerging economies seeking to build capabilities in advanced technology reinforces this behavior. Of course, in a global marketplace, we would not expect all investment and all parts of a supply chain to be located within the United States. But it is the crucial point in these firms' development that raises concerns about important capabilities migrating offshore.

The knowledge in firms at this critical point is mainly tacit or at best loosely codified. In our sample, firms are trying to demonstrate viability of their product while also building it at scale. The two activities are inseparable—as people say of bioprocessing—"The process *is* the product." This process by which the technology is scaled from pilot to commercial production creates opportunities for learning by building. When this learning takes place outside the United States it is likely to lead to the generation of new or enhanced innovation ecosystems outside the United

States. The consequences of this are evident—greater knowledge generated overseas of critical production capabilities that lead to greater capabilities upstream abroad.

It is possible to look even more deeply into this issue, as Erica Fuchs and her colleagues at Carnegie Mellon University have, with an analysis of the divergent R&D trajectories of U.S. optoelectronics firms after some of these companies moved production offshore.[26] Within a few years, they found sharp divergences between the technological paths of those who remained or emerged within the United States and those who had moved either assembly or fabrication and assembly offshore. The new optoelectronics technologies that integrated function on a single chip flourished only in the firms that operated in the United States, while those that had moved offshore tended to work on optimizing the model of the standard discrete chip technology.

While some might argue that the iterative process of innovation that we describe is not critical to the United States as long as the country continues to drive the idea generation and early stage research and development, we believe this is a mistaken view of the risks and stakes involved. The transfer or sharing of this advanced knowledge across national borders, knowledge that often took years to develop, risks the potential loss of the national competitive advantage these capabilities have created in three ways. First, the loss of this learning by doing deprives the country's innovation ecosystem of new learning and thus reduces the accumulation of knowledge and capabilities, ultimately diminishing the potential for future and as yet unknown innovation. The "industrial commons"[27] is made poorer for it. Second, as we have seen in other industries, loss of learning by building tends to shift the center of gravity for established and new industries away from the country, with implications for future industry growth. Finally, it limits the benefits the country could gain from the economic growth generated by the downstream activities these firms will create with scaled production in terms of investments and jobs.

Many of these companies have benefited from U.S. R&D programs, research grants, shared production facilities, or preferential tax treatment. Should the country develop policies that raise the likelihood that these investments will pay off in the long run?

4
Main Street Manufacturers and Innovation

To see what innovation does for the United States, most of us look to Silicon Valley, Seattle, Cambridge, Massachusetts, Research Triangle in North Carolina, or Austin, Texas. These are meccas of high technology creation, the hometowns of Microsoft, Apple, Biogen, Google, and Amazon. In close proximity to them are many other new companies that glitter in the constellation of America's latest industries. How does the light radiating from these stars reach across the country? In one recent analysis, that of Berkeley economist Enrico Moretti, it is innovation in these high-tech clusters that creates new zones of growth, wealth, and prosperity.[1] Throughout much of the rest of the country, wherever mid-tech manufacturing dominates regional economies, Moretti and others who share his views see stagnation, low wages, and unemployment. He calls the geographic patterns three Americas: an America of the brain hubs, like Seattle; an America of declining, decaying cities that once led the country in physical goods production, like Detroit, Flint, and Cleveland; and an America of places in between. In this chapter we look at the places in between, and at the innovative potential of Main Street manufacturers located in those regions.

Moretti maps the great innovation hubs in the country by tracing out the geographic concentration of patenting and finds an extraordinary clustering of patent-holders in cities like Seattle, San Diego, and San Francisco and Boston on the coasts and a few clusters in the middle of the country in places like Austin, Texas. As he describes it (figure 4.1): "The map shows a cluster of intense innovative activity (the dark areas) surrounded by an ocean with almost no innovative activity (the light gray and white areas). The states that generate the most patents are California,

New York, Texas, and Washington, with California producing the greatest number and with New York a distant second."[2] These locations attract college-educated workers in disproportionate numbers. The concentration of skilled and creative people within close geographic proximity creates an environment in which start-ups flourish. The more skilled people there are in town, the better the matches in the labor market between jobs and talents, and out of this fit grows even greater creativity and productivity. The salaries people in these cities earn are far higher than those in the rest of the country—even multiples greater than for people in the same occupations but who live elsewhere in the country. By a diverse set of social criteria, too, like schooling, lower crime rates, and lower divorce rates, these look like great places to live. Spillover effects of this virtuous circle of innovation and growth accrue even to less well educated workers in those cities, because their services can be better utilized and rewarded.

As Moretti shows, these great innovation hubs rarely have been created by deliberate decisions or policies. Even though these cities end up with more educated people, more cultural institutions, and greater social

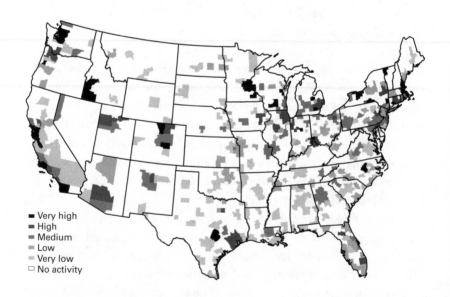

FIGURE 4.1
Great innovation hubs
Source: Moretti, *The New Geography of Jobs,* p. 84.

amenities, simply pouring those resources into a city does not create the desired effect. Moretti's key story is about Microsoft and Seattle, and he uses it to demonstrate the almost accidental way in which Microsoft located in Seattle and Seattle took off.[3] Bill Gates and Paul Allen started Microsoft in Albuquerque, New Mexico. The company was growing well. Both Gates and Allen came from Seattle, and they decided to return there and bring the company along. In 1979, when they moved back to Seattle, Seattle and Albuquerque were cities with almost identical demographic and economic profiles. Seattle had only 5 percent more college-educated workers, relative to population, than Albuquerque; today, Seattle has 45 percent more college-educated workers than Albuquerque, and on almost every other dimension, it is doing far better.

Innovation in Main Street manufacturing

Moretti's analysis left us wondering, though, what the rest of the United States might do better to promote innovation to drive growth and good job creation. What is the potential for innovation outside the brain hubs? This question matters for at least two important reasons. First, only a small fraction of the American population lives and works in those booming cities, and if we follow Moretti's line of reasoning, we have to recognize that we do not know how to create de novo more Seattles. If we are concerned to maintain and improve the standard of living of the majority of Americans, we need to look beyond the Bostons and Seattles and consider how the water level of innovation and growth could be raised elsewhere. Second, if we are concerned with the overall rate of growth in the American economy, we need to look well beyond the R&D intensive, high-tech manufacturing industries, which have much higher rates of product and process innovation and much higher rates of growth than non-high-tech manufacturing.[4] (See table 4.1.) But the high-tech industries account for only 21 percent of U.S. manufacturing.[5] If it were possible to increase the potential for innovation and growth in the rest of manufacturing, there could be big gains for the economy.[6] While the output of U.S. high-tech manufacturing is still the largest in the world and accounted for $390 billion of global value added in high-tech manufacturing in 2010, the U.S. share of this world market declined, from 34

TABLE 4.1

Relationship between R&D intensity and real output growth in manufacturing
Source: Gregory Tassey presentation to PIE Commission (September 12, 2012),
calculations based on data from the NSF, *Science and Engineering Indicators*, 2010,
appendix table 4-14, and US Bureau of Labor Statistics for real output.

Industry (NAICS Code)	Avg. R&D intensity, 1999–2007	Percent change in real output, 2000–07	Percent change in real output, 2000–09
R&D Intensive:			
Pharmaceuticals (3254)	10.5	17.9	4.9
Semiconductors (3344)	10.1	17.0	1.1
Medical equipment (3391)	7.5	34.6	39.5
Computers (3341)	6.1	109.9	147.0
Communications equip (3342)	13.0	−40.0	−59.7
	Group Avg: 9.5	Group Avg: 27.9	Group Avg: 26.6
Non-R&D Intensive:			
Basic chemicals (3251)	2.2	25.6	−7.8
Machinery (333)	3.8	2.3	−22.4
Electrical equipment (335)	2.5	−13.4	−33.4
Plastics & rubber (326)	2.3	−5.2	−28.0
Fabricated metals (332)	1.4	2.6	−23.6
	Group Avg: 2.5	Group Avg: 2.4	Group Avg: −23.1

percent in 1998 to 28 percent in 2010, as others like China pushed ahead into this market segment.[7] In contrast, rather surprisingly, U.S. medium-low-tech manufacturing industries (like rubber, plastic, and metals), which produced $3.0 trillion global value added in 2010, have almost held their own in global markets over the period 1995–2010, falling by only 1 percent, to a global market share of 18 percent.[8]

High-tech manufacturing companies may be the soaring towers of the cathedral, but the medium-low-tech firms that account for almost eight times more value added in production certainly look like the weight-bearing foundations of the economy. So it is not just a question of how to make more American manufacturing into high-tech manufacturing, but of how to make more American manufacturing at all levels of technology more productive. That's why we need to figure out how to raise the level of innovations of all kinds—product, process, repurposing, business model, incremental, or radical—in these companies and how to increase the likelihood that the necessary inputs—like skilled labor, capital, and suppliers—will be available to these firms as they try to commercialize their ideas. As we started the MIT research on innovation and production, we realized how little is known about the kinds of innovation that emerge outside the high-tech sectors—that is, in most of manufacturing. And we know even less about how manufacturers bring those new products and processes to commercialization.

To recognize innovation, we usually look, as Moretti did, for intellectual property protected by a patent. Patents may be the gold standard of innovation, but if we use them as the sole measure, we risk missing much of the contribution of small and medium-sized manufacturing companies to transformation and growth of the economy. In the solid core of U.S. small and medium-sized manufacturers, patents are not common. Getting a patent is expensive; protecting it in court can be prohibitively expensive for a small company. From the interviews we learned that even when they have patents, most established small and medium-sized manufacturers do not rely on them as key elements in their business strategies. Indeed, a number of the companies explained to us that patents can be dangerous, for they may reveal too much of your hand to your competitors. They told us that trade secrets that they jealously guard against all outsider eyes and tacit knowledge that resides in hands-on experience and practice in the company are their real competitive assets.

Even in the interviews with small high-tech firms—all firms that originated from patents—we heard that patents can be a double-edged sword. Not only may they show too much about the company's secrets; even the shadow of doubt about the origin of a company's new products can lead to suits. One founder CEO claimed he no longer read the literature on patent filings in his specialty in order to pre-empt any future charge that he might be intentionally intruding on others' territory. We did hear a few tales of small firms triumphing in suits against patent infringers. For example, Medinol, an Israeli medical device start-up firm, whose founders had been MIT graduate students, won a $750 million payout from Boston Scientific, and that sum funded much of Medinol's subsequent development of heart stents.[9] The litigation went on for five years. It's a great story of David winning out against Goliath, but we wondered how many small-business owners would have had the relentless drive and willingness to risk all that Kobi Richter—Medinol's founder, a former Israeli ace airforce pilot—did to pursue the suit so long.

As for R&D, only rarely do the novel activities in the well-established small and medium-sized manufacturers correspond to the OECD's *Frascati Manual* and "Oslo" definitions of "research and development" as "creative work undertaken on a systematic basis in order to increase the stock of knowledge, including knowledge of man, culture and society, and the use of this stock of knowledge to devise new applications."[10] Indeed many of the manufacturers told us at the start of the interview that while they were willing to answer our questions and proud to walk us through their plants, they did not think their experiences were relevant to our research on innovation and production. In one way or another, many of them echoed the sentiments of a CEO who, in response to our inquiry about how he brought new ideas along through development into the market, said: "No, no, we don't do R&D; we're just a machine shop. We're just metal benders." Daniel Berry, the head of MAGNET, the Ohio program for supporting manufacturing, told us that so many people in its target audience see innovation as a "loaded term"—something expensive that happens only in a lab—that MAGNET now substitutes for "innovation" the phrase "making a unique and distinctive product."[11] Viewed through the lens of these definitions—patenting and expenditure on activities clearly identifiable as R&D—many successful small and medium-sized American manufacturers appear to receive the same verdict as that pronounced by the report of the 2012 Advanced Manufacturing Partnership on the 300,000 average manufacturing companies in this country: that they are "outside the American innovation system."[12]

That's not what we found in the PIE research. By digging deep in the experience of the Main Street manufacturing companies and tracing out the relationships between them and the firms to which they supply components and services, we discovered quite a different story. Many of these manufacturing firms *are* integral to the American innovation system—just not in ways that can always be systematically registered in patent filings.

Basically, what makes R&D and patents valuable is the creation of "unique and distinctive" products and processes that are difficult to copy. What's new becomes the source of value and profit for the innovator only if others cannot quickly replicate it. A patent makes it harder to copy an innovation, for to the inherent difficulty of figuring out how to repeat someone else's discovery it adds the daunting hurdle of legal protection. But while a patent is a definable and marketable source of value, it is not the only important barrier to extraction of value in the form of profit and wages from new ideas. Indeed, economists increasingly recognize that innovation involves long sequences in which many inputs that may not be counted as R&D contribute to the emergence of new products and processes.

The ability to protect and capitalize on new ideas for a product or a process or improvements on old ones depends not only on the intrinsic value of the concepts (as embodied perhaps in the value of a patent) but also on mastering the capabilities for developing them. The difficulties of replicating the capabilities for development are an integral part of the process of extracting and protecting value in the form of profit and wages. In firms that have significant in-house manufacturing we could track the creation of these capabilities as new products moved back and forth between the designers and the production engineers. At Festo, for example, a German company that makes components for automation systems and develops automation "solutions" bundling customized hardware and software, we saw how innovation and the capabilities for developing it into a marketable product could be joined in a single firm.[13] Festo has 2.1 billion euros a year in turnover and 15,500 employees world-wide. Typical of Festo projects are a robot that picks up and places a solar cell on a module after testing it for purity and a robot for a pharmaceutical company that fills vials with medication. We visited Festo's experimental "ramp-up plant," where we saw workers trying to assemble new products in the middle of the floor. Around the sides of the plant floor were seated the quality and test engineers. When workers came up against problems in assembling the new product, they walked over to the quality and test engineers and tried to solve the problem. If they could not, they brought in (from an adjacent building) the design engineer responsible for the project. There are 1,000 design engineers on site (and 400 elsewhere in the world in Festo facilities). The design engineer is personally responsible for each of his projects and for seeing it through until it works. This "ramp-up" phase goes far beyond prototyping into pilot and mass production. Once all the hitches in producing the product have been solved through these iterations, the product is ready to be transferred to a regular Festo production facility—somewhere else, possibly not in Germany.

As we discovered in many of the interviews, though, value grows not only out of the stand-alone capabilities of individual firms like Festo, but also out of the combinations of capabilities that emerge from repeated interactions and reiterated experiences of joint problem-solving among multiple parties. When firms are able to combine their capabilities with others over a number of product generations, they become more efficient in new product introductions. They also become more capable of warding off competitors, who cannot easily step into the longstanding relationship or quickly replicate it. The repeat collaborations that emerge out of combining capabilities thus come to be effective barriers to a rival newcomer's entry into a market segment—arguably as powerful as patents. Firms do not necessarily even need explicit advanced arrangements for collaboration in order to gain the benefits of the complementary capabilities that others provide, though joint planning may well facilitate matters.

Geographic proximity makes it easier for resilient combinations of capabilities to emerge and persist. The Italian industrial districts specializing in such sectors as ceramics, packaging machines, apparel, textiles, and eyeglasses represent highly developed forms of this phenomenon. The industrial district is a local labor market with higher-than-average manufacturing employment in one sector. By this definition, there were about 240 of these districts in Italy in the 1990s. Research carried out by the Bank of Italy showed that a firm located within one of them was likely to have higher productivity and profitability than a matched firm that was in the same industry but located outside a district.[14]

The superior performance of these firms seems to come from colocation. It helps the innovator to work through problems that take special skill sets, unfamiliar equipment, and different kinds of experience if she can find a machine shop nearby that has made components similar to the ones she thinks will be needed for the new product. As the entrepreneur and the supplier go back and forth in each other's shops, handling each other's drawings and mock-ups and early prototypes and watching early models come off the line, tacit knowledge from each side gets exchanged, which enhances each party's capabilities. As we heard from the company founders in many of the interviews, being across the street, or in the lab across the way, or just a short drive away from suppliers was critical during the early years in which they were moving their idea toward a prototype and into pilot production.

Studies of the industrial districts and clusters both in the United States and abroad leave many important questions unanswered about the impact of having industrial activities in the same sectors located in close geographic proximity. There is a recent large-scale data analysis of clusters that suggests strong positive effects for productivity, profitability, employment, new enterprise formation, and innovation. In a July 2012 National Bureau of Economic Research working paper, Mercedes Delgado, Michael Porter, and Scott Stern present results of a systematic examination of performance metrics from clusters across the United States that produce traded goods and services.[15] The findings indicate that even beyond the spillovers that one might expect from having specialized producers and suppliers located in close proximity, there are greater gains from having regional groupings that include a wider set of complementary industries. The researchers illustrate the point with a contrast between Raleigh-Durham and Greenville, North Carolina. Both localities are specialized in the pharmaceuticals industry. Raleigh-Durham, however, also has related industries like medical devices and a number of universities and community colleges with research and education programs. As a consequence, employment growth in the industry in Raleigh-Durham has far outstripped that in Greenville.[16]

The overall findings of the Delgado–Porter–Stern research show that it is the interdependencies among complementary activities, not narrowly specialized clusters, that produce higher rates of growth and job creation, and they do so across a broad range of industries, not just in high-tech or manufacturing. In the PIE interviews, researchers observed that the complements entrepreneurs found locally had often been deployed in the past in quite different sectors than the ones in which they would be put to use by today's innovators. For example, the semiconductor equipment cluster on the North Shore of Massachusetts could hardly have emerged without the precision machinists who had originally been employed by the United Shoe Machinery Company, a firm in Beverly, Massachusetts, that once had had 4,000 workers. Like the vertically integrated companies described in chapter 2, United Shoe Machinery had a wide range of functions within its four walls, including divisions that acquired and produced raw materials for making its machines and divisions that serviced the machines that they leased to shoe manufacturers. United Shoe Machinery ran a vocational school for training its mechanics. From the fifties on, as the shoe industry declined, the company branched out into making other kinds of equipment, including equipment for plastics and electronics. The company was bought up and finally disappeared in the eighties. But workers who had been trained in it went on to work for other companies and also to open their own machine shops. These are the firms we found that today produce components for new companies like Varian, Brooks, and Axcellis.

There's no longer a shoe industry of any importance in the region, but the human and material resources it once created now support new industrial activities. Conversely, where old capabilities have died or migrated, it may be difficult to build new industries. When the consumer electronics industry moved off shore, U.S. battery makers had no incentive to upgrade their capabilities to making rechargeable batteries. So today, when radically new batteries are being developed by start-up firms, the newcomers cannot find the suppliers and partners they need to develop the new business within the United States. Discovering the importance of industrial legacies in the emergence of new sectors obviously does not mean that old industries should be protected and preserved in the hope that someday something new might grow out of them. It may suggest, though, that public policies focus on enhancing and extending capabilities already present in a region, rather than trying to build new clusters from scratch

Offshoring and outsourcing over the past decade raise the question of whether today physical propinquity may be less important than in the past in building collaborations to scale up innovation. As local industrial ecosystems in the United States have thinned out and capabilities have disappeared, we have seen managers looking abroad to find the necessary complements to allow them to develop new products. In chapter 5, we will present some of these new relationships between U.S. innovators in the energy industry and Chinese suppliers who work together on scaling the U.S. innovation to market. Drawings get sent over the Internet; Mechanical Turk finds helpers; companies send engineers abroad to work with suppliers. In analyzing these new relationships that involve coordination of the inputs needed to bring a product to market, we ask some of the same questions we posed in the industrial districts: Does the combination of capabilities through cooperation bolster an individual manufacturing firm's ability to realize value from its capabilities? Does colocation matter—or could the same collaboration take place at a distance? Does colocation make the new creation more difficult for others to emulate, and thus ward off competition? And to those old questions we added new ones: How do relationships between innovators and suppliers and manufacturers evolve over time when the actors are located in different countries? When more of the capabilities that the innovator needs to access are located abroad, do returns on innovation remain as high as before? Will innovative activities shift abroad to follow the capabilities to commercialize them? Before turning to patterns of collaboration, though, let us start with the actors.

Bringing innovation to market in Main Street manufacturing

Some of the small and medium-sized manufacturers we visited are clearly innovators in their own right, turning out new products, new processes, and new services that they sell to a diverse set of customers. Combining new services and solutions with "hardware" is a strong trend in many of these firms. Other firms' chief innovative activities can best be described as repurposing: taking products and processes from one industry or specialization and figuring out how to translate them for new uses, as Medinol, the Israeli medical device company, did when its founder saw that the lithography processes used in etching silicon wafers could be used for making heart stents on flat metal sheets that would then be rolled into tubes. In that case, repurposing gave rise to new patents. But much valuable repurposing does not.

Other Main Street manufacturers *enable* innovation by selling critical prototyping, manufacturing, and services to customers—whether fledgling start-ups or large companies or confirmed fast track innovators—who do not know how to do these things or cannot afford to do them on their own or are organizations that have downsized their own workforce and no longer have these capabilities within their four walls. Often these services and products are honed and redesigned through repeated exchanges among engineers, technicians, and workers in the customer's facilities or at the supplier's plant, in which case being a manufacturer located in close proximity to an innovator is important.

In order to understand the full range of innovation in manufacturing—from manufacturers who in their own plants produce novel products, processes, and services; to repurposers; to those who excel at blending manufacturing and services; to ones who enable the innovation of others—all usually unknown to official innovation statistics—we identified a particular group of manufacturers and visited their plants to ask them about recent innovations. We targeted manufacturing companies (with one or more plants) with revenues that had doubled over the period 2004–2008 and with employment numbers that had also grown. The names and addresses of these manufacturers were extracted from the population of 350,000 American companies in all sectors "whose sales have at least doubled over a four-year period and which have an employment growth qualifier of two or more over the same period."[17] The identification and designation of these "high-impact companies" was the work of Spencer L. Tracy, Jr., at the Corporate Research Board, in a contract for the Small Business Administration.[18] He provided PIE with a list of all the manufacturing companies out of the population he identified as "high-impact" firms, that is, all the firms with North American Industry Classification System (NAICS, or "nakes") codes corresponding to manufacturing that had doubled their revenues and increased employment in the years 2004 to 2008.

From that list, we extracted the names of all 3,596 manufacturers with one or more plants, more than $5 million in annual revenues, and more than 20 employees. By Tracy's calculations, each of them had doubled its revenues and headcounts between 2004 and 2008. Since these are private companies—many of them family-held businesses—we had no reliable way of verifying Tracy's claim about their vital statistics. When we tried to check these facts with the CEOs we interviewed, many of them were rather vague on financial details. In part this may have been due to the reluctance of private companies to share financial information. But in many cases we realized that they actually did not know. (The lack of good financial data was particularly evident at another point in the interviews: when the companies tried to explain how they figured out costs and priced new products and services. The most common answer was: whatever the market will bear.) These are not very big companies, since very big companies rarely double their revenues over four-year periods; and they are not start-ups, because to be on the list at all they had to have been in Dun and Bradstreet books for quite a while longer than any-thing qualifying as a start-up. They have higher than average revenue per employee (for their industry sectors). They are also companies that man-aged better than most to survive the 2008–2010 economic crisis. In the interviews we learned that many had had what they termed "near-death" experiences in 2009. Thirty-nine of them have disappeared since 2008; the current status of another hundred is unclear.[19]

Tracy considers these firms as successes. For the purposes of the PIE research on innovation and manufacturing, it was not so much "success" we sought but a clear indication that the firms we studied would be, at a minimum, viable, not moribund. We wanted to conduct our study in firms that were in shape potentially to seek out new opportunities. We have taken this pool state by state, and in four states thus far—Massachu-setts, Ohio, Arizona, and Georgia—have been interviewing owners and managers and walking through their plants with them. Fifty-three of the small and medium-sized manufacturers we visited came from the pool of 3,596. The firms we interviewed were quite representative of the numbers of firms in the total population of "viable" manufacturers.

TABLE 4.2
Firms in dataset and firms interviewed

Manufacturing industry (according to NAICS category)	Interviewed firms (in percent)	All firms in dataset (in percent)
Chemical products	7.4	5.9
Computer and electronic products	11.1	9.1
Electrical equipment	5.6	4.7
Fabricated metal products	31.5	17.5
Furniture	1.9	3.0
Medical equipment and supplies	5.6	2.2
Nonmetallic mineral products	1.9	2.8
Plastics and rubber products	16.7	5.1
Machinery	18.5	12.0

To those Main Street manufacturers that came from the Tracy list we added another 43 companies in the same sectors that we discovered as suppliers to some of our cutting-edge innovators. In the analysis, we have called them all "Main Street companies."

In each of the interviews with these Main Street firms, we made the same requests and asked the same questions: tell us about two or three new ideas—new products, new processes, improvements on old products or processes—that you have tried to bring to market over the past five years. What have you done to try to move it from an idea into the market? Where do you find the right skills, capital, suppliers, and expertise that enable you to scale that innovation up to market? Where are the obstacles? What would it take to expand your ability to develop new products? Where do you locate the production, and why? National Science Foundation statistics state that in 2006–2008, 22 percent of all U.S. manufacturing firms reported "a new or significantly improved product, service or process," but beyond those working with patents, we do not really know what they are doing or how they are doing it. With the interviews we have carried out in these 21st-century "Main Street companies" we hoped to see inside the black box of American manufacturing innovation.

Innovators in their own plants

When we started studying the manufacturing companies that had doubled sales between 2004 and 2008, we had no idea whether any of them had patentable innovations. In contrast, in the "scale-up" research, we started with companies that had grown up out of patents (see chapter 3). But among the "Main Street" companies we interviewed, we did find some remarkable innovators in the familiar form of companies created on the basis of new knowledge and patents. One was QD Vision, in Lexington, Massachusetts, practically in the back yard of Edward Steinfeld, one of the PIE faculty researchers.[20] When Steinfeld met with Jason Carlson, the president and CEO, he learned that the company grew out of research by two MIT professors, Vladimir Bulovic and Moungi Bawendi, pioneers in "quantum dot" nanotechnology. QD Vision produces nanomaterial that has special light-emitting properties. It is produced in a process similar to one used by pharmaceutical companies in chemical synthesis batch manufacturing. The quantum dots can be embedded in a glass substrate, and when used with LEDs they can down-convert the color of the light to produce better color performance. When used as a component in flat-panel displays, it greatly enhances color and clarity.[21] QD Vision has nine patents with another 120 pending, and it has received about $55 million in venture capital funding. QD Vision has 74 employees, more than half of them with masters and doctoral degrees.

For a business like QD Vision to grow, Carlson reflected, it needs to provide an essential and differentiating component to customers that are market leaders in large markets. The goal is to create consumer awareness similar to "Intel inside" for big electronics companies like LG, Samsung, and Sony. Carlson felt that in the electronics industry it is difficult to achieve a balance between having your own manufacturing facilities and an integrated production system—with very high capital costs—on the one hand and giving up all manufacturing capacity and becoming dependent on outsourcing production to manufacturers like Taiwan Semiconductor Manufacturing Company (TSMC) on the other. The danger was that as one of TSMC's smaller customers you would always be at the end of the line in boom times. In a sense, the nature of QD Vision's product helped ease this trade-off, for it involves making very small amounts of substances that are inexpensive to ship because of their size, and both capital costs and labor costs can be reduced as volume increases, owing to the scalability of a batch process. The real challenge over time is continuing to innovate on the basic product and controlling the intellectual property.

QD Vision faced a more immediate challenge in its early years: to find suppliers with manufacturing expertise. It needed chemical and glass suppliers and experts with the kind of experience that could be found in the Massachusetts biotech industry. QD chemists first had to figure out how to produce the quantum dot liquid solution in experimental batches. Then they needed to learn how to produce it in much larger production batches—a step requiring complex research and intellectual property. Massachusetts suppliers have been important in helping QD Vision reach these benchmarks. It helped that some of them were nearby, allowing for faster collaboration.

As QD Vision builds out its full-scale production the face-to-face interaction with suppliers will be as critical as ever, but it is likely to have much more of an international footprint. The Massachusetts suppliers may not be big enough or low-cost enough once production builds out to full commercialization. QD Vision has already partnered with a contract manufacturer in Taiwan capable of incorporating the quantum dot nano-material produced in Lexington into a glass optic. There are no contract manufacturers with that experience in the United States because there's no high-volume display industry here. QD Vision is already working on the next generation of quantum dot products called QLEDs, and as this work continues, more may shift to Asia as QD Vision is likely to enter into strategic partnership with one of the leading flat-panel display companies located there. But whatever the future development of the company, a key lesson from its history is that in the long stretch between the lab and market, local suppliers can aid in the early development phase of bringing the product to market.

Another of the promising and innovative companies we visited may have to move offshore—not for lack of potential customers in the United States, but because its access to retail channels is blocked by large established brands. The story of MicroBlend, a company that fell into our Arizona sample of manufacturers, starts from an inventor, Danny McClain, whom his colleagues remember as a "true genius."[22] MicroBlend is in Gilbert, Arizona, but aside from the location of its founder, we could see no local origins; it looks like a company that could have started anywhere. MicroBlend began from McClain's 1998 invention of a system to produce paints in ten different types, and in any amount, from a compact unit occupying much less space than the long aisles that latex paints fill in a typical hardware store or Home Depot or Walmart or Lowe's.

The MicroBlend unit connects six tanks of architectural "pre-paints," which get combined with a tint when a customer chooses from a menu of colors and paint qualities. The customer touches a computer screen and then collects his paint by placing a bucket under a nozzle dispenser. Knowing how to keep the pre-paints homogeneous is MicroBlend's "pixie dust," as Mel Sauder, the CEO, calls it. In the model they propose, MicroBlend would own the equipment it places in retail stores. Sensors would monitor the level of product in the tanks, and MicroBlend would replenish supplies as needed. This is truly a game-changing technology and business model.

One great advantage of the MicroBlend system is its small footprint: about 100 square feet in a store as contrasted with the 3,000 square feet of water-based latex paints in an average Home Depot. It would also greatly reduce shipping costs, since only the pre-paints would be moved around, and not a large and bulky cargo of paint cans. There would be more choice for a consumer, both of product and of the minimum quantity of product that the consumer has to buy. It would reduce inventory costs for the retailer, since MicroBlend would manage inventory, with sensors in the tanks monitoring the paint levels and signaling when replenishment was needed.

MicroBlend has fourteen patents on the process, the hardware, and the business model. They told us that there's much beyond what you can learn from their patents to making the system work, and while Micro-Blend has gone to court at great expense to protect its patents, it also tries as much as possible to keep the key processes a trade secret. The first prototype was built out of an old refrigerator; they have brought in suppliers to help fund building subsequent versions. As MicroBlend has moved from "innovation for innovation's sake" to scale-up, it recruited a chief operating officer whose previous experience was at Fuji Film, rolling out digital printing operations at Walmart and other major retailers. Despite the scarcity of venture capitalists in Gilbert, Arizona, and its distance from the venture capital communities of the two coasts, MicroBlend has managed to raise more than $40 million to fund its development.

MicroBlend has had successful pilot runs in big-box stores, Sauder claimed, and there are real chances for adoption. But the huge problem the company has experienced in the United States and has not been able to solve is pushback from established paint brands that in several instances, according to Sauder, have threatened to pull their products and logos from any store that dares to let in MicroBlend. This is too big a risk for a retailer to make on a small new company with no established brand or reputation. For this reason, Sauder told us, MicroBlend has not been able to sell in the United States. MicroBlend now is staking its future on a partnership with a large Latin American retailer. While the immediate plan is to supply the pre-paints to Latin America from Arizona, as the Latin American operation proves successful, it's not hard to guess where production would be likely to take place in the future. Of all the Main Street innovators we studied, MicroBlend was one of the few selling (or proposing to sell) a product to consumers, not to businesses. In the power of the brands to resist entry by a newcomer with a disruptive innovation, we could see why most successful new manufacturing ventures are ones selling to businesses and not attempting to compete with established brands for shelf space in the big-box retailers.

Most of the Main Street manufacturers we visited had production that was more firmly rooted in the United States than QD Vision or MicroBlend because their customers are still predominantly American. A good example is U.S. Endoscopy, a medical device company in Mentor, Ohio, that employs 380 workers.[23] U.S. Endoscopy was started by a "street engineer," who had a natural talent for building things but not much formal engineering training. One of the key early products started with a suggestion from a doctor about a way to catch tissue that had been cut away by a surgical catheter, a table in a warehouse, and two men with no previous experience with medical devices. The jack-of-all-trades founder has now turned the business over to a professional manager, and the improvisation of the early days has given way to product development by design and process engineers recruited from Ohio universities. The proximity of great hospitals in Cleveland and easy access to surgeons is a local asset. While U.S. Endoscopy talked about Ohio's great supplier networks, and how important these local suppliers were in early days of the company when they had fewer in-house capabilities than they do today, they emphasized that they are not willing to turn design over to design houses or manufacturing over to contractors. They are committed to keeping manufacturing in-house, near to the design facilities, in order to get new ideas and products out fast. The CEO told us: "U.S. Endoscopy is a new product development machine. If products are so price-sensitive that outsourcing would make a difference, that's the wrong line of business for us. We make Porsches." In July 2012, the owners' family sold U.S. Endoscopy to an Ohio neighbor, Steris, a medical supply and services maker with 5000 employees.

Repurposing as innovation

Alongside these companies with patents at their core we found a group of innovative small and medium-sized firms whose main innovative talents were taking products and processes and translating them into a whole new set of activities or even transposing technologies from one industry to another, as the Medinol example at the start of the chapter illustrated. Some of the most focused examples of repurposing leading to new business lines emerged in the interviews we conducted in Germany. In German manufacturing the proximity between R&D people and production seems to create exceptionally fertile terrain for stimulating such innovation. One example comes from Alfred H. Schuette, a machine tool company founded in Cologne, Germany, in 1880, and still run by the same family. Their two principal lines are multispindle automatics for high-volume turning parts, used to make 80 percent of the world's spark plugs; and five axis grinding machines. As Carl Martin Welcker, the CEO, told us: "Our strategy is we build the most complex of complex machines. If they were simple, we could build them in Taiwan." He recounted how they had "repurposed" their multispindle turning machines to make a new machine for fabricating medical devices—a sector they had never been involved in before. The idea came from one of his staff, who saw a machine for making artificial knees at a trade show and thought it was just too big and expensive. He was called over to look at it, and they decided they could use machines Schuette already had to make these knees for a fraction of the cost of the machine they were looking at in the show. They also wanted their machines to do it better—by milling, grinding, belting, polishing, and cleaning the knee. The first machines they shipped to a UK customer needed a lot of reworking, and Schuette sent over teams of engineers to debug problems they had not even imagined, like dust from the polishing clogging the filters. Six years after the project started, this part of the business became profitable.

The basic repurposing story was the same at a German equipment supplier to the solar cell business. They started in the early nineties by making machines for the semiconductor industry. Wet chemistry was their strong suit. One of their old customers, who had shifted out of semiconductors into photovoltaics, asked for their help fixing some machines. At that point everyone in the solar cell business was using "dry chemistry" methods. As our interviewee tried to help repair his old customer's machines, he realized that he could use his "wet chemistry" machines for the same process and do it cheaper, faster, and with better quality. Another of the German companies described how the skills they now use for making gearboxes for windtowers that are far quieter than others derive from trade secrets in making special steel that they have been perfecting over a hundred and fifty years, as a metal casting firm founded in the middle of the nineteenth century.

Repurposing-driven innovation of the kind we saw in one after another German company also appeared in some of our strongest Main Street U.S. companies. The MIT researchers visited an Ohio metal fabricating company founded in 1940.[24] It has 220 employees, and the third-generation owner expects it to grow by 30 to 40 employees a year, even as automation and robots and laser cutting machines reduce the number of workers needed on any single operation. In the 1940s, the company made boilers and pressure tanks. By the 1970s, the firm was mainly fabricating metal for construction. At the start of the Iraq war (2002) the firm grew rapidly as it made metal plates to reinforce military vehicles that had proved vulnerable to improvised roadside bombs. Once the armor boom was over, the company explored other uses for its unique capabilities in forming 20- to 30-ton components. It took steels that were lighter and stronger and had been developed for the construction industry and was figuring out how to use them in making components for a new generation of aircraft carriers. Lighter steel would greatly reduce the Navy's energy bills, but the foundry would have to do extensive development and testing to prove to its shipyard customer (and to *its* customer, the Navy) that the new materials were as tough and resilient as the traditional structural steel they would replace. The Navy encouraged the company to experiment with hybrid laser welding to produce thinner, lighter welds with less deformation. With both the special steel and the hybrid laser welds this company is taking technologies still in early prototype stages and working with customers and other suppliers to pilot them and bring them to market.

As the owner described his capabilities, they are to "take a technology that someone else has come up with, find a way to incorporate it into some existing or new product line, scale it, and find different customers in different markets to sell it to. Our innovation is to introduce new materials into different industries and to do testing for our customers." He told us: "We may not drive the technology, but we're scaling it up." As the owner reflected on the differences in strategy from his grandfather and father's times, he pointed out that they had mainly connected with others in the same trade. In fact those connections had been very thin: they met competitors in trade associations and at trade shows. But there had been practically no information sharing and a lot of concern for keeping trade secrets and keeping customers out of the reach of competitors. Today, the owner focuses on building connections in industries with potential customers. It's still an open question for him whether more information about the firm's capabilities would attract more customers or whether the net effect would be to attract more competition.

Building solutions: Combining manufacturing and services

One of the strongest trends we saw in the Main Street firms was adding services to activities that had once been straightforward manufacturing. In the most innovative companies we visited, the distinction between manufacturing and services is becoming more and more blurred, and value derives from the ability to bundle these capabilities. In a way, even a traditional machine shop provides a "service" when it customizes a component for a specific customer and works with the customer to modify and improve the customer's original drawing and specifications. Manufacturing firms have always provided "services," when they send technicians along with the component to install it, or to instruct the customer in its use, as for example, the Ohio company we visited that makes half-sleeves to repair leaks in oil pipelines and sends workers along with the part to stand on the oil platform coaching the divers on how to position it.[25] That company has just short of a hundred workers, has $10 million in backlogged orders, and exports 70 percent of its products. Repairs are another service that manufacturing firms have often offered. We do not have measures across the economy of how significant a fraction of manufacturing company revenues derive from repair services, but the interviews suggest it may be substantial. The CEO of a New England company that makes tanks and piping for biotech firms estimated that about a quarter of his revenues derive from repairs on equipment—from all makers, not only their own—and fully one half of his profits.[26] The CEO told us that the capabilities he needed to do the repairs were ones he acquired in the course of manufacturing parts. And the same certifications that qualify his parts for use in sensitive biotech manufacturing extend to his repairs as well. Why he makes more on repair services than on manufacturing new products is quite simple, he explained: customers needing repairs are desperate for speedy solutions and haggle less over cost; customers buying new equipment can afford to wait out bidding wars from competing suppliers. All these services, which are associated with manufacturing because the manufacturer is uniquely qualified to provide them, are quite traditional ones.

What we were seeing in many of the Main Street firms, though, was something new: firms that were not just modifying one or another dimension of the customer's drawing, but firms taking over more and more of the design functions their customers used to have in-house. There is a broad shift of engineering design services from the "mother ships"—the brands, the original equipment manufacturers (OEMs), the large multinationals—to suppliers who, from doing work on "spec" and contract manufacturing, now are selected exactly because they can offer design services. The CEO of an Ohio machining shop (86 employees, up from 57 in 2007) working mainly with aerospace firms said bluntly: "Today our customers have no experience with machining. They have no knowledge. They don't recognize what's required to produce the kind of precision they require."[27] Modern Industries, an Arizona Main Street company (with 500 employees) makes equipment for the semiconductor industry and "builds to print."[28] But what does build to print mean these days? Andy Yahraus, the CEO, told us that many of his customers have gotten rid of most of their manufacturing engineers and transferred functions they used to carry out in-house to contract manufacturers. In the process they have reduced their ability to produce detailed engineering designs. Many of the new Asian contract manufacturers have scant experience in the industry, and while they perform well when provided with complete detailed designs, they are not yet capable of producing such designs, particularly if the part is radically different from previous models. The CEO sees this as a great opportunity for his own company:

> Once components are decoupled from design, there's a reduction in the latent knowledge of how things are made. The process has to be simplified when things are "leaned out." So, when there is a game-changing design, there is no latent knowledge base that allows 3rd world manufacturers to make it. Those of us American and European

companies that stay competitive are then in great demand. The expectation is that we'll contribute to design in manufacturing. The OEM may give us a terrible drawing—so you have to fix it. OEMs have few people who can read blueprints. Sometimes they give us blueprints; sometimes they just give us a solid model, and we detail it out. We then pass drawings back and forth. There's a shortage today of people who understand what every component needs; and without engineering experience in a factory, you can't learn how to do the interpretation necessary to making a drawing into a product.

We observed in this company, as in a number of the others, that suppliers hesitate between all-out commitment to nurturing these design strengths and just making things cheaper in order to compete with Asian suppliers. It's time-consuming and expensive to develop or improve components for customers, and like many others, this company cannot even claim R&D tax credits, so all the development costs come out of retained earnings. The firm ends up tugged in opposite directions. Even while it recognizes that design capabilities bring them customers, it also worries that pure survival requires competing on price and might take moving some production to Mexico to get lower-cost labor that can be hired and fired easily.

There's a major shift underway toward raising the demands that customers make of suppliers—but this process advances very unevenly. When lead firms still had a greater range and depth in their own teams of design and manufacturing engineers, they selected suppliers who excelled simply at making things reasonably well and cheaper, and that often led to making them overseas. As lead firms have focused on core competence and shed manufacturing and detail design capabilities, they have become increasingly more dependent on suppliers for providing these functions. This creates the possibility that suppliers who offer design services or new and improved products and processes can command higher prices, but it's still a very chancy bet for the supplier. The tug and tension between competing with the lowest-cost rivals and advancing process and product innovation is a constant preoccupation and involves choices fraught with uncertainty. As one CEO in put it: "It's a bloody competitive battle. Low-cost regions have gained on the warfront, but now we're seeing counter-forces. The OEMs that leaned out their own capabilities are demanding more from us suppliers." What we observed in the trenches of Main Street manufacturing looked like a struggle between competing by race to the bottom and growing the economy through innovation. How the odds in this fight could be tilted toward more innovative strategies across a broad swath of American manufacturing firms is the true challenge for public policy.

Enabling innovation

Searching for suppliers with the right capabilities to move innovation from the lab into production through all of the different phases of development was an issue frequently raised in the interviews. What the start-up needs in the way of a supplier changes as the company grows. As it builds a prototype and then moves into pilot production phases, having the right kind of supplier locally available at the right time can be critical for scaling up fast enough to meet investors' expectations. Tracing out the growth trajectory of Ambri, a new battery producer, we found different suppliers all along the route and yet other suppliers the company anticipated in its future.[29] Ambri's cofounder was Donald Sadoway, an MIT professor of materials engineering. He worked on aluminum and other metals, and realized that some of the processes he observed in smelting could be harnessed to store power cheaply for electricity grids in a liquid metal battery. The battery consists of three liquid layers that act as the electroactive components, with a liquid metal positive electrode, a fused salt electrolyte in the middle, and a liquid metal negative electrode. The cells are enclosed in modules; the modules are stacked in a truck-sized container. Each of the units would generate about a half megawatt—enough to power 200 homes. As Sadoway moved his innovation out of the lab into a start-up company, he received venture funding from Bill Gates,who had discovered Sadoway via an MIT OpenCourseWare on-line class, Introduction to Solid State Chemistry, and from Total, the French oil company, which met Sadoway in an MIT international program, and from ARPA-E, the Department of Energy's Advanced Research Program Agency. When a new round of financing was sought, Khosla Ventures came on board to lead the Series B round. Subsequently, the firm changed its name from Liquid Metal Battery Corporation to

Ambri—paying homage to its origins in Cambridge, where the firm is located, a few blocks from MIT.

But Ambri needed more than capital. It needed vital resources from the industrial ecosystem in order to be able to make the modules and containers at a high level of quality, fast, and efficiently and to connect with suppliers, regulators, and the utilities who would be eventual customers. The first of the local resources Ambri acquired was the CEO, Phil Giudice, who was the Commonwealth of Massachusetts Under-Secretary of Energy and who from his state job, from earlier stints at a successful energy management start-up, EnerNOC, and from 20 years as a management consultant to energy companies, had deep experience with all the players in the energy ecosystem. It was Giudice who knew local suppliers able to work with Ambri on developing the module enclosures and the container. Everyone recognized that PhDs with welding sticks, despite MIT's claim to educate people with hands-on skills, were not the path to go forward to successful commercialization. And so Ambri has been working with metal working suppliers in the Boston region to develop prototypes. Here again, as in the Kiva Systems example discussed in chapter 3, the entrepreneurs emphasized the importance for their companies of locating and working closely with nearby suppliers with the right specialized skills.

When we explored how the suppliers themselves were developing new capabilities and acquiring the inputs in equipment, facilities, and expertise that they needed, we learned that these firms have to operate with whatever resources they can generate in-house. Their innovative efforts do not qualify for R&D tax credits. As local banks have been bought up by large national banks headquartered out of state, their enthusiasm for building up the local economy has diminished. Local bankers—where there still are local bankers in the United States—regard manufacturing suppliers as risky bets. A number of the interviewees explained that virtually the only opportunity for getting outside resources to develop their new projects is when they have some piece of a defense contract. Then they can acquire new equipment, and they buy machines that have functionality beyond what is strictly speaking needed for that job. The idea is to use the equipment later on to move into new products for new civilian business. This point was made often enough in the interviews that we came to see the elevated cost of defense procurement as an indirect subsidy to technology upgrading in the civilian economy. Piggy-backing on military contracts may or may not be the most efficient way of providing public support for new capabilities in Main Street firms; at the moment, it is one of the few ways open to many of them. The effects of reducing the defense budget will therefore ripple out across the civilian economy and cut off one of the few viable routes to funding technology upgrades in small and medium-sized manufacturing firms in sectors in which venture capitalists only rarely invest.

In the interviews there were also references to other ways of raising capital. For the high tech start-ups, venture capital played a major role, and government stimulus spending, private equity, and the SBIR grants came up occasionally. These have been analyzed in depth by the PIE "scale-up" project and are discussed in chapter 3. But in the interviews with the Main Street firms, those sources were rarely mentioned. There's a conservatism, too, about borrowing that even the younger members of family-owned businesses have picked up from grandparents and parents: "Never borrow" was a rule of thumb for many of the founding genera-tion. Family and rich friends sometimes help fund development. During the economic recession, one Ohio firm had literally mortgaged the family farm to pay off new equipment purchases—and in the aftermath, decided to sell half the company to a Japanese parts supplier in order to insulate the family against any such future vulnerabilities. Usually, the Main Street companies fund development and upgrading out of pocket from last year's profits. Since most of these small and medium-sized enterprises pay taxes as subchapter S corporations taxed at the owner's personal tax rate with estimated taxes based on the prior year's earnings, they are extremely cautious about new equipment purchases and about projects that run over multiple years.

Why Main Street innovation does not take off

If the contributions to innovation of fairly successful small and medium-sized manufacturers are as significant as the above examples above suggest, why don't these companies grow bigger, faster, or more profitable? The sample of manufacturers we interviewed in Massachusetts, Georgia, Ari-zona, and Ohio was by design drawn from companies that had done very well in the recent past having doubled their revenues over the period 2004–2008 and increased their headcount. If any Main Street manufacturers should be capable of expanding rapidly, we reasoned, it would be these firms. But the numbers of new or improved product and process introductions we observed in these companies were modest. Only a few of the companies had plans to expand their physical facilities; and few showed signs of imagining a future very different from the company in its current state. True, almost all of these firms had been severely hit by the 2008–2010 financial and economic crises. The words "near-death experience" came up again and again in the interviews, with managers telling us of orders that fell by 50 to 70 percent over the course of the *annus horribilis* of 2009. By the time we interviewed them in 2011 and 2012, however, most had returned to or surpassed the levels of activity of pre-crisis years.

What expectations might we reasonably have for growth in Main Street manufacturing? A machine toolmaker is not going to take off like Microsoft or Facebook, but we could not help wondering why these companies did not look more like the German firms we interviewed that, like the Americans, were mostly selling capital goods to other businesses. Chapter 5 will discuss German production in some detail, but here we note one striking and important difference. The American company stands alone. The German firm has access to a rich and diverse set of external resources—to which it contributes, but which it does not have to generate on its own. It hires employees who have been educated in technical schools and universities linked to hands-on experience and credentialing within companies. The German system has no R&D tax credits, but firms collaborate in R&D consortia which receive some government funding, and individual firms can get some funding to implement these projects. When the German family business goes to a bank, it deals with local bankers who know the region and who are committed to supporting local economic development. For a price that seems acceptable even to small and medium businesses, the German firm can get expert advice and use of expensive equipment at parapublic institutions like the Fraunhofer Institutes. Many of the German manufacturing firms are located in dense regional networks of suppliers and competitors where information circulates easily; as the British economist Alfred Marshall said of the industrial district, "the mysteries of the trade become no mysteries; but are as it were in the air." In American clusters like Silicon Valley, these "mysteries" often diffuse along with people, as they move around from company to company. In Germany, there is much less job mobility. Rather it's the sheer density of participations in trade associations, trade fairs, industry-funded applied research institutes, and employer-union joint councils that creates a continuous updating and upgrading of knowledge and practice.

On each of these points, the companies we visited in Massachusetts, Ohio, Georgia, and Arizona were in a very different kind of situation. On Main Street, the company operates with those resources it can generate itself. It finds few complementary capabilities in the environment on which it can draw. Even fifty years ago, in the heyday of manufacturing, the stand-alone company may have been more typical of American industry than of manufacturing firms in many other countries. Even when the MIT *Made in America* study was conducted at the end of the 1980s, there were strikingly lower levels of common resources available to U.S. companies than in Germany or Japan. For example, there was much less corporate and public investment in educating for workforce skills. Very often the answer to the question of how they trained workers was simply: "We tell them to follow Joe around—he's doing the job now." The strongest industry groups were ones that organized for trade protection. There were few industrial consortia that pooled efforts on innovation, and those institutions that did try to provide precompetitive technology research services to their industry had trouble raising funds. Companies were often more concerned to shield their new activities from competitors for fear of being copied than they were willing to participate in industry association projects on new technologies.

In the interviews we conducted in Ohio, young generations of family-firm leaders told us that their parents and grandparents had never visited a company in the same line of work nor opened their plants to anyone. Today there's still the worry about what a competitor could learn. There's still the fear that if word got out about things going well, that union organizers would move in. Even in the past, there were low levels of collaboration across lead firms and their suppliers. While Japanese corporations worked closely with their suppliers, like Toyota with Denso, big American companies tended to keep their production plans to themselves and to force their suppliers to compete with each other to get to the lowest possible price.

But even if there was no golden past of industrial collaboration within recent memory, twenty-five years ago there was a thicker network of connections among firms, as well as a denser industrial population, and there were public goods being spun off by large vertically integrated corporations in the course of their ordinary internal activities. Among the public goods that the large corporations provided was championing and funding associations operating across a wide range of industry concerns. For example, Milliken & Company, a private textile company in Spartanburg, South Carolina, with annual sales in the 1990s estimated at about $2.5 billion, played the key role in the establishment of the Institute of Textile Technology, an applied research facility for the industry; in ATMI (American Textile Manufacturers Institute), an industry association mainly focused on lobbying Congress for trade and tax policies; and in the AMTEX Partnership, created in 1993 with the Department of Energy to bring researchers at the national laboratories to develop new technologies for the textile industry. Milliken also was a big supporter of regional universities and trade schools. Motorola, a large vertically integrated electronics corporation, organized programs for diffusing "six sigma" and other Japanese lean manufacturing practices, and many companies well beyond the set of Motorola suppliers sent employees and managers to be trained in them.

As vertically integrated enterprises (as described in chapter 2) transformed themselves into "core competence" companies, as they began to transfer manufacturing functions abroad and to expand abroad, they changed their practices in ways that had serious consequences for the local industrial ecosystem. First, they shifted some of their purchasing away from local suppliers, and the negative impact rippled out across the local economy. Second, and equally important, they ceased producing many of the public goods that had once benefitted participants in the local economy beyond the big firm. An example is the provision of skills. New corporate structures were no longer oriented to lifetime employment, so companies had less incentive to invest in training their employees, many of whom would be moving on to work in other companies in a few years. At the same time, firms were expanding in markets outside the United States, and found less reason to focus on training new workers at home. Some of those trained in apprenticeships and vocational programs within the large corporations had always leaked back into the general labor pool, and so when the big firms cut back on their in-house training, the smaller firms in the region could no longer dip into a local reservoir of trained workers for their own hires. Finally, across big and small companies in which we conducted interviews, there was a concern about "legacy" skills, ones employees had brought in with them from prior employment but that were not being reproduced in the workforce. At a semiconductor maker specializing in analog chips and chips for cell phones, for example, the plant managers pointed out that most of their engineers were in their late forties or fifties and had skills that dated back to work they had done in defense contractors twenty years earlier. When this generation retires, it is not apparent where replacements will be found.[30]

Corporate restructuring affected the local ecosystem in yet another way after deregulation of the banking system and the 1999 repeal of the Glass–Steagall Act. Local banks were bought up by national and international banks that had much less interest in and knowledge of any particular locality. In Arizona, one well-connected interviewee mournfully recalled the good old days when local bankers, local businessmen, and politicians huddled in smoke-filled rooms behind closed doors and plotted out the future of the Arizona economy. As he described it, those networks produced the investment in irrigation that made the Sonora Desert bloom in citrus and cotton fields and built the Palo Verde nuclear plant, the interstate highways, excellent public schools, and thriving companies. Today, those networks have unraveled. As he explained it, the introduction of partisan primary elections threw open the doors of the political arena, and polarization resulted. Bank of America and JP Morgan Chase bought all the local banks; the biggest companies in town now are ones like Intel and Raytheon, with headquarters out of state. In this new environment, he said, the only agenda on which everyone can agree is cutting taxes. As outsiders, we could not evaluate whether the Arizona scene had changed as drastically he described. But across the states we visited, the evidence we collected did suggest an increasingly fragile industrial ecosystem with gaping holes at points where globalization and the transformation of corporate structures have eviscerated old institutions.

5

Lessons in Scaling from Abroad: Germany and China

Myths about manufacturing die hard. Two in particular are proving resistant to contrary evidence, and they weigh heavily on our thinking about the future of manufacturing in the United States. Even when these ideas are not explicitly stated, they still invisibly orient views about what is and is not possible in the United States. The first myth is that in an advanced high-wage economy, manufacturing can be only a sunset sector, since manufacturers make commodities most profitably produced in low-cost, low-wage economies. The second myth is that the real advantages of emerging countries in the global economy today come only from exploiting low-cost labor. Whenever we find successful companies doing more complex and high-tech production in developing countries, it must be because companies are getting government subsidies, protection, or some other special deal that would not exist in a more open economy. These two notions do contain some kernels of truth. But as in all myths, the elements of truth here are blown up and built into a picture very different from reality. However distorted the picture, though, it has real impact. These two myths blind us to the genuine strengths in the ways other countries scale up innovation to commercialization. These ideas make it difficult to understand how countries use policies and institutions quite different from our own to gain full benefit from their innovative capabilities. They handicap our ability to learn from best practices elsewhere. In short, to take advantage of lessons from abroad, we need first to reconsider two strongly ingrained beliefs about the global economy: one about whether an advanced country might still have a sizeable and flourishing manufacturing sector and the other about whether a developing economy might already possess real technological capabilities.

The Production in the Innovation Economy project decided that the best way to explore these issues was to send our research teams to Germany and to China. In most respects, those two countries could hardly be more different from each other. Germany is one of the world's richest and most advanced industrial societies. China, for all of its remarkable progress, is still a poor-to-middle-income country with rather low productivity and few companies that compete in world markets on the basis of unique products or processes. Yet both of these countries have companies that excel in scaling up innovation to market. In both Germany and China we found compelling examples of innovative manufacturing and scale-up that challenged many of our ideas about why innovative companies in the United States so often falter before attaining the size and capacity to reach large numbers of customers. In interviews with senior managers in the two countries, as in our interviews in the United States, we tried to track how a company advanced new ideas from the earliest stages of development through to prototyping, test and demonstration, pilot production, and large-scale commercialization. Which of its innovations had made it to market and which had not, and why? We asked the same questions in American, German, and Chinese firms, in the same or similar industries.

In all countries, many—probably most—new ideas fall by the wayside en route to the market because they turn out to be less good than they had originally seemed. Sometimes the market was just not there for the new product. Or someone else got there first. Or, as an investor said of Advanced Electron Beams, a promising Massachusetts start-up in low-energy electron beams for sterilization processes that had attracted $50 million in venture funding before it closed its doors in 2012: "The technology just proved to be too difficult to commercialize."[1] With hindsight, it is almost always possible to argue that if a new product or process had really been promising enough, the market would have attracted investors to fund the commercialization of the product. If it failed to scale-up, it must just not have been a valuable enough innovation. This may well be true much of the time, but the evidence that PIE researchers have collected from the analysis of the trajectories of the start-up firms and from PIE interviews with CEOs and entrepreneurs in a broad range of established industries suggests that this is too simple and circular an explanation. As we suggested in chapter 3, there are obstacles to scaling up innovation in the United States that cannot be dismissed by reasoning that the ideas would have made it to the market if only they had been good enough. Even thirty years ago, when innovation mainly grew out of research and product development in large companies well able to finance scale-up out of their own cash, it seemed that Americans were better at inventing things than at commercializing them. The spectacular rise of the Japanese electronics industry, for example, took off from products like digital cameras and active-matrix liquid crystal display panels, which had been invented in the United States but never found commercial successes in this country.

Today, when high-tech innovation is far more likely to emerge in small start-up firms with no established footprint and with high degrees of dependence on high-risk venture and corporate capital for their growth, the issues surrounding scale-up to market have become even more challenging. As the research presented in chapter 3 shows, one of the most difficult of these points of passage is the transition to large-scale commercialization, moving from a stage where a company has demonstrated the workability and value of a product and shown its ability to make a few for a limited number of customers, to a stage where the product can be made at a price the market will bear and sold to a large enough number of customers to generate revenues that will sustain and grow the company. In the not-so-distant past, IPOs offered a vehicle for bringing in new capital at this stage and growing a company. Over the past decade, the number of IPOs has sharply declined. It's still too early to know whether new legislation that loosens the legal requirements for forming and listing new companies, the April 5, 2012, Jumpstart Our Business Startups Act (JOBS Act), will lead to a new wave of IPOs. Potentially, lowering the legal hurdles might enable a substantial backlog of candidates for IPOs to move forward. But as of today, the possibilities for traversing this pass to commercial scale—the "valley of death" for many promising ventures—still lie mainly in merging with a big partner or being acquired by a large already-established company.

As we examined outcomes at the stage at which companies engage upon large-scale commercialization, we found cause for concern about the future of the innovation. Although we have not been able to measure this with any precision, the technological potential of innovation in small companies bought up by large corporations often seems to be cut off by absorption and integration. In our meetings, innovators frequently lamented the fate of their creations once they were brought into large bureaucratic organizations. In a fairly typical account, one founder of an aeronautical components company that had been acquired by a large corporation summarized his experience by saying that everything that had made his firm a success was squashed. "They bought the spirit of the company and destroyed it. It was like Pac-Man: they matrixed everything into the divisions of [the acquiring company]. They stopped our innovation." Of course, company founders are very likely to be biased about the value of their innovation, and disappointed by the failure of the acquiring firm to build out the technology's potential. But what was surprising was how often the accounts we heard in the large firms that were the acquirers mirrored the same sentiments. In interviews in the large corporations, managers regretfully talked about how in trying to integrate the small firms they bought they had, as one expressed it, "hugged them to death."

In the Main Street manufacturing companies we visited, in contrast to the high-tech start-ups coming out of MIT research, the innovations that firms came up with were often incremental improvements or ways of repurposing technologies that had first been developed for another set of uses and customers. The amounts of capital these companies needed to find to make it work were in no way comparable to the sums the start-up firms needed to scale up to commercialization. Yet in company after company what we could recognize as innovative projects seemed to stall before taking off. The great puzzle about these firms is why even ones that had done reasonably well in recent times were not bringing new products into the market faster and on a grander scale. (The sample, after all, had been biased toward more successful small and medium-sized companies, ones that had doubled their revenues and head counts between 2004 and 2008.) The conclusion in chapter 4 suggested that the blockage arises from the fact that these companies have to develop all the resources for growth internally and can find few complementary capabilities outside the company to support them. They're on their own.

Americans have historically valued self-reliance and autonomy, but today's extreme isolation of individual manufacturing enterprises is in many ways a new situation. The transformation of corporate structures since the 1980s has greatly reduced the footprint of large vertically integrated companies across the heartland of American manufacturing (see chapter 2). With these changes in corporate structures, there has been a

great attrition of the public goods and connective tissue that big companies once supported. Regional pools of skilled workers, dense supplier
networks, and institutions like vocational schools, local banks, unions,
and trade associations have all shriveled and shrunk. The holes in the
industrial ecosystem that these changes in corporate structures opened
over a thirty-year period then suddenly grew dangerously deeper over the
past decade, as large numbers of companies were wiped out by low-wage
competition from Asia. As we heard again and again in the interviews,
when the ecosystem thins out and becomes more fragile, companies start
to wonder whether they will even be able to find replacements for key
suppliers when the current generation retires or dies.

These were the American dilemmas we had in mind as we moved our
research teams to Germany and China to investigate how companies in
these countries manage to bring new products and processes to market.

The German manufacturing economy

German manufacturing represents an outstanding example of high-wage
jobs, strong employment security, and powerful export performance in an
advanced industrial country. In Germany in 2010, manufacturing still
contributed 21 percent of value-added to GDP, and 22 percent of the
workforce was employed in manufacturing. In the United States that
year, in contrast, manufacturing contributed 13 percent of value-added
in GDP and just under 11 percent of the workforce was in manufacturing.[2] Manufacturing jobs continued to decline in both countries, but in
Germany today they still represent close to 20 percent of the workforce.
The explanation of why German manufacturing thrives can hardly be low
wages: in fact the average hourly compensation of German manufacturing workers is 66 percent higher than that of American manufacturing
workers. While the United States has had a trade deficit in manufactured
goods ($41.7 billion for three months ending in October 2012), German
trade has a surplus (in October 2012 of 15.8 billion euros)—a surplus
even in exchanges with China.

There are certainly multiple factors at work in accounting for why
German manufacturing remains so strong, and experts do not agree.
Skeptics about the prospects of manufacturing in high-wage economies

tend to discount the German example; they argue that Germany does so well because its currency is undervalued as a result of membership in a euro zone that includes economies like Greece, Spain, and Portugal, whose export capacity suffers from using the euro, a currency valued higher than theirs would be if they went it alone and were free to devalue. Were Germany to leave the euro, or if the euro zone fell apart, an independent German currency—a new mark—would rise in value and the price of German exports would also rise. In this debate over the role of the euro in supporting German exports, it is useful to remember that Sweden—another strong manufacturing exporter—is not a member of the euro zone, and Sweden, too, has maintained strong manufacturing performance.[3] A recent report by the McKinsey Global Institute (2012) has parsed the factors that account for the differential between manufacturing in the American and German economies. They include differences in industrial specializations, current account balances, consumption and savings behavior, and outsourcing patterns.[4]

What this snapshot of the two economies does not show, though, is how German manufacturing managed to withstand radical shocks—the high costs of German reunification in the 1990s, competition from Asia, the financial and economic crises of 2008–2010—and to bounce back as an export powerhouse and a dynamo of innovative production in sectors like wind and solar energy. Even a decade ago, Germany's prospects did not look very bright. At the end of the 1990s, as globalization opened national borders to capital mobility and trade, Germany was mired in slow growth and burdened with a stagnant demography and the high costs of a generous welfare system, early retirement pensions, and strong job security. The outlook for German manufacturing in a far more competitive global economy appeared grim. In a 2003 book entitled *Can Germany Be Saved?* Hans-Werner Sinn, a leading German economist, predicted that even in the unlikely event that politicians would be courageous enough to initiate radical economic and cultural reforms, "it will take years before these produce any notable results."[5] Many shared Sinn's pessimism. Contrary to these negative forecasts, though, the German government did carry out a far-reaching set of labor market reforms (Hartz I–IV). Reforms introduced from 2003 on brought far more flexibility into employment contracts and tightened the conditions for receiving unemployment compensation.[6]

On the downside, the new legislation accelerated the emergence of a dual labor market, with job security provided to the "permanent" workforce, and with far greater possibilities for the company to bring in workers on fixed-term contracts with much lower wages and with few of the employment protections of the regular workforce. In 2010, about 15 percent of the German workforce was on such fixed-term contracts, with the incidence falling heavily on younger workers, women, and foreigners. In the interviews the PIE team carried out in German manufacturing companies, managers recounted that these "temporary" workers were the first to be laid off during the crisis and only now (2011) were being rehired.

The critical value of these reforms for the economy emerged during the 2008–2010 economic crisis, when employers and the unions were able to agree on a scheme (*Kurzarbeit*) for keeping workers on the job by cutting their hours but not firing them. For employers this meant not having to lose workers with valuable and company-specific skills in which the firm had heavily invested. For workers it meant a precious form of job security. The "short-time work" arrangement was complemented by unemployment benefits which workers received to top off the reduced hours and wages on the job. At its peak in 2009, about 1.5 million workers were on short-time work.[7] In large measure because of this scheme, while unemployment skyrocketed in other Western economies over the course of the financial and economic crisis of 2008–2010, German employment held steady, with unemployment rising only 0.2 percent between 2008 and 2009.[8] In a survey conducted by the German Engineering Federation (VDMA) of 500 of its members, firms reported that the most important outcome of the 2008–2009 crisis was that despite a 25 percent drop in orders, short-time work contracts made it possible to shrink the workforce by only 5 percent.[9] In the same survey, respondents commented on the importance of an innovation focus, a shift reflected in the increase in the share of engineering graduates on their staff from nine percent to 17 percent over recent years. Beyond the crisis, the labor reforms have also created flexibility in responding to more normal periods of low and high demand. With flex-time arrangements employees bank extra hours they work in busy times and draw on their "accounts" during slow periods.

Labor market reforms clearly were important in containing costs in German manufacturing and in buffering employment against shocks from the crisis. They made it possible for German manufacturers to push forward into higher value-added product lines and to expand production abroad for new customers—even while maintaining high levels of employment and wages at home. But while these reforms helped pull German manufacturing out of a slump, they cannot account for the difference between manufacturing's long-term performance in Germany and the United States, since even with these changes, German wages, social benefits, and job security are still much higher than American. We need to dig deeper into the structures of German manufacturing to analyze how companies across a range of sizes and industries have been able to stand up to stiff international competition by continuous innovation in high quality and high value-added products and processes.

As we compared the German manufacturing companies we interviewed with the American manufacturers we were studying, we saw systematic variations across three domains: their business models, their paths to innovation, and the industrial ecosystems in which they operated.

Business model

The first major difference lies in property relations, with family ownership playing a far greater role across businesses of all sizes in Germany than in the United States. Even in the hundred largest German companies—most of which operate in global markets with production sites both in Germany and abroad—family control is important. In very large companies, the share of businesses with concentrated family ownership has held steady over the past twenty-five years at about 20 percent.[10] In a study Christina Lubinski conducted of 310 companies with over 250 employees, she found family ownership and control in over half. Two-thirds of them had passed through at least one generational succession. In smaller-sized companies, family control is ubiquitous.

Family control matters in many ways. In virtually every interview that PIE conducted in Germany, managers emphasized that the longtime horizons of their R&D projects and of their calculations on payback periods for operations overall depended on the family owners' commitment to the company as a business to be managed for generations to come and a business to be carried out mainly in its home region. One among many examples is STIHL, a world leader in chain saw and outdoor power tool products. We met with the CEO and the director of engineering at the headquarters and main production facility in Waiblingen, a small town near Stuttgart.[11] In 2010, STIHL's sales were 2.36 billion euros. Eighty-nine percent of its sales were made outside of Germany; but a third of its workforce (3,874 employees out of 11,310) remained in Germany. When we asked why, the CEO replied that STIHL has strong roots in the region and it was important to be a good corporate citizen and protect the family's good name.

At STIHL as in other German family businesses, there are strong cultural norms and traditions at work, but they persist and can be sustained in face of stiff global competition because they are tightly associated with other distinct financial and production features of the German business model. The finance of German business depends far more heavily on self-financing than in the United States, where companies are more likely to go public early and to derive more of their resources from equity capital and bank loans. This makes German businesses less vulnerable to stock analysts' focus on quarterly earnings. Public policy also supports family businesses, for German estate taxes give a privileged status (and lower rates) to family wealth in inherited businesses.

The link of family ownership to corporate structures and strategies is critical. As the STIHL managers told us, retained profits and no bank debts allow them to focus on long-term growth and on a production strategy of vertical integration for premium quality products. The cash reserves of the company also buffer it in hard times. When the PIE researchers asked whether STIHL had experienced difficulties with its bankers during the 2008–2010 financial crisis (a common experience reported in our American interviews), the STIHL executive shook his head, and noted the firm's resilience, not only to economic shocks, but to the pressure of demands for short-term returns. In other interviews we conducted in German enterprises, we did hear about close links with local banks that proved important in weathering bad times. These local links between banks and manufacturers stand in sharp contrast to the situation of American manufacturing in many communities where local banks have been bought up by giant national banks with no particular local knowledge or commitment and where companies find few banking interlocutors with minimal understanding of their business.

The larger significance of STIHL's family ownership and financial autonomy is the way it supports a corporate structure of vertical integration. STIHL focuses on producing high quality chain saws and handheld outdoor power tools for professionals and do-it-yourself customers. Their products command a significant price premium, and customers are willing to pay because of the reliability of the tools and the exceptional service that is bundled in the sale along with the product. The managers told us: "If you're a logger out in the woods somewhere and your chain saw fails, you'll lose a few days by the time you've driven somewhere and gotten it fixed." STIHL customers are willing to pay extra for the reliability of the product and for the guarantee that if the worst comes to pass, that the STIHL dealer who sold the tool will be able to repair it. In order to achieve the levels of quality that STIHL incorporates in the tools it sells, the company uses vertical integration in two key domains: first, in organizing R&D and the manufacturing of its high-end professional tools and second, in retail sales.

STIHL spends a significant amount of its revenues on R&D, and to do it efficiently, the executives said, requires centralizing all R&D in Waiblingen next to their most advanced professional tools production facility. A high-performance chain saw can have 130 to 200 parts, and developing a new one can take as long as developing a new model of a car. For STIHL it can take two to four years to bring an innovative new product to market. It starts with a product idea; then its specification; then conceptual design; then moves to detailed design; simulation, tooling, testing, and finally production and market introduction. For rapid prototyping, they use a variety of techniques and technologies to speed the process. But even during the early stages of product development and prototyping they are constantly receiving feedback from manufacturing to ensure that design and production are compatible. The steps carried out in the development process are executed not only sequentially but also in parallel, so that the more product-oriented R &D engineers are interacting with more manufacturing-focused production engineers. The links to manufacturing also work to provide information that they feed back into their simulation software, and that allows them to adjust their models. Keeping R&D next to manufacturing makes it possible to continuously bring innovative products into the market.

The second domain in which STIHL integration stands in sharp contrast to its competitors is retail sales. STIHL insists on selling its products only in independent servicing STIHL dealerships, and not in big-box stores. STIHL believes that only through this network of dealers can they provide the high level of service to customers giving advice, instructing customers and providing after-sales service that is an integral part of the sale of the tool. One of the STIHL ads we saw pinned to a headquarters wall read: "What makes this handheld blower too powerful to be sold at Lowe's or Home Depot?" The answer spelled out was service provided by the network of STIHL dealers who stand behind the product. STIHL also sees its independent dealers as outlets in which the wide range of STIHL products can be displayed. STIHL is willing to fill in even very small gaps in its product line in order to satisfy a broad range of outdoor tool needs. They told us about making olive tree shakers for the olive harvest and tools for stripping cork trees of the bark for corks, both small but important markets. The completeness of the line and the quality of service are the promises bundled in with the purchase of each piece of equipment.

This vertically integrated business model at STIHL coexists with globally-distributed production and sales. STIHL has established manufacturing plants in Germany, the United States, China, Brazil, Austria, and Switzerland. While in the 1970s the foreign plants were set up because of import barriers and tariffs, today the main rationale for STIHL's foreign direct investment is to benefit from local cost advantages and to locate near their largest customer markets. The United States, for example, makes up a large part of the worldwide STIHL market, and the majority of the STIHL products sold in America are built at its facility in Virginia Beach, Virginia. The "Built in America" message is an important one for U.S. customers, they said, and locating in the United States also helps them hedge currency fluctuations between the dollar and the euro. STIHL's U.S. plant employs a workforce of over 1,900.

In a number of the German companies we visited, the managers observed the differences between the vertical integration of R&D and manufacturing in their own plants and the separation of these activities in the operations conducted by their close competitors. We talked with Dr. Theo Freye, the speaker of the Executive Board and also responsible for marketing and strategy of Claas, a 100-year-old family-owned agricultural machinery company that is Europe's leading producer of harvest combines.[12] Claas in 2012 had sales of 3.4 billion euros and a workforce of 9,077. Like STIHL, Claas has production plants in all of its major markets: in the United States (in Omaha, Nebraska), in Russia, India, and all over Europe. For the largest business unit producing grain harvest machines, the most advanced manufacturing production plants and the main Claas R&D center are in Harsewinkel, a town in North Rhine Westphalia. When Dr. Freye told us that an increasing share of the improvements in the future in the operating efficiency of farm machinery will come from electronic control systems and software, we asked why Claas would need to keep R&D near the machinery production. Dr. Freye agreed that the product cycles and the technology cycles are more and more disconnected. Modularity and the separation of R&D from the manufacturing facilities were trends he could see in the industry. But Claas thinks it needs to keep the parts together. Dr. Freye commented: "If you give up on learning how to manufacture, you've given up on learning how to gain value from the whole value chain. The broad product offer creates a certain complexity, which needs to be managed along the whole supply chain in order to gain flexibility and maintain competiveness. Yes, we do have a factory in Hungary—but we are very well-connected and also have R&D there. We need to be playing piano on the whole keyboard—on the full value chain." He described the very different approaches of the engineers who design the "hard envelope" of the farm machinery and of the electronics engineers. The development cycle of the hardware is six to eight years; that of the electronics far shorter. Even the mentality of the engineers is different, since the machine designers typically grew up on farms around heavy machinery. Keeping the two groups together in the same place—even eating lunch together—forces them to mutually adjust their rhythms.

Paths to innovation

Studies of industry have often observed that innovation in German manufacturing leads to incremental improvements in existing processes and products rather than the creation of radically new products and businesses, where the United States appears to do better.[13] Apple iPods, Facebook, and early generations of drugs personalized for an individual genome are not the kinds of products likely to emerge first in Germany while new generations of high-end capital equipment and production machinery, highly engineered luxury cars like BMWs and Mercedes, and high-performance textiles are more likely to come out of German factories than out of American plants. In part, these differences have to do with different industrial specializations with longer life cycles for goods and services sold to businesses and shorter life cycles for goods and services sold to consumers. They also reflect differences in business models, with the German firm's access to finance that is less demanding of immediate returns thus making it possible for management to invest in longer-term development projects.

Incremental innovation also draws on complex skills in the workforce, since many of the potential improvements grow out of hands-on experience and direct observation of production. When, for example, Teamtechnik, a company specializing in automation equipment, was ramping up production of machines to make solar photovoltaic stringers, it took weeks to assemble the first machines. The assembly workers—all of whom have "Facharbeiter" skill qualifications—provided feedback on design for manufacturability and for more efficient use of materials, and now it takes only one day to make it. The ability to learn from direct involvement in production is strong in the German workforce, both because of initially longer periods of worker education and apprenticeship and also because firms continue to invest heavily in the capabilities of workers.[14] The demand for apprenticeships among the school-leaving population has remained quite steady over the years, even as access to university education has widened. The average length of apprenticeships is three years, having increased over the past twenty years.[15] These workforce training patterns stand in sharp contrast to American practices. As the *Made in America* 1980s research comparing U.S. and German company involvement in apprenticeships and training showed, even twenty-five years ago, American companies were investing less in training than the Germans.[16] With the break-up of vertically integrated companies and the virtual disappearance of "lifetime" employment career ladders, U.S. companies have further cut back on training. Today the tendency is to satisfy the need for new skills by going back into the labor market and hiring new people rather than retraining the old ones already on the job.

This familiar comparison between the strengths of American industry in radical innovation and of German industry in incremental improvements highlights important differences. But by describing the German advantage as one in "incremental innovation" it fails to capture how these capabilities are used by German companies to create new industries. What the PIE researchers saw in company after company was the *repurposing* of key technologies to develop wholly new products and services. One German company had started as an equipment supplier to the semiconductor industry, and their specialty was machinery for wet-chemical processes. One of their old customers who had shifted from making semiconductors to making solar cells had a problem in its production plant and asked for help. In the course of helping the customer, they realized that if they applied their core wet chemistry technologies without much change to solar cell equipment, they could make far better equipment than the current standard. Initially it seemed like a simple transposition of technology from one field to another. But as solar took off and they had to ramp up production tenfold, they had to come up with a whole new manufacturing process. Assembly was so complex that they needed to control the entire value chain from design to manufacturing in order to get speed, quality, and efficient use of materials. They start with a standard machine to which they add customized options. These machines are tested and optimized on the customer's shop floor for months, while design engineers observe their performance and modify them. Every year they release a series based on incremental improvements; every three years they come out with a completely new product line developed from scratch, with a ramp-up that presents a whole new challenge.

VEM, the second largest manufacturer of electrical machinery in Germany, makes rotating electrical machines, and in the 1990s decided they needed to shift away from ship-building. They brought their technical skills into wind turbine production, and about half the sales revenues of their Dresden facility now come from wind.[17] Eickhoff Wind Power makes wind gearboxes.[18] The company was founded in the middle of the nineteenth century as a metal caster, and today the proprietary casting technologies they use still give it a competitive advantage. A manufacturer of robots that started in the auto industry as a supplier of machine tools for coating the glass for cars repurposed its technologies for solar modules. They started from technologies that were critical to their old specialization and ended up modifying them radically for the new business. Because solar module customers have different requirements for the architecture and dimensions of their production lines, the machine supplier turns out a large number of almost custom products. Here again we found a firm with a high degree of in-house integration and production. Their R&D department is right next to the production facility. The customers inspect the machines while they are being made. And this supplier's engineers accompany the machines to the installation at the customers' plants making final changes all along to accommodate conditions in the customers' facilities. Today this supplier's revenues are about half from its old auto business and half from solar.

We saw other auto component suppliers who had also "repurposed" technologies for the renewable energy business. Teamtechnik is a company that had specialized in automation systems for flexible production. It was founded in 1976, and worked mainly for the auto industry.[19] Stefan Rosskopf, Teamtechnik's second-generation head, decided it would be wise to diversify the company's business across a number of sectors and to reduce exposure to cars. As he recounts it, he ideally wanted a sector where he could use 70 percent of what the company already knew how to do and where they would need to innovate for the 30 percent required to develop new products. They realized that in wind and solar thermal, their previous auto industry capabilities were not relevant. For solar cells, he could see that semiconductor companies were already in there and had strong legacy knowledge to draw on. With solar modules, however, there was as yet little automation and there was a huge demand for large-scale production equipment. So over a two-year period Teamtechnik started working on machines for making solar modules. Ultimately they were able to repurpose about 70 percent of their technology from the auto industry. The innovations came in infrared and laser welding and also in creating a system that combined previously separate steps for spraying flux fluid on the cell.

Rosskopf reflected that the knowledge they had transferred from the auto industry, for example in assembling and testing valves, was extremely valuable in advancing technology in the new industry. In developing the new lines, Teamtechnik also learned from working with suppliers. He mentioned working with Festo, an automation company PIE researchers had also interviewed. (See chapter 4.) Rosskopf said: "People are really good at developing solutions. We'll tell them: I've got this part and it needs to move from here to there, but it's very fragile. And it needs to happen in two seconds. Festo is just down the road, so they come over and we play around and figure out what parts we need from them. They are a real enabler."

Customers usually ask Teamtechnik to start working on a machine for assembling a part even before they have completely finished developing the part. So changes are inevitable. But as Rosskopf explained, it has to work this way because if customers take a few years to develop a gearbox and then Teamtechnik took more years to develop the machine to assemble the gearbox, the lead time would be too long. So these processes need to take place in parallel. It usually takes the company about one and a half or two years to make a prototype for the customer. Three different kinds of engineers will work on it: mechanical engineers; electrical engineers; and then the software team. As Claas told us, too, each of these disciplines has its own rhythms and ways of doing things, and so having them together is critical for getting them into synch.

Rosskopf told us he could not imagine not having their R&D take place right next to production, since the machines cannot be developed in a simulation or on a computer. CAD and similar programs cannot simulate the conditions of the machines—the friction and the stress on materials when surfaces are covered in oil. Nor can the simulations work to figure out the stability of cell connections at different welding temperatures and pressures. When Teamtechnik consulted with the Fraunhofer Institute and several university labs, they learned it would still be too expensive and too inaccurate to try to resolve these issues with simulations. So for now, they build the machine, test it, tweak the parameters, and try again. Their engineers bring experience they've gained on the job. Most of them did apprenticeships before college, so they have real practical skills. There is a lot of tacit knowledge about what does and does not work—that is why they expanded into industries where they could apply knowledge they already had and combine it with something new.

When there are big customer markets abroad, it's necessary to be physically present in those locales, even if production costs are not much lower there. It's important for relationships with the customers and for showing commitment. When assembling systems that are custom-designed, engineering as well as production technicians will need to be present, Teamtechnik found from their Polish and Chinese experience. In some of these markets, the company may even have to start making standard components, if they are not available locally at the right quality. But R&D needs to remain in Germany if the company is to continue to bring out innovative products.

Innovation in Germany builds on legacies: in industrial specializations, longstanding relationships with customers, workforce skills, and proximity to suppliers with diverse capabilities.[20] The potential of German patterns, however, extends well beyond defending existing niches against low-cost competition with incremental advances in process and products. New businesses are being created, not usually through start-ups—in contrast to the American model—but through the transformation of old capabilities and their reapplication and repurposing for new ends. In tracing out the trajectories through which the companies we interviewed developed wholly new lines of business—moving from autos to solar modules, from semiconductors to solar cells, or from machines to make spark plugs to machines that make medical devices like artificial knees—we saw not only innovation, but scaling up to market. In the Main Street manufacturers we interviewed in the United States, companies usually had only their own internal material and human assets to draw on when they tried to scale up an innovation; in the German case, companies not only had their own legacy resources, but also found a wide and diverse set of complementary capabilities in the industrial ecosystem. It's impossible to understand the different fates of manufacturing in the United States and Germany without comparing the density and richness of the resources available in the industrial ecosystem across much of Germany to the thin and shrinking resources available to U.S. manufacturers across much of the country—outside of some very lucky regions, like Silicon Valley, Cambridge, Massachusetts, Raleigh-Durham, and a few other hot spots that have been well chronicled in the literature on clusters and on the "new geography of jobs."[21]

The German industrial ecosystem

As PIE researchers visited companies in Germany, the technologies we saw them developing were familiar, but the industrial landscape they inhabited appeared to be an entirely different universe from the one we saw around the companies in the United States. By industrial ecosystem, we mean the territorial base of resources and relationships outside a company's four walls that it can use in developing its business and, of particular interest to our project, in bringing new ideas into the market. Some of the complementary capabilities that reside in an industrial ecosystem come from suppliers. In the PIE interviews in Germany, managers frequently volunteered that when they are thinking about developing something new, they first just go down the street and ask a supplier: Can you do it? Companies referred to learning new technologies from suppliers who had acquired them working in different industrial sectors. In the U.S. interviews with start-ups like Kiva, Q-D Vision, and Ambri, we had also heard how important it was for innovators to find nearby suppliers and to work through initial phases of scale-up together. But failures to find the right suppliers in the right place and anxieties about the resilience and viability of critical suppliers were frequent themes in the American interviews—and not in the German.

Other complements to internal-firm resources in Germany are provided by institutions already discussed earlier in this chapter: local and regional banks and the dual vocational educational system. But what's especially striking in Germany is the large presence in the ecosystem of institutions whose specific function is to enrich the terrain for industrial innovation.[22] These organizations include trade associations, industrial collective research consortia, industrial research centers and associations, Fraunhofer Institutes, university-industry collaboratives, technical advisory committees, and more. A few examples of each of these types of organization can be found in the American states in which we conducted the PIE interviews. But the sheer numbers and density and reach of these organizations in Germany have no real equivalents in the United States. One survey of a sample of 744 industrial collective research projects undertaken in Germany between 2003 and 2005 found 293 different organizations involved in just those programs.[23]

The role of the government in supporting innovation through these institutions comes via specific technology programs that receive both industry and public funds. Germany has no R&D tax credit. Although some of the groups in Chancellor Angela Merkel's coalition favor such a credit, others oppose it, in part at least out of concern that it would supplant the current mode of funding innovation through grants to research institutes together with businesses.[24] The sums the government provides for programs may not be very large. The industrial collective research networks program, for example, received 123 million euros from the German federal government in 2008.[25] Private business picked up about 85 percent of the total cost of the program. In interviews, companies described receiving government R&D funding for participating in research consortia that ranged from 20 percent of development costs in a project on measurement to 50 percent of costs for participants in a photovoltaic group.

But even for the projects that received the largest share of government funding, participants describe the greatest benefits as ones coming from the cooperation that the funding incentivizes. Government acts here as a convenor, and uses funding sweeteners to encourage collaborations that will end up providing companies returns far beyond the lowered R&D costs. The photovoltaic cluster Solarvalley Mitteldeutschland received 40 million euros of funding from government to match 40 million euros from industry for a five-year project on grid parity. It brought together universities, research institutes, and companies. One of the industry leaders of the cluster described his company's experience in the cluster:

> Of course we had difficulties. It takes a while until people are on the same wavelength and trust each other. There's a lot of competitiveness and people don't find it easy to collaborate. But over time, things work out. We each pick our own partners and the ideas are developed in joint brainstorming sessions.
>
> We would never be able to come up with all of these ideas ourselves, but even more important, there are too many ideas to be tested all by ourselves and to discover which are promising and which are not. That's where companies that do not participate and only use in-house research are missing out. Competition is important, but these processes we are testing in collaboration with others are still three or four years from mass production so there is no direct product collaboration. If we can cut down development time by a year, this cluster will have been successful in helping us be ahead of international competition. Companies need to realize that the real competitive threat is

not the other firms in the cluster, but our foreign competitors, especially in East Asia.

He observed that the sums the German government has invested in the Solarvalley fall far short of the billions he believes the Chinese provide to the industry through cheap land, loans, and subsidies.

In order to target government research funding on areas thought to be significant for the economy in the future, the "Projekttraeger" or "project-bearer" system was created, with government determining the priorities and handing off the selection of grantees and administration to independent research organizations with expert reviewers on their staffs. Government ministries identify the programmatic themes and priorities and then choose a "Projekttraeger" organization to administer the program and select grantees. The funds can be given to encourage establishing a cluster, as long as the funding is directed to pre-competitive activities. In medical devices, for example, funding might go to supporting R&D collaborations between research institutions and companies in exploring alternative technologies for hearing aids—but not to development of a new hearing aid. The boundary lines between precompetitive development work and work on commercialization may be blurry but they are somewhat constrained by European Union bans on direct subsidies to firms.

Institutions that support the innovation and its scale-up in the ecosystem work through diverse mechanisms. They diffuse information that small and medium-sized companies would have difficulty obtaining by themselves. They bring companies together in research consortia to discuss roadmaps for new technologies and to work collaboratively on precompetitive stages for these new technologies. They build equipment and facilities to be used by multiple firms who could not afford to buy these themselves. They distribute some public funds through competitions. In the case of Solarvalley, the cluster even funded basic research and education by funding chairs at the universities in Halle and Ilmenau and degree programs in collaboration with industry at those universities. In general, these are institutions that lower the cost and the risk of innovation and increase the likelihood that innovation that plays off new combinations of specializations will actually come to life.

Scaling up in China

In the spectacular rise of Chinese industry over the past three decades, the similarities between Chinese capabilities and those of German manufacturers are hardly the points that come first to mind. The standard explanations of the extraordinary growth of Chinese economy and of the role of exports in that growth focus on factors very different from anything in the German economy, now or in even the distant past. Analyses of Chinese growth emphasize low-wage labor, foreign direct investors bringing capital and manufacturing export experience from Taiwan, Hong Kong, and the West, and the facilitating role of government, which provided political stability, cheap land, cheap loans, and a protected and undervalued currency. Underlying all of these factors is China's huge population, with seemingly inexhaustible reserves of low-wage workers and the vast potential of more than a billion new consumers—a field of dreams for investors. China experts may differ on exactly how much each of these factors mattered over the past thirty years, but there is general agreement on the basic story.

What's new, though, is that over the past ten years firms have been emerging in China with remarkable innovative capabilities in manufacturing. As in Germany, a number of companies in high-tech sectors like wind, solar, medical devices, and batteries show signs of mastering the scale-up of complex products and processes in new industries by bringing down the heavy capital costs of commercialization, accelerating time to market, and turning out new-to-the world goods. Even in these high-tech sectors, the "legacy" of low factor costs still matters. While wages have been rising rapidly in China in relation to productivity, for the most part they remain far lower than Western wages even in high-tech industries.[26] The prowess of a firm like Foxconn, Apple's principal supplier, in rapid and cheap product introductions of new generations of iPods, iPhones, and iPads still depends heavily on employing and disciplining vast numbers of low-wage workers.

But low-wage labor alone cannot account for the capabilities that companies in high-tech sectors like wind, solar, medical devices, and batteries are demonstrating as they innovate in manufacturing by converting processes of scale-up into a terrain of value creation.[27] Indeed as PIE researchers learned, in a number of the most successful renewable energy companies in China, wages for the upper tiers of the engineering work-force are not significantly lower than they would be in the West, and wages for lower levels of the engineering technicians are on a path of convergence. For example, at JA Solar, a privately owned Shanghai company listed on NASDAQ and the world's largest producer of solar cells, the CEO told the PIE team that all of the senior management through the vice president level are engineering PhD returnees from the United States, Australia, and Europe who earn salaries corresponding to their equivalents back in the West.[28] Down through the JA Solar hierarchy, the pay differential between returnees and locally trained engineers has been eliminated.

More important, though, PIE researchers saw examples of Chinese firms that have developed innovative capabilities in manufacturing that have allowed them to excel in scale-up to mass manufacturing not because of labor cost advantages, but because they are able to translate between advanced product designs and complex manufacturing requirements. Like the German firms we examined, the Chinese companies are creating knowledge that derives directly from their own manufacturing experience. Some firms use this knowledge to transform manufacturing processes and existing product designs, other firms are able to use this knowledge to create new-to-the-world products and components.

Dan Breznitz and Michael Murphree have described in *Run of the Red Queen* (2011) how the Chinese excel at all those forms of innovation that incorporate, enable, and rapidly deliver products and solutions at the technological frontier—but do not themselves initiate the path-breaking innovations at that edge.[29] Like Lewis Carroll's Red Queen, they race to keep up, and staying in there takes speed, determination, and clever short-cuts. Their unique capabilities in the race derive from being able to rede-sign for manufacturability, from finding less expensive materials than those the inventor may have originally considered, from hands-on experience of bringing successive product generations through to the market, and from easy access to a surrounding industrial ecosystem replete with qualified suppliers who can provide every component needed at the drop of a hat. While a company like Foxconn may originally have won its Western customers by providing the lowest prices thanks to the labors of hundreds of thousands of compliant, low-wage workers, today it has rein-forced this initial advantage by gathering around itself a dense network of suppliers. A *New York Times* report on why Apple makes iPhones and iPads and iPods in China quoted an Apple manager: "The entire supply chain is in China now. You need a thousand rubber gaskets? That's the factory next door. You need a million screws? That factory is a block away. You need that screw made a little bit different? It will take three hours."[30] The extraordinary abilities of Foxconn for rapid product innovation depend on being able to marshal the experience and capabilities in manufacturing complex new products of scores of subcontractors around it. Even as wages rise in China, Foxconn will still have an enormous advantage in bidding for the work of the world's innovative design houses since its commanding position in a rich ecosystem allows it to offer customers like Apple and Hewlett Packard a complete range of the productive assets needed to bring complicated and demanding products to life rapidly and at relatively low cost.

This ecosystem now allows firms like Foxconn to offer unprecedented capabilities in scale-up and innovative manufacturing to its large, American customers, and also provides infrastructure that attracts foreign start-ups. In a gray, faceless business park on the outskirts of Shanghai we met a group of Silicon Valley engineers who had come to China to commercialize a radically new type of solar cell that offers efficiencies similar to traditional technologies but relies on much cheaper materials. The many reasons that had brought this group to Shanghai certainly included the typical tax breaks, and deals, and permitting processes that make it easy and fast to open a manufacturing facility in China. But the CEO also pointed to a rich local supplier base and the presence of an engineering workforce specialized in scale-up and mass manufacturing as a reason to leave California. "There is an entire supply chain here locally and everything we need can be bought in the vicinity of the plant. Even production equipment can be purchased very easily from local suppliers and the abundance of local solar firms means that we can source used equipment, which much reduces the cost of setting up our operation. Our local R&D engineers know how to re-engineer and adjust inexpensive standard equipment to meet the production requirements of the new cell."

These capabilities in innovative manufacturing are an important part of the explanation for why Chinese firms in some sectors have become indispensable partners for many Western start-up firms on a path to commercialization as well as for more established companies who no longer have manufacturing in-house. The new innovative capabilities of the Chinese enterprises are not, of course, the sole factor at work in any of these cases. In many of these partnerships, as PIE research on the trajectories of start-up companies discovered, the relationships between U.S. innovators and Chinese companies have as a starting point the willingness and financial ability of the Chinese companies to sink large amounts of capital into the final stages of scaling up production to full capacity in industries that require heavy bricks-and-mortar investment. A start-up like Boston Power, a start-up that pioneered in batteries for electric cars, received $155 million in Chinese government and private funds for a factory near Shanghai.[31] For Great Point Energy, a seven-year-old Cambridge start-up, it meant a $1.25 billion deal for its first commercial-scale plant for making natural gas from coal.[32] The plant will be located in the far west of China. The investor is Wanxiang Holdings, the same firm that bought up the patents of A123, another Massachusetts start-up, one that went bankrupt when it was unable to scale its technology successfully.

But while many of these partnerships may start because of finance that Chinese public and private sources can provide and that innovators do not find elsewhere, the shape of the trajectory of the relationship as the innovative start-ups work to commercialize production in China with Chinese strategic partners is not determined only by money. In part, these relationships evolve in response to the enormous expansion of the China market. In the energy sector, for example, there is explosive new demand in China, while in the West demand is flat, and there are entrenched firms that have little reason to bring new supplies of energy into the market. In the absence of a carbon tax, incentives to invest in new sources of energy in the West are few and, like feed-in tariffs, liable to disappear in new policy cycles. The boom in natural gas has made it even less likely that major utilities in the United States will make major investments in renewable energy scale-up. So selling to the Chinese market is certainly an alluring prospect for some of the Western start-ups and a reason to partner with cash-flush Chinese firms. But even in those industries in which the main customer markets are still in the West, as they are for consumer electronics and for photovoltaic cell and module production from the inception of this industry in China in the mid-2000s to today, American and European innovators are turning to Chinese partners. Increasingly the reason for choosing Chinese manufacturers has to do with their specific capabilities in knowledge-intensive scale-up.

For the PIE researchers, studying the evolution of these capabilities was a unique opportunity to observe the different ways that value can be created through innovation in different kinds of manufacturing. Across a diverse set of firms, some in supposedly mature commodity businesses, others in new emergent sectors, like renewable energy, in product industries and process niches, the researchers identified a number of common patterns:[33] reverse-engineering and re-engineering mature products, making a design into a new-to-the-world product or process, and indigenous innovation.

Reverse-engineering and re-engineering a mature product

Chinese firms, like those in economies like Taiwan and Korea in the take-off phases of their industrialization, are mastering the art of reverse-engineering existing products and doing it in ways that are cheaper and faster, while still turning out goods of acceptable quality. What often emerges from this process, however, is a product resembling the original and with close to the same functionality, but incorporating simplified components, cheaper materials, and an altered product design that makes it easier to manufacture. A number of these companies indeed advertise "Japanese quality at Chinese prices." And even when the products do not exactly reach the level of the advertised claim, they are often of *good enough* quality to do the job.

The Chinese ability to combine existing designs and components and produce expensive equipment at a lower price can be of great value to American companies. In a U.S. metal fabrication firm we visited in the Midwest, we saw a team of five Chinese technicians installing a gigantic Yawei single ram press brake. With it the U.S. company will be able to make pipes or crane arms or transmission poles up to 60 feet long as single pieces. To make these parts today, the firm needs fifteen people working on that job; with the new press, only three or four workers will be needed. But this will not mean cuts in the workforce. This company now has over two hundred employees. Business has been expanding rapidly, and they expect to grow by thirty to forty new workers a year for the foreseeable future. The machine had been custom-made in Hebei province in China from a Dutch design with key components coming from Germany and Japan. Most of the value of the press, the CEO explained, comes from the Chinese "cobbling together global capabilities." He commented: "Certainly if they could pump out machines like the one we bought from them on their own, we'd be in real trouble in the U.S.!" Whether or not that's true, at present, these Chinese capabilities are allowing an American company to afford expensive new equipment to accelerate its expansion.

The PIE interviews in China provided a picture of what's taking place at the ground level between Western high tech companies and Chinese manufacturers that gives rise to these capabilities. In the wind industry, for instance, PIE researchers visited a Chinese firm that had obtained a license for a generator from a German wind turbine supplier. The licensed design was a state-of-the-art generator model, of the type used in thousands of wind turbines around the world, but the design was incompatible with the most cost-effective fan model available on the market. While the German engineers had been unable to fix this problem, the Chinese firm redesigned the original generator to work with the cheaper fan and then licensed back this innovation to the Germans. The reverse-engineering capabilities of the Chinese firm allowed it to produce an alternative, and the Germans recognized the value of this by paying for a reverse license.

In this case the Chinese firm collaborated with a Western company through a contractual arrangement, but in some cases, the Chinese use these capabilities to compete head-on with the Western producers. They have bought key components from foreign suppliers, licensed technology, and sometimes bought up smaller foreign competitors. Then, using cheaper materials, simplified designs for manufacturing, and some domestic components, they have been able to push prices down. In part because of these capabilities, they have been able to engineer wind turbines costing as little as 75 percent of the least expensive 4,500 RMB/watt models of their foreign competitors. Foreign wind companies have taken note of these capabilities, and one European wind turbine firm we visited went as far as setting up a complete supply chain in China, poaching Chinese engineers from local competitors, learning about alternative materials available domestically, and changing architectures of its European-designed products to ease scale-up and mass manufacturing. The European firm was eventually able to match the cost of its Chinese competitors, yet the market had evolved and customers were demanding larger turbine types. The firm's Chinese competitors were able to redesign their products to cut costs while simultaneously reacting to rapidly changing market conditions, now offering cheaper and larger wind turbines than the European firm. Speed, therefore, is at least as critical as cost-cutting in this process. The speed advantage of the Chinese firms at least in part derives from an improvisational trial and error approach to testing feasibility and design that prioritizes rapidity and cost over a formal stage-gate innovation process or any standardized procedures. The Chinese head of a large foreign wind turbine manufacturer acknowledged that if he brought the firms' latest and most advanced wind turbines to China, the turbines would not be able to compete on cost or technology, even if they were to be proven more reliable than those made by Chinese competitors.[34]

Making a design into a new-to-the world product or process

To explain the location and distribution of activities between firms in advanced industrial countries and those in developing economies, analysts frequently refer to the concept of a product cycle. This idea was first laid out by Raymond Vernon in 1966 and more recently reformulated by Pisano and Shih to distinguish early years of production of new products—when the complexities of scaling them from labs and from prototypes to full commercialization are still significant—and more mature industries.[35] The complexities of early years of production are thought to constitute natural barriers to the migration of these activities abroad. Only when production processes mature, that is, when they are more completely understood and can be standardized and codified, can they be transferred into countries with less sophisticated engineering capabilities, and with lower costs of production.

PIE researchers found in China that the product cycle model no longer works to explain many of the emerging relationships between Western innovative firms and their Chinese partners. Nowadays U.S. and European companies often arrive in China with a design and rely on the production know-how of the Chinese firms to fill out the commercialization processes. Sometimes the foreign firm has no manufacturing capabilities at all, or it may be unable to make a product at a viable price, or it may be deterred by the capital and tooling costs of commercialization. In the case of Great Point Energy, as the *Boston Globe* reported, the firm had received $155 million in U.S. venture funding, but needed far more to bring to life its technology for converting carbon feedstocks into pipeline quality methane gas using catalytic hydromethanation (catalytic process) instead of the thermal processes used in synfuels production. The environmental impact is lighter than with other processes; costs are lower; lower-quality coal can be used; and it is possible to capture or sequester the CO_2. But with "fracking" and the natural gas boom in the United States, American utilities were just not interested. In China, there were not only willing big investors, and enormous energy needs, there were also real capabilities for novel approaches to accelerating start-up time for the plant and lowering costs.

PIE researchers learned that while Great Point will be doing the front-end design work in the United States they have found valuable design expertise and knowledge they could draw on from their Chinese partners for making the Great Point technologies into a commercially viable project.[36] In plants that do coal gasification, the cost of the basic originating technologies may account for only 10–15 percent of overall costs. The balance of systems costs are huge, with an extended period of development and numerous players involved. A global engineering firm has to be brought in to design the overall plant in which the technology package will be embedded. There has to be close collaboration with fabricators on what's feasible to build, how to change design in order to facilitate fabrication and lower costs, and how capabilities in fabrication might enhance the basic technology design. Multiple forms of knowledge are involved, from technology design on the part of the originator, to project management on the part of the engineering construction firm, to manufacturing know-how once the plant is built, and to the continuous improvement of the technology on the basis of plant operation. Given the number of gasification plants that are under construction or that will be built in China over the next decade, access to this cumulating expertise will be essential for any company wishing to enter this industry. In the case of Great Point Energy, bringing its design to life in the western deserts of China will represent a true combination of Western and Chinese innovative capabilities. This is not a mature operation being transferred to a developing economy, but a new-to-the-world technology reaching commercialization for the first time.

Such cooperation in the commercialization of innovative technologies occurs even in licensing relationships, in many ways the model of technology transfer from advanced to middle-income economies that the product cycle envisions. Take the example of Vensys, a German wind turbine manufacturer that in 2000 had spun off from a local university research group. Vensys had developed a gearless "direct drive" wind turbine, eliminating the need for a gearbox, one of the most expensive turbine components to purchase and maintain and a component notoriously prone to breakdown and malfunctions. By using a novel type of generator, the rotation of the blades can be transmitted directly to the generator without transmission through a gearbox in between.

Unable to find the capital to invest in a production facility and unfamiliar with scale-up and mass manufacturing, Vensys licensed its core technology to firms around the world, including to China's Goldwind in 2003. Subsequently, optimization of the wind turbine technology as well as design adjustments for manufacturing occurred in cooperation with the Chinese partner, for the initial 1.5MW turbine as well as for larger turbines that followed in later years. In 2008, the relationship between design engineers in Germany and production engineers in China had become so beneficial that Vensys sold a 70 percent stake to Goldwind. Although Vensys had higher offers from other bidders, they partnered with Goldwind precisely for the production capabilities and the know-how in innovation manufacturing essential for the long-term viability of their turbine technology.[37]

In 2009, more than 1,000 Vensys turbines were manufactured in Goldwind plants in China; in 2012, nearly 12,000 megawatts of turbines using Vensys's innovative direct drive technology were operating in China, compared to 70 megawatts in Germany.[38] While basic research and development functions have remained in Germany, where Vensys employment has more than tripled since 2007, design changes relating to cost reductions, manufacturability, and technology optimization occur in China, where R&D centers have been established in close proximity to production facilities.[39]

Indigenous product innovation

The capabilities of Chinese firms to use knowledge that they have acquired from experience in manufacturing to bring new products to life may lead to innovations that can be patented, PIE researchers found. In these cases, the strengths of the Chinese companies are not just in enabling a foreign design to be implemented and commercialized, but in actually developing Chinese innovations that will be introduced both domestically and abroad. LP Amina is a Charlotte, NC based energy and environmental company that focuses on sustainable coal utilization for power generation and innovative coal-to-chemicals production processes.[40] As LP Amina was working with Chinese power plants to improve combustion efficiencies, it realized there were real constraints on the efficiencies it could achieve because of the limitations of the standard equipment being used to filter and segregate coal particles by size before they pass through to the combuster. This equipment, which stands outside the plant several stories high, is called a *classifier*. The mostly commonly used classifiers are based on old U.S. and German designs; they allow coal particles that are too large to enter the combuster to pass through, and they also strain the plant's fans by forcing air through the classifer. LP Amina tackled these issues with its in-house engineering staff based in China and its engineering consultants based in the U.S. The result was a retrofit that LP Amina patented in both the United States and China in 2010. By reducing the number of wrong-sized particles reaching the combuster and reducing fan pressure, the efficiency of the plants with the retrofitted classifier technology improved significantly. The payback period for such a retrofit can be as short as eighteen days of plant operation.

The real breakthroughs that allowed LP Amina to get to its patented retrofit design came from the knowledge gained in the course of making and installing twenty retrofits in China after the initial conceptual modeling. Each retrofit required some tailoring to individual plants, with a few basic variants. This experimentation allowed the company to learn by doing. When LP Amina had proposed trying out its retrofit to U.S. utility companies—for free—it had found no takers, even though the potential efficiency gains were high. Today, the U.S. utilities are very interested, and pilot projects are in progress. As Will Latta, LP Amina's founder and managing director, reflected on why the Chinese firms had been willing to experiment with the retrofits, while the U.S. utilities had not, he identified two factors. First, the retrofit classifiers would have to be built locally, because of their bulk. And the cost of making one in China—because of low wages, speed, and streamlined licensing and certification—would be only about one-quarter of the cost of making one in the United States. So potential U.S. customers did have to envisage a larger outlay and presumably a somewhat longer payback period. But even more important, there's an inherent conservatism in the behavior of utilities serving the stable U.S. market as contrasted with utilities in China, who are in explosive growth mode. The strength of the Chinese engineers is in rapid breakneck technology deployment, so they are willing to try out lots of new things.

PIE researchers heard similar comments from Western wind turbine manufacturers operating in China. In that industry, it was the government pushing to increase installed capacity as quickly as possible—even before there were systems in place to take the turbines off the grid in a controlled way in the event of grid accidents and instability. The observer noted: "The mentality here in China is: Try things out. Push the limit. Find your mistakes. Then fix them. Germans would never accept all this uncertainty—but one advantage of the Chinese system is that it's very fast and you learn quickly." For all the concerns about reliability and quality of Chinese-made products, Western wind firms have realized the benefits of this mentality. They are taking more design work to China and working with Chinese suppliers for components that need to be developed from scratch. Interviewing Western wind firms, we learned that Chinese suppliers of central turbine components such as generators and transmissions, which few manufacturers develop in-house, take roughly half as long as those developed in Europe or the United States. Particularly in markets such as renewable energy, which are highly volatile owing to their dependence on government policy and regulation, speed and improvisation can make the difference between successfully bringing an idea to market and missing the window of commercial opportunity.

Where do scale-up capabilities lead?

Much of what the PIE researchers saw in Chinese firms that drew on strong innovative capabilities—and not simply on using low-wage workers or low-cost land and capital—is of recent creation. In earlier MIT research projects (1996–1997; 1999–2005) in which some of the same researchers had conducted hundreds of interviews in factories and R&D centers in Hong Kong, Taiwan, and mainland China, they had not found significant innovative capabilities.[41] Low factor costs and the managerial skills of the foreign owners of the mainland-based manufacturing seemed to account for the successes we observed in producing goods for export. Even the efforts at technology transfer from advanced Western firms to Chinese partners (most of them technology transfers mandated by the Chinese government) did not seem to be taking off.

Enormous change has taken place over the past decade, and at the leading edge of Chinese manufacturing there are firms whose innovative activities are clearly adding significant value to the commercialization efforts of Western companies. These phenomena are so recent, though, that we do not know how profitable these new competencies are for the Chinese firms themselves. How are the returns from these new partnerships distributed between Western innovators and the Chinese manufacturers? If the capabilities provided by the Chinese are indeed ones that are unique or at least very difficult and expensive to replicate, the margins of the Chinese firms should be higher than those of the Chinese manufacturers who simply make standard commodities to the specifications of the Western firms. The Chinese firms with these innovative capabilities would then be winning a larger share of the gains from their relationships with the Western firms. We do not know if this is the case.

The only one of these relationships for which we have systematic analysis of the returns to producers carrying out various functions is the creation of goods and services between Apple and its subcontractors. Pioneering research papers by Dedrick, Kraemer, and Linden have explored for the consumer electronics industry how the distribution of profits varies both by industrial sector and by the architecture of the product. System architects like Apple and those component suppliers like Intel with capabilities and intellectual property that are essentially irreplaceable are the ones that capture the lion's share of rewards.[42] What this means for the bottom line of Chinese contract manufacturers is a very small share of the profits. With "tear-down" analysis, experts at iSuppli have calculated that in 2010 on a $600 Apple iPhone 4, Apple's profit was $360.[43] Assembly in China accounted for $6.54 of the costs. It's obvious that Foxconn (Hon Hai), Apple's principal subcontractor manufacturer, could have earned only razor-thin margins. Given the enormous volume of work flowing through Foxconn, even with slim margins the company has been able to thrive.

But a low-margin high-volume business model is not one that is likely to be profitable or sustainable for China's new innovative manufacturers like the ones described above—if only because the volumes they are producing will never approach Foxconn's. For these companies to prosper over the long term they need to be able to continuously generate innovation in manufacturing and to be able to capitalize on this by reaping high(er) profits. The remarkable accomplishments the PIE researchers have documented need to be but the earliest entries in a steady stream of innovative creations. The question for the future of these companies, then, is whether they can extract and invest enough of the value of their current production to be able to generate high levels of innovation as a regular part of their operations. Will these companies turn out to be "one-trick ponies," or will they evolve into enterprises capable of continuously reinventing ways of closing the gap between the innovator and customer?

For the Western partners of the Chinese companies, too, there are high stakes in the future of the relationship. The key question is whether it's possible to retain their capacity for innovation. Often this is framed as a matter of whether innovation that is shared with China or that is developed with Chinese firms will eventually be wrongfully taken over by the Chinese. There are enough cases of that happening that virtually no company working in China discounts such a possibility. In some of our interviews, companies simply recognized that they would have to accept the loss of whatever intellectual property they deployed in China and race to be ahead with the next generation of products and services. Others specified particular technologies that they are unwilling to move into Chinese plants. Yet others have devised particular organizational strategies for trying to shield their technology. One large U.S. company with several plants in China, for example, described setting up their Chinese plants entirely differently than their U.S. plants. In the United States, they have not had a one-man one-machine organization since the seventies; today a worker operates across the entire front of the line. In China, in contrast, each of the functions is compartmentalized, and the employee sees just the information he needs to do his job, rather than the big picture. Given the high annual rate of employee turnover in China, this makes it easier to replace a worker and to train his successor; and it also limits the amount of knowledge a departing worker could bring to a competitor. But protecting their IP by compartmentalizing functions, the manager ruefully acknowledged, has a big downside: it means they cannot get innovation out of their Chinese plants. The manager explained: "Most innovation results from repurposing ideas from one place and applying them to another. If you can't see the bigger picture, you're not going to come up with new things."

For U.S. innovators the long-term risk in their China relationships is far greater than the loss of any particular proprietary technology or trade secret. And it's a risk for which the greatest responsibility is American. When U.S. companies transfer the commercialization of their technologies abroad, their capacity for initiating future rounds of innovation may be reduced. Chapters 3 and 4 have laid out some of the reasons that innovation fails to build into companies and jobs here in the United States: the lack of finance for large scale build-outs of capital-intensive activities, the holes in the ecosystem that leave small and medium-sized firms totally dependent on internal resources when they want to develop new ideas, the structure of incentives that favor radical innovation over incremental innovation, and, indeed, the availability in China and elsewhere of alternatives to monetizing one's own innovations at home. Yet as the discussion here of German and Chinese manufacturing suggests, the potential losses for American innovation of continuing down this track may be very large. In part, that's because much learning takes place as companies move their ideas beyond prototypes and demonstration and through the stages of commercialization. As the interviews and plant visits in Germany illustrated vividly, learning takes place as the engineers and technicians on the factory floor come back with their problems to find the design engineers and experiment with new approaches; learning takes places as users come back with problems. And in the challenges of large-scale production, even of commodities like diapers and razors, companies like Procter & Gamble find a terrain for innovation that allows them to reap higher profits.

6
Trends in Advanced Manufacturing Technology Research[1]

Nineteenth- and twentieth-century manufacturing was a long process of transforming the raw materials provided by nature through stages of fabrication, assembly, and warehousing into finished goods for sale in markets. From its origins until today, this has been a production process divided into distinct steps separated in time and space. Raw materials from forests, fields, and mines are transported to a manufacturing plant and temporarily stored in warehouses until needed for fabrication. The warehouse serves as a buffer to ensure that the production line will never be starved of inputs. Next in sequence comes the manufacture of individual components that are the fundamental building blocks of the finished products. Parts are then used for final assembly, which may occur in multiple stages involving subassemblies if the product is particularly complex. Completed assembly involves final inspection to check that the product meets all requirements and works as intended. Finished goods are then stored for distribution to markets through the outgoing supply chain.

There have been some significant changes to this process as changes in corporate control and advances in information technology have led to the deverticalization of companies. Companies used to keep many of the functions involved in production within their own four corporate walls. Ford once even owned rubber plantations. Today, firms purchase an increasing amount of the materials and components on the market from suppliers instead of making them in-house. The parts ordered from suppliers remain until needed in intermediate buffer stations either at the supplier or in inventory at the final assemblers. Assembly may take place in multiple phases involving subassemblies put together on parallel preassembly lines that feed into the main production line. Manufacturing today also draws on major technical advances in statistical process control to monitor quality continuously, rather than allow defects to slip through to final stages.

Through the first century of mass production, companies emphasized maximizing throughput by making a relatively small assortment of standard products. Since the late 1980s, however, mass markets have fragmented, and firms increasingly turn out a greater variety of products that respond to specific customer demands in different market segments. This responsiveness to demand has led manufacturing plants to reverse a traditional linear organization oriented to pushing out product and scheduling output on the basis of sales forecasts and, instead, to organize assembly in response to real-time orders—"pull." This requires sophisticated integration of production planning and scheduling of plant operations and supply chain management.

But even with these changes of the past decades, manufacturing today still closely resembles its mass production ancestors. We now stand on the edge of radical changes in this system, as a set of new technologies emerging in laboratories and research centers across the United States promises to completely transform the traditional linear manufacturing organization. First, our ability to synthesize new materials has now advanced to a point where human design of these materials will become as critical a step as fabrication and assembly. The downstream implications of engineered materials have great potential for combining and eliminating subsequent fabrication and assembly steps. Coatings, for example, may become less necessary. Second, the boundary between fabrication and assembly has blurred with the introduction of ultraefficient processes, automation, and even continuous manufacturing in batch sizes of "one." Third, the product is often not just a physical artifact or widget but an integrated solution that involves bundling of physical products with services and software. Finally, there is a trend toward the systematic return of recycled materials to fabrication or even material synthesis.

These changes are part of a wave of new technologies that we call *advanced manufacturing*. Some definitions of advanced manufacturing limit its range to the utilization of specific technologies and to the end-products of manufacturing that employs such technologies. For example, the President's Council of Advisors on Science and Technology (P-CAST)'s *Report to the President on Ensuring American Leadership in Advanced Manufacturing* (June 2011) calls advanced manufacturing "the

1. New Materials   3. Integrated Solution
2. Fabrication/Assembly   4. Recycled materials

family of activities that (a) depend on the use and coordination of information, automation, computation, software, sensing, and networking, and/or (b) make use of cutting edge materials and emerging capabilities enabled by the physical and biological sciences, for example nanotechnology, chemistry, and biology. It involves both new ways to manufacture existing products, and the manufacture of new products emerging from new advanced technologies." The report of the Advanced Manufacturing Partnership (July 2012) uses the same definition.[2] The 2012 report from the Institute for Defense Analyses, *Emerging Global Trends in Advanced Manufacturing,* employs a definition that is more comprehensive but that also covers much of the terrain of quotidian good business practices: "Advanced manufacturing improves existing or creates new materials, products, and processes via the use of science, engineering, and information technologies; high-precision tools and methods; a high-performance workforce; and innovative business or organizational models."[3]

Sharp delineation of the boundaries of a phenomenon are useful, but PIE observations both of technologies in the making in university, corporate, and public laboratories and of the actual operations of innovative manufacturers suggest a broader definition than one limited to particular technological fields or industries while still focused on cutting-edge technical change. We see advanced manufacturing as the creation of sustainable capabilities to make successive generations of integrated solutions

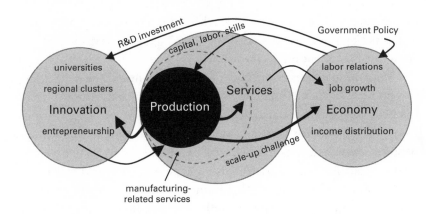

FIGURE 6.1

Structure of PIE study and position of the innovation-production interface coupling production of physical artifacts with services and software. The sustainability, efficiency, and rapidity of producing these generations will increasingly draw on custom-designed and recycled materials. We may find advanced manufacturing in new biotechnology production, but it can also transform even the oldest industries, like textiles. We conceive advanced manufacturing technology as an interface between the innovation system and industrial production. This might be depicted as a system of feed-forward and feedback mechanisms, as shown in figure 6.1.

Scanning new technologies

Our findings on a range of new manufacturing technologies that hold promise for increasing productivity, efficiency, and accelerating time to market are based on an internal scan of research at MIT, a survey of U.S. university programs in manufacturing, and a literature search. Out of the data collected in these inquiries, we identified three main families of technological opportunities in manufacturing that may be within reach even within the next five years. First, there are technologies that are truly enablers of classes of products that do not yet exist. Examples of these include nonsilicon-based semiconductors, wearable electronics, new drugs and fuels from biology, and new microsatellites with propulsive capabilities. Many of these have the potential to create new niches—even possibly new industries—that may generate substantial demand and economic activity. A key question is whether these new products will generate sufficient value and interest over time to coexist with or partially substitute for current products.

Second, there are opportunities for "programmable" manufacturing processes that do not rely on capital-intensive tooling and fixtures. One of the big trends is to counteract the need for expensive and unique manufacturing equipment with technologies such as 3D printing and maskless nanolithography. Several critical questions arise regarding these new flexible manufacturing processes: Can they guarantee the required tolerances? Will they catalyze distributed manufacturing—manufacturing in smaller, more agile, and more flexible production facilities, closer to end-users?

Third, there are new opportunities that derive from technologies that can enhance productivity and flexibility in existing large-scale manufacturing processes. Technologies like RFID tracking of parts during manufacturing and distribution and human-robotic collaboration are enablers of greater efficiency and productivity at key points along the value chain in existing manufacturing, even if they are not in and of themselves game-changers. If we develop these possibilities, the critical question may be whether there will be uptake by a wide diversity of actors in the U.S. industrial base.

Looked at in greater detail, the data collected in our investigation can be grouped into seven technology categories as follows:[4]

1. *Nano-engineering of materials and surfaces*   This involves the synthesis and structuring of functional and multifunctional materials at the nanoscale [10^{-9} m] and microscale [10^{-6} m] from the ground up. The materials include inorganic metals and composites and also biological materials and complex polymers. These technologies do not simply modify materials as they exist in nature, but create synthetic materials that may not have direct counterparts in the natural world. Respondents in our survey of U.S. manufacturing programs identified large area graphene production, roll-to-roll manufacturing, 3D integrated circuits for semiconductors, nanoengineered fiber-composite materials, and nanoetching of surfaces as especially promising targets for incorporation into commercial production.

2. *Additive and precision manufacturing*   This category of technologies includes new manufacturing processes that build up macroscopic parts layer by layer and achieve complex three-dimensional shapes starting from ingredients in powder or wire form. Often these processes are completely numerically controlled and avoid the need for expensive custom tooling. The creation of compliant actuators and sensors that can operate at small scale also fits into this group. Here the areas of research most frequently mentioned were 3D printing at home, rapid prototyping integrated with computer-aided design (CAD), next-generation injection molding, advanced electrical discharge machining, MOSIS-like foundries for prototyping, laser-based manufacturing, and metal sintering and forming of custom parts.

3. *Robotics and adaptive automation*   This group of technologies focuses on the intelligent use and adaptation of robots and automation equipment in manufacturing. These technologies either replace or augment human labor during manufacturing, particularly where very high precision is

needed, where tasks are easily standardized and repeatable, and where large forces and torques are required. New ways of programming and reconfiguring human-robotic teams and building in adaptability are also being actively pursued in this category with intelligent automation, embedded sensors in products and processes, reconfigurable robotics, wireless real-time sensing, and networked control for telerobotics and remote operations. These robotic and automated features could be made "smart"—coupled with systems of embedded sensors that continuously inform evaluators of the performance of each stage and element in the production, distribution, and product life cycle process. This continuous feedback could lead to better design, better products and stronger life cycle performance on an ongoing, real-time basis.

4. *Next generation electronics* Semiconductors based mainly on rigid silicon-based substrates may be reaching physical and economic limits by 2020 or so. The next generation of electronics is currently under development using other materials such as GaAs-based semiconductors, maskless lithography processes for "printing" circuits—avoiding the need for expensive masks—and the development of organic or flexible substrates. We found ultraviolet nanolithography, multifunctional devices with integrated sensing and controls, new computer interfaces, and wireless factories among the new areas being actively explored.

5. *Continuous manufacturing of pharmaceuticals and biomanufacturing* Significant efforts are underway to scale down the chemical production of small molecule drugs while providing more flexibility and real-time monitoring and control. This may not only improve the efficiency of manufacturing for "blockbuster" mainstream drugs but also enable economic manufacturing of niche or so-called "orphan" pharmaceuticals. Parallel research is underway to turn cells and bacteria into small programmable factories that have the ability to produce custom-designed proteins and compounds on demand. Both pharmaceutical manufacturing and biomanufacturing are included in this group. For example, Professor Bernhardt Trout and colleagues in chemical engineering at MIT, in collaboration with Novartis, are working on developing a continuous process for pharmaceutical manufacturing. Stem cell–based manufacturing, human organ engineering and manufacturing, personalized medicine, and tissue manufacturing are other new directions.

6. *Design and management of supply and distribution chains*   The sixth category of research involves planning and managing large and distributed networks of suppliers in multiechelon supply chains. There are major efficiencies to be gained from innovation in the product distribution system. Reducing distribution costs domestically could change calculations about where to locate production. The enabling technologies include standards, information technology, algorithms, and database management techniques for planning and tracking millions of individual items that are flowing through factories, distribution centers, and retail stores. The role of the Internet in creating real-time traceability with RFID, UID, and other technologies is constantly growing. Besides the ability to efficiently handle the logistics of less-than-truckload shipments, one of the functions of these technologies is to prevent fraudulent imitations from reaching the consumer.

7. *Green sustainable manufacturing*   The scarcity and difficulty of access to materials such as rare-earth elements have increased the premium on efficiency and sustainability in manufacturing. Rising transportation costs and new environmental regulations are other drivers of sustainability in manufacturing. New research efforts in this domain center on closing material loop cycles through reuse and remanufacturing and recycling of materials, as well as the minimization of energy consumption during manufacturing. There is important research underway on photovoltaics, concentrated solar energy, and battery storage.

Toward a world of distributed small-batch manufacturing?[5]

How these new technologies will be built into new production systems is the critical question for the future of advanced manufacturing in the United States. Just as we saw Japanese "lean manufacturing" techniques adopted in the 1980s in the United States and Europe in very different ways than in their country of origin, so, too, do we think these new technologies may be incorporated into very different new manufacturing "worlds." Advances on the frontiers of technology do not determine any single pathway for economies. Consider, though, how some of the novel possibilities identified in the survey summarized above might come together to create radically new opportunities for manufacturing in the United States. Imagine a manufacturing world of distributed small-batch manufacturing. This is, of course, only one possible outcome, but we suggest it to provide a more concrete picture of how a new technology paradigm could transform manufacturing. At first glance this may appear as a back-to-the future utopia of artisanal producers that is impossibly distant from today's large-scale, centralized, and globally organized production. But in fact, in a number of economic sectors, we are already seeing a major process of fragmentation at work that involves many of the same mechanisms and technologies that we can conceive as having the potential of transforming manufacturing. In retail, once dominated by giants such as Walmart and Target, there is a growing trend of fragmentation. Consider, for example, the extraordinary success of Inditex, a clothing manufacturer and retailer based in La Coruña, Spain, whose flagship brand, Zara, is the fastest-growing women's apparel retailer. In a world dominated by behemoths that manufacture garments in long runs in far-flung labor markets—China, Bangladesh, Honduras—Inditex makes about half of its fast-selling products in small lots in first-world Spain. The Zara store managers watch what's selling and report back to La Coruña daily. Designers at La Coruña rapidly determine if a "trend" has emerged, and if so, design and cut fabric for this latest fashion. Local manufacturing shops pick up the fabric and quickly deliver finished products to La Coruña. Small lots—only a few garments at a time—are then shipped to stores. If the store sells out, it may order more in a classical "pull" system of manufacturing. More often than not, new fashion trends are sensed and Zara moves on.

This model has placed many competing retailers at a disadvantage. Manufacturing far away has the problem of long lead times. By the time their products get to the shelves, trends have already been shifted by fast-fashion Zara, and customers have moved on. In an industry driven by margins, Zara bucks the trends by manufacturing in more expensive locations—banking instead on agility and speed to market to make up for labor costs. To be sure, Inditex does manufacture its stable, slower moving products in the Far East, but it does not handicap its "fast fashion" with long lead times.

Two upstart retail companies, both less than 20 years old, are now challenging other retail industry leaders. Founded in 1995, eBay is the poster-child for business fragmentation. By allowing a range of small to medium-sized vendors to sell to a global market place using auctions, eBay has leveled the playing field to some extent, and created a thriving granular retail economy that would have been inconceivable only a few years ago. Amazon, founded only a year before eBay, may be seen as an online version of big-box retail. But Amazon, too, provides a marketplace for small retailers who can sell through the amazon.com website. Amazon Marketplace contributed about 9 to 12 percent of Amazon's total $48.1 billion annual revenues in 2011.

Disruptive companies that fragment existing business models have been emerging at a faster pace over the past decade. Zipcar, founded in 2000, is a members-only car sharing service that has affected not only traditional auto-rental sales but also new car sales to consumers and to businesses.[6] Zipcar fragments the way in which consumers acquire personalized transportation. One of the founders of Zipcar, Robin Chase, is now trying to further fragment the car sharing business with GoLoco (www.goloco. org), which enables Internet-based carpooling, and Buzzcar (www.buzzcar. com), which enables peer-to-peer car rentals. A few years ago it might have been inconceivable to fragment the hotel industry. Yet there is now a new business that permits nonprofessional, private individuals to rent space in their properties—a room in a house for example—to visitors, using the Internet. AirBnB (www.AirBnB.com), for example, enables anyone to rent space for lodging on a flexible basis and has signed up over 1,000,000 hosts in over 26,000 cities and 192 countries since its founding in 2008.

Software development, too, has been affected by fragmentation. Software development, initially internal, experienced a major shift in the 2000s with outsourcing. The development process continued to be monolithic, even when transferred to an outsourcing company. Fragmented software development has emerged in the last few years. oDesk (www.odesk.com), founded in 2003, enables individual contractors from around the world to bid on small software development jobs. The range of tasks has since expanded to include writing, sales, administration, and business support. Professor Sanjay Sarma's lab used oDesk twice in the last year. A coder in Pakistan charged them a mere $11 an hour to write firmware for a new logging device they had designed. oDesk contractors also helped them design a website. The speed and the cost were an order of magnitude better than if they had worked with a dedicated business.

The principles underlying these new businesses and their success in competing with industry giants are ones that have long been identified in management theory. Delays cause instabilities. Forrester described the bullwhip effect in the supply chain, where small variations in the end of the supply chain can cause whiplashes at manufacturing.[7] Little's Law tells us that in steady state, the amount of inventory in the supply chain is proportional to the length of time the inventory spends in it.[8] The Toyota Production System showed that small-lot, responsive manufacturing enables agility and better quality.[9] The dot-com crash and then the economic crisis of 2008–2010 exposed the mortal dangers of unsold inventory. All the lessons of the past fifty years tell us that inventory must be minimized, and manufacturing must be responsive. Yet the trends in manufacturing over the past thirty years have driven it in precisely the opposite directions: toward bulk and toward distant locales. With massive offshoring to countries with lower labor costs and the growth of new markets in emerging economies, manufacturing plants have become bigger and manufacturing has become more consolidated.

Bulk imposes its own tyranny: local ecosystems can wither away, and, over time, reshape themselves around offshored manufacturing. Offshoring provides real economic advantages that many companies leverage today. It is reinforced by the fact that manufacturing and shipping today are best at scale. Suppliers, supply chains, and logistic systems slowly warp around the gravitational field created by distant manufacturing hubs. Small-lot manufacturing becomes more difficult, local small-lot shipping becomes expensive, and the vicious circle picks up momentum.

Toward a new manufacturing system

What would it take to drive into manufacturing these new economy-wide trends we observe that are reducing scale, shortening the path between the producers of the goods and services and their consumers, and customizing output? In a world of fragmented production, when a company needs a part, it does not build a factory. Rather, it taps into a national network portal and places a computer-aided design (CAD) description of the part it desires, and the numbers it needs, on the portal. To protect its intellectual property, it may perhaps modify the part somewhat. Meanwhile, software systems from small manufacturers around the country prowl the portal looking for parts to bid on. Each manufacturer has a rating, not unlike the system used by eBay, and provides a capacity and response time. Small manufacturers can produce only small numbers of parts, so many small companies might be necessary to meet the customer's total needs. Software in the portal, perhaps with manual selection from the customer company, selects the ensemble of companies that will manufacture the run. Perhaps representatives from the customer companies also talk to the prospective small manufacturers to ensure that there is a fit.

Companies that are chosen then receive detailed CAD files. The files contain everything from dimensions to tolerances to surface finish requirements. The small manufacturers swing into action and rapidly bring their own special techniques into play to manufacture the parts. Some companies may have jigs from a previous job that fit just right. Others may have faster or more powerful machines better suited to manufacture the parts in question. In this massively distributed, massively parallel way, parts are rapidly manufactured around the country.

The parts are electronically verified for quality. A verification file, in the form of a scan or an electronic response, is sent back to the customer company, which examines and certifies the part for shipping. Parts are then shipped back, not with point-to-point couriers, but with a loosely knit peer-to-peer shipping network whose vehicles plying across the country sell every last empty cubic inch of space to a "shipping passenger." Rather than going through a predetermined shipping route, parts reach the final customer through a dynamic route. The shipper and the customer can track parts and know where they are at any point in time. In this world, factories would usually be virtual, not captive. Capacity would be flexible. Small businesses would compete by innovating and anticipating better. Like the Internet, this would be a resilient and adaptive system.

Some of the pieces that would enable this model already exist. Over the past thirty years, computer-aided design and automatic manufacturing using technologies such as computer numerical control (CNC) machining have reduced the uncertainties in describing parts. The Internet has made communication inexpensive and quick. Just as we email Word or PDF documents today to the likes of Kinko's, designers can email IGES or ProE files to manufacturers. There are already some models of distributed manufacturing. On a website like Alibaba, an online marketplace connecting customers and manufacturers, the customer can identify possible suppliers and chat with them online. Once a potential partner has been selected, the designer sends CAD files to the manufacturer. Manufacturers are increasingly willing to entertain small order sizes—even 100s or 10s.

Several U.S. companies today sell prototyping and small-lot manufacturing for integrated-circuit manufacturing, machined metal and wooden parts, injection molding, 3D printing, and printed circuit board manufacturing. The MOSIS service (Metal Oxide Semiconductor Implementation Service, www.mosis.com) was the forerunner of small-lot Internet-based manufacturing. Starting in 1981 at the University of Southern California, MOSIS enabled researchers to upload designs for integrated circuits using the file transfer protocol (FTP) of the Internet. An effort in the early 1990s at the University of California, Berkeley, to create a "mechanical MOSIS" enabled users to design and upload files to an open architecture CNC milling machine, which would then manufacture the part automatically.[10] After a lull of a few years, new services have started cropping up with slick interfaces and increased capabilities. Ponoko (www.ponoko.com) describes itself as a "personal factory." After users upload designs, Ponoko assigns them to one of many manufacturing hubs. The parts get made and shipped back to the user. Proto Labs (www. protolabs.com) takes the model a step further. Selling itself as "jumpstarting innovation," Proto Labs uses its own facilities to custom machine parts using CNC and to injection mold small runs of parts. Already, several hardware startups are using services like Proto Labs to quickly produce functional prototypes. Though some of the elements of the vision of distributed manufacturing are in sight, a major and concerted effort will be required to kick-start a manufacturing ecosystem that takes the fragmented manufacturing approach to the next level. Many elements of the vision are still missing. Alibaba, for example, connects a single manufacturer in an ad hoc way with a supplier. It falls short of the creation of an adaptable, open manufacturing community that self-organizes around the customer. Shipping, too, remains traditional.

Some of the constraints on moving away from large companies seem, at the present time at least, irreducible. Large entities do have an advantage in procurement because of bulk purchasing. So for certain large-quantity products, such as toothbrushes, the costs of the plastics and injection molding machines and tooling, such as dies, will be more favorable to a bulk manufacturer. The cost of manufacture of an injection molding die, for example, is significant and can only be recouped if the number of products manufactured is relatively large. For this reason, it is unlikely that distributed manufacturing will ever be feasible for commoditized bulk products like toothbrushes. Distributed manufacturing is more likely to be viable for smaller lot products that form the "long tail" of product types or for complex products where customers seek special features.[11]

The vision we paint, therefore, is unlikely to appeal to the manufacturers of large-volume products in which variation is limited. The manufacture of precision products such as integrated circuits and LCD glass panels requires special operating environments in which contaminants such as dust and chemical vapors, and ambient conditions such humidity and temperature, are carefully controlled. It is often cost-effective to consolidate such facilities, called clean rooms, and share equipment and building costs.[12] We will therefore leave such demanding high-technology products out of our present discussion.

But other constraints that have in the past militated in favor of large-scale production may today be relaxed by new approaches and new technologies. One possibility for distributed manufacturers to counter the disadvantages of their small scale is purchasing consortia. In the past, farmers and retailers formed coalitions to achieve purchasing power through cooperatives (co-ops). Since the 1990s formal purchasing consortia have begun to find a footing in the corporate world. Antitrust concerns have limited these developments and most cases are from not-for-profit entities such as universities.[13] If the antitrust issues could be resolved, purchasing consortia could reduce the handicap of small businesses, though they would not eliminate the advantage of bulk manufacturers.

Clean rooms: The case of battery packs

While today it seems unlikely that distributed manufacturing can be applied broadly to products that require clean rooms, there may be opportunities for some classes of products. Consider lithium cells. Cells today are manufactured in very controlled environments with highly automated equipment and to relatively tight tolerances. Our research shows, however, that for some applications, tolerances for lithium cells may be overspecified, exaggerating the need to build expensive, consolidated clean rooms.[14] Lithium cells today are manufactured to have very low variations in DC internal resistance (DCIR) because variations within a cell can lead to localized heating. Variations across cells in a parallel connected battery-pack lead to "run away," in which one cell ends up taking increasing portions of the load of the battery pack and wearing out rapidly. In his master's thesis, though, Radu Gogoana showed that matching cells with similar DC internal resistance across a battery pack (rather than manufacturing all the cells to the same tight tolerance) could have a significant benefit for manufacturers. Capacity fade of cells is more correlated to mismatches across cells than to the initial DCIR of the cell. Yet the clean-room environments and the heavy equipment used in battery manufacturing is at least in some part assumed to be required simply to control initial DCIR values. In other words, our research shows that manufacturers may be able to loosen tolerances on individual cell manufacturing and instead merely measure and match cells across the pack.

Quality assurance remains perhaps the most difficult obstacle blocking realization of a distributed manufacturing system. There are two broad approaches to assessing quality for manufactured products: physical inspection and functional inspection. Physical inspection of a printed circuit board (PCB), for example, might involve careful visual examination or more precise approaches such as x-ray fluorescence. Functional inspection of the same printed circuit board might involve electronic testing to see if the circuit is performing as expected, and perhaps measuring temperature increases using infrared thermography while the circuit is in operation. Visual inspection might be automated and performed in a distributed fashion, with high-resolution photography and advanced image processing. Functional inspection could also be distributed with standardized testing circuits. Electronic testing can also be applied to batteries and other electrical components.

The inspection of complex 3D mechanical parts, however, is more challenging. Tolerances are specified for mechanical parts in a complex and intricate way. Manufactured parts must be measured for compliance. The field is referred to as *metrology*. Traditionally mechanical parts are inspected using a variety of technologies ranging from calipers to go/no-go gauges. Three recent digital technologies have emerged that, if

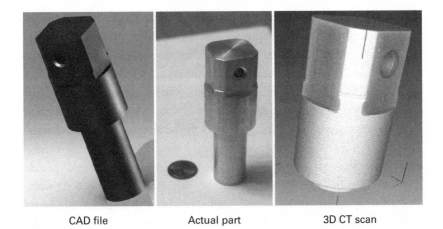

| CAD file | Actual part | 3D CT scan |

FIGURE 6.2
Industrial CT scan experiments

widely adopted, might change the practice of metrology and quality assurance: coordinate measuring machines (CMMs), 3D laser scanners, and industrial CT scanning. CMMs have been used for many years, mostly for advanced and detailed measurement of high-end parts. The technology consists of either a touch-sensitive probe or an optical probe attached to a very precise 3D motion stage. By touching the part at different points the CMM is able to reconstruct and verify the dimensions of the part.

Recently, 3D laser scanners have shown promise. Using a laser triangulation system, the scanner essentially reconstructs the shape of the part as a "point cloud." Although primarily used today for computer animation and for reverse engineering, the accuracy of these systems is becoming high enough to contend as a serious solution to remote digitization of precision parts. Industrial computer tomography (CT) scanning machines are essentially x-ray machines that create 3D reconstructions of both the insides and the outsides of parts. CT scanners are unique in their ability to provide details of the insides of the part. Accuracies of these systems are now high enough to be a serious contender routine for 3D metrology.[15] The accuracies achievable by high-end scanners is now in the 1μm range—that is, good enough for precision machining.

All three technologies have limitations. The machines are expensive, and 3D scanning is not yet precise enough. CMM operation requires careful path planning so that the probe does not collide with the part—but touches it gently. CT scanning machines are expensive and do not measure surface finish adequately. Moreover the computational processing of the point cloud is expensive today for high-quality images. All three technologies, however, digitize metrology and enable the possibility of distributed quality assurance. In the world we are imagining of distributed production we can conceive a "magic metrology machine" which examines not only the outside of the part but the inside as well. Distributed manufacturers would simply scan the part in their magic machines and "fax" the shape to the client. The client would be able to subject the parts to a much higher level of scrutiny than is possible today. Once the client has accepted the part, it would be shipped out by the manufacturer. If the "magic metrology machine" is too expensive, perhaps a "Kinko's-like" quality service center in the local town would allow the manufacturer to qualify the part before shipping it to the supplier. The creation of such a magic box, which promises to be no easy task, would enable much higher quality while also liberating manufacturing from the aggregating force of pressures to ensure quality by having "one throat to choke" at the producer end.

A new supply chain: Peer-to-peer shipping

The networking underlying the Internet is based on a concept called *packet-switched-networks*. Data are broken into packets, which are then routed along networks by *routers* based on the end-address of the packet. Packet-switched networks are flexible, resilient, and scalable—and have revolutionized communications. The use term *packet* borrows from the supply chain, and was coined by Paul Baran of Rand Corporation, the 1991 Marconi Award winner.[16] Baran also, rather aptly, referred to packet switching as "hot-potato routing." Prior to packet switching, communication was largely based on circuit switching, in which two parties established a dedicated, rather than ad hoc, communication circuit for transmitting data. In other words, the modern communication industry has moved to a large extent from dedicated routing to more unpredictable ad hoc routing. Supply chains used to be ad hoc and disorganized at the turn of the last century. Ironically, with the growth of large corporations and bulk shipping, it can be argued that the supply chain has since become more dedicated.

Consider a possible future state in which the supply chain mirrors the Internet. Call this a Supply Internet. A supply carrier in this world would be a vehicle that happens to have capacity to carry goods: an individual truck or a car, for example. A supply router would be a drive-through warehouse that can quickly identify and deliver packages to a carrier.

Traditional warehouses are simply not designed to achieve single-packet delivery functions but rather to deal with large lots coming in or going out. The growth of electronic commerce over the past two decades challenged traditional warehousing. Amazon, for example, had to receive large shipments of books, clothes, or toys, and then ship single items to individuals ordering them on line. Amazon warehouses have one aspect of what we would call a supply router: quick response. But developing the real functionalities of a supply router emerged only with Kiva Systems, founded in 2003, with the goal of automating "pick, package and ship." Kiva Systems uses autonomous robots to move specialized shelving and greatly increases the speed of receiving, picking, shipping goods. In a sense, Kiva Systems has developed a shipping router.[17] Kiva Systems was acquired by Amazon Corporation in 2012.[18]

In the world of distributed manufacturing we imagine, supply carriers can be corporations that own trucks, individual truck owners, and per-haps even individual car owners. Consider a truck owner who has finished delivering goods from Boston to New York. Her truck is equipped with radio-frequency ID (RFID), a technology that automatically tracks inventory, and with GPS, which determines her location. She is a member of the peer-to-peer shipping service of our new world, and her truck communicates with the service headquarters to indicate how much room she has on her truck, where she is, and where she is heading next. As she turns to head back to Boston, she receives a message on her smartphone alerting her to a new shipment opportunity for taking goods back to Boston. The message indicates that a supply router warehouse on the Bruckner Expressway has a package that will fit in her truck, to be delivered to Boston. She heads out of New York and pulls into the specified supply router warehouse, which has several pickup lanes not unlike a drive-through restaurant or a gas station. The package she will be picking up has already been positioned at Lane 8, and as she arrives, an arrow on her dashboard directs her to Lane 8. A worker at Lane 8 quickly opens the back of her truck and carefully places the inventory in the truck. The RFID systems in the truck and the warehouse confirm the transfer. The driver now leaves the supply router warehouse, heading toward Boston with her "hot-potato" inventory. As she approaches the greater Boston area on Route 90 E, a signal on her dash reminds her to take the exit for the supply router warehouse in Framingham. There, the process is repeated in reverse—the package is removed and RFID systems confirm the transfer. A fee for the transfer is meanwhile automatically credited to the driver's account.

The key technologies for supply carriers are also already in existence. GPS, of course, is ubiquitous. RFID is also now in wide deployment. Many of the key technologies in the RFID used in logistics today were in fact developed in a research effort that Professor Sarma led.[19] The vision we have described requires large-scale coordination, logistics standards, pricing standards, and an overlay software system for routing and tracking goods. The costs of the key components—RFID readers, RFID tags, and GPS—are today well within the range for a system such as the one proposed to be economical.

The industry that comes closest to the peer-to-peer approach described above is the less-than-truckload (LTL) industry. LTL shippers usually handle shipments larger than parcels but smaller than full truckloads, as shown in figure 6.3. The LTL industry has faced several problems over the years. Increased offshoring has meant that some volume has moved toward bulk shipping by the full truckload. The growth of e-commerce, meanwhile has bled other volume parcel shipping. According to the U.S. Bureau of Transportation Statistics, the percentage of LTL shipping, measured in dollars, has dropped from 39 percent to 29 percent of the total shipments between 1993 and 2003.[20] There has been a great deal of consolidation in the LTL industry since deregulation in 1980.[21] Anecdotal evidence suggests that LTL shipping is significantly more expensive in the current climate. Furthermore, LTL pricing remains volatile and complex.[22] Yet as shown in figure 6.3, LTL shipping occupies a key position for distributed manufacturing. Peer-to-peer shipping is a way to "democratize" shipping and to provide a cost advantage in the bulls-eye of

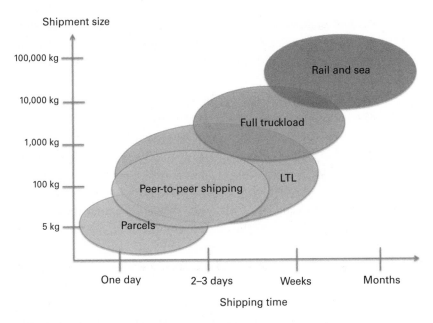

FIGURE 6.3
Peer-to-peer shipping in the context of LTL shipping

distributed manufacturing. In addition, local peer-to-peer shipping has a significant advantage: speed. Unlike offshore bulk manufacturing, local shipping can enable a much more responsive supply chain and enable the type of business practices that Zara has pioneered.

Putting the pieces together in a manufacturing system

Let's consider the following scenario. A large company of the future, LCOF, seeks to manufacture 5,000 housings within four weeks for a new motor in response to a sudden order from South America. Its engineers create a CAD file, properly toleranced, and post it on the New Manufacturing World (NMW) website. The housings will be made of a standard grade of cast iron. Small manufacturers around the country, perhaps around the world, are constantly perusing the website, either manually or using software agents, looking for promising orders. One hundred companies are interested in the motor housing and see that the order is for 5,000 parts, and the lead-time is specified as two weeks. They all respond with bids. Procurement officers at LCOF review the bids. The bidding companies have eBay-like ratings, and each bid is associated with a number of parts as well as basic manufacturing plans. The parts will require sand casting followed by finish machining. Based on a complex algorithm that calculates costs, distances, ratings, and the manufacturing plans presented by the small companies, LCOF officials pick fifty companies that can together provide the 5,000 parts needed. The small suppliers can provide between 10 and 200 parts each. LCOF may speak to the companies, check references, and provide additional information such as quality control details before finalizing the orders.

The suppliers now get to work. Each has its own "secret sauce." Some suppliers already have cast-iron ingots available from a previous job that they are keen to use. In fact they were able to place lower bids because they have this excess inventory. Others immediately go to their purchasing consortia and order cast iron. Some manufacturers have sand-casting capabilities in-house while others have friendly partners across the street that can provide the service. Some have three-axis routers in-house with which they can quickly machine slices of the mold patterns in 2D, which they assemble into 3D patterns and then hand finish. Others have five-axis machines with which they can machine the pattern in one go. Once they have the molds, they make their castings. The castings require post-machining. Here too each supplier has a trick. One happens to have a modular fixture and can immediately set each part up for finishing. A few have two machines of adequate size, and they set up ad hoc assembly lines to perform the finish machining—one for the first setup and another for the second. This gives them efficiency. It is this efficiency that they had anticipated and priced into their bids.

When a supplier finishes machining a few parts, say six out of the hundred in their bid, the owner loads them into the back of his pickup truck and drives down to the local quality-control service center. The QC service center has all the equipment necessary to run the tests that the customer, LCOF, had requested. In this case, LCOF requested that the part be placed in a certain orientation in a CMM machine, and that the CMM perform certain dimensional verification checks. LCOF was also worried about voids within the castings, so had also requested an industrial CT scan on the part. The service center performs all the tests and uploads them to the LCOF site. An electronic response from the LCOF site confirms that the parts are good to go. The QC service center also happens to be a shipping center in the national Supply Internet. The worker at the QC service center packs the castings on three pallets and slaps RFID labels on each pallet. The RFID labels contain electronic product code (EPC) numbers, which are unique "license plates." Each EPC is then associated with the address of the small supplier and the end address, which is that of LCOF. The EPC is also associated with the test results, so that they can always be pulled up. The QC service center worker uploads the shipping request to the national Supply Internet server. The owner of the manufacturing supply company returns to the shop, now confident that he can proceed with the remaining 94 parts he needs to make.

Meanwhile, a truck in the vicinity of the QC service center, which has just finished a delivery and is contemplating returning to its home city, receives a request for a "passenger"—the six housings, in three pallets, that were just qualified and are waiting to be shipped. The truck driver is on the Supply Internet and is always ready to leverage his journeys. He accepts the assignment. He drives toward the QC service center. The worker at the center receives the confirmation from the truck driver, as well as the location, type, and license plate of the vehicle. She quickly moves the three pallets to the loading dock. When the truck shows up, she and the driver move the pallets into the truck, shake hands, and part ways. The truck driver now heads home. Instructions in his dash indicate a small diversion he will need to make as he approaches the city. He drops the pallets off at the supply router warehouse in the city and heads off for a well-earned night's rest.

Both the supplier and LCOF had to constantly monitor the shipments as they head to the receiving location of LCOF. The three pallets parted ways at one point because there was an opportunity to fit two pallets into a truck leaving the same night. The third pallet heads to a different intermediate point the following morning. No one is worried because each pallet has an RFID tag and each supply carrier has a GPS system, and the hot-potato routing works. In two days, all the pallets arrive at LCOF.

The supplier, meanwhile, continues to churn out more housings, steadily working toward his target of one hundred. He does not wait for a full truckload, but often drops single pallets off at the QC service center, which then get qualified and enter the supply Internet individually. LCOF starts receiving daily shipments. It performs additional quality checks. In week two, torrential rains from a storm wash out a bridge and shut down a segment of highway. Fortunately, the ad hoc routing of the supply Internet immediately reroutes the pallets that are stuck through a different, more southerly route, ensuring that LCOF still receives supplies with just a two-day delay. Unfortunately, the same storm causes a major power outage further north. One of the suppliers, which is on the hook for fifty housings, shuts down. The supplier calls LCOF and informs them of his predicament. LCOF immediately reaches out to the other suppliers and asks for bids for additional parts. The other suppliers are able to absorb this extra demand, and in 2.5 weeks, LCOF receives all the housings it needs. Fortunately, it now has a 1.5-week buffer to meet the demand from the South American customer.

The Supply Internet network is fast and resilient. It is also tolerant of small lots—promoting just-in-time delivery and reducing bullwhip.[23] It is in fact very much like the Internet. Medium-sized suppliers refuse to join the supply Internet network early on but after a few years see the value to them as well. Over time, various new technologies are developed to further assist this new world. A 3D printing company offers three-day turnaround for patterns for sand castings. It sends patterns to manufacturers using the same supply Internet. A manufacturer of industrial CT scanning machines offers a low-cost unit that is affordable for smaller shops. A telematics provider creates a combined RFID/GPS/voice system that can easily be integrated into vehicle dashboards. A major automaker announces that this telematics unit will be standard in all its trucks. A flourishing mobile application industry emerges around the Supply Internet with productivity apps that enable everything from mobile inventory alerts to opportunity tracking.

This could be a new, fragmented, and democratized manufacturing world. The path from today to this future will not be easy. It will require several technology advances, some policy advances, but, perhaps most important, critical mass to nucleate the ecosystem. In the case of the Internet, the push and the critical mass came from the Department of

Defense. Once again a convenor will be needed to provide some of the resources but above all to organize some of the coordination and risk-pooling that will convince others to make their own investments in change. In a world of small firms and new technologies, risk reduction is key to advance. It remains to be seen where the push for the next major stride in systems technology will come from.

This chapter has described a series of technology advances that could put us on a pathway toward advanced manufacturing and transform production. These technologies are not specific to particular industrial sectors, but could apply across a number of sectors, from medical devices to aircraft production. Across the history of American economic advance, new combinations of technologies, production processes, and business models have led to dramatic production efficiencies and industrial leadership. We see on the horizon new paradigms that could create an advanced system of 21st-century production.

The second section of the chapter explored in depth one of these possible new manufacturing paradigms. While the history of production has been characterized since the industrial revolution by ever-greater mass production at ever-greater scale, there are in the making technologies, processes, and business models that would enable a *scale-down* of production, with goods produced at an efficiency and cost comparable to mass production. This scale-down could result in a relocalization of production with customized products aimed at the specific needs of specific customers. If we can create the supporting R&D and industry-academic regional cooperation to bring these possibilities to life, they could transform the future of U.S. manufacturing.

7

Jobs, Skills, and Training

When Americans think about the economy, their deepest anxieties are about work: Where are the jobs going to come from? What kinds of jobs will be there for their children? While the economy is slowly recovering from the financial crisis and the economic recession, unemployment in 2013 still remains high and the stagnant incomes for most American workers in the last decade show no sign of change. Understanding this situation is a huge challenge for research and for public policy. There are many conflicting explanations of the causes of today's employment problems, and as many divergent views on the future of work.

PIE researchers have tackled one of the most contentious issues around the persistence of unemployment: the claim that the problem stems from a shortage of skills in the workforce so that employers cannot find and hire people with the right capabilities. Establishing whether or not there is a skill shortage is critical to our focus on how innovation moves to market. When innovative entrepreneurs in start-ups or in long-established companies cannot find the quality and quantity of skills they need nearby to develop a new product, they are more likely to look abroad for partners or, if going abroad is out of reach, simply look back to their current lines of production to squeeze out and sell more of what they are already making. The question of whether there's a skill gap is thus crucial for the pathway of innovation in the American economy. To arrive at an objective finding based on data on plant hiring and vacancies, PIE researchers carried out a nationally representative survey of plant managers in close to 900 U.S. manufacturing establishments and conducted dozens of on-site interviews with employers and training institutions in "old" manufacturing regions like Rochester, New York, and western Massachusetts, as well as in new hotspots like Raleigh-Durham, North Carolina. In virtually all of the PIE company interviews carried out in the United States, Germany, and China, the researchers asked managers about how they find workers and technical personnel with the skills needed to develop, test, and bring into large-scale production the new ideas that emerge from R&D centers or from the shop floor. This chapter describes the results of this research and, in particular, the work carried out by Paul Osterman and Andrew Weaver. Osterman and Weaver analyze the data from the survey and from training institutions and community colleges in fuller detail in their papers in *Production in the Innovation Economy*.[1]

People worry that innovation may simply wipe out manufacturing jobs, with robots at home and large pools of low-wage labor abroad eliminating them. The concern that automation reduces employment for human beings with average intelligence and capabilities has been a recurrent fear in the United States, as successive waves of technological change and productivity growth have over and over again transformed the structure and content of jobs. In 1964, the U.S. Congress established a National Commission on Technology, Automation, and Economic Progress to consider evidence on whether technological change was a major source of the unemployment of the time (1954–1965). In terms close to those heard today, the report acknowledged that some believe that "technological change would in the near future not only cause increasing unemployment, but that eventually it would eliminate all but a few jobs, with the major portion of what we now call work being performed automatically by machine."[2] The report concluded by finding that unemployment was largely due to failings in fiscal and monetary policy. Twenty years later, another national enquiry, launched this time by the National Academy of Sciences, addressed the same issue, and concluded: "Technological change is an essential component of a dynamic, expanding economy. Recent and prospective levels of technological change will not produce significant increases in total unemployment, although individuals will face painful and costly adjustments."[3]

A strong formulation of today's concerns about automation and work comes from researchers who have studied the impact of the digital revolution on the workplace. Erik Brynjolfsson and Andrew McAfee describe an acceleration of technology setting off a "race against the machine." They think the jobless recovery of the past decade is evidence of digital technology's having changed the relationship between economic growth and employment, with fewer jobs overall. They conclude: "The losers are not necessarily some small segment of the labor force like buggy whip manufacturers. In principle, they can be a majority or even 90 percent or more of the population."[4] What's different this time, they argue, from the technical advances that were studied by the national commissions in the 1960s and the 1980s is that Internet and digital technologies are general-purpose technologies with great impact across all sectors of the economy. We do not know if Brynjolfsson and McAfee's predictions about work will ever come to pass, or even if their theory can explain much of the current employment situation. As chapter 2 discussed, the re-evaluation of evidence on productivity gains and on manufacturing output carried out by Susan Houseman and other economists shows no evidence that over the past decade automation played a major role in job losses.

For assessing the claim that the introduction of new general-purpose technologies leads to large-scale job losses, we do have careful research on a previous episode in American history at the entry moment of another powerful general-purpose technology with impact across the economy: electrification in the early twentieth century. Studies have found that electrification of the workplace did lead to profound changes in the distribution of skills, but it did not produce an overall disappearance of work, or even a bias to skilling or deskilling that was constant over time.[5] The shifts in skills from the introduction of electrification resembled, in fact, shifts discussed in current research on changes in the distribution of skills in the labor market—a hollowing out of jobs held by workers with midlevel skills.[6] The patterns of change in labor markets as waves of new technologies transformed the economy in the past cast some doubt on the plausibility of Brynjolfsson and McAfee's scenarios. With technological change, as with the financial market bubbles that Reinhart and Rogoff analyze, it always seems to contemporaries that "this time is different," and it's true that a possibility of radical discontinuity can never be wholly ruled out.[7] In looking toward the jobs of the future, the PIE project, however, has taken a different approach and has searched for signs of change in the current experiences of employers. Rather than starting from technologies and trying to deduce their impact on jobs, the researchers have started from what plant managers report about changing skill requirements in their own establishments and the ease or difficulty they experience in filling positions. The results of this inquiry are reported here.

Finally, the PIE researchers working on jobs and skills have tried to identify the sources of the problems about skill formation in the United States. Here again, as through much of the analysis earlier in this book, the role of changes in American corporate structures from the 1980s on emerges as a central point. When large vertically integrated enterprises dominated the United States corporate landscape, they tended to carry out more internal training than companies do today. The training carried out in the large firms had spillover benefits for the workforce as a whole, as companies tended to train more apprentices than they needed in order to identify and retain the juniors they saw as most promising. Some of the workers trained in large companies moved into jobs at suppliers and to small and medium-sized firms in the region. Large companies often supported vocational schools in local communities in order to educate a population from which they could recruit in the future. In part the vanishing of apprenticeships and the reduction in training within firms reflects the fact that the average size of today's manufacturing establishments is smaller than in the past.[8] Long job tenure, let alone lifetime employment, has become rare. And more turnover and less job security have become regular features of work life. Smaller companies are less able to afford training. Companies of all sizes have less incentive to train workers who are not likely to be working for them for many years, since there's less chance to recoup internal investments in skills and more likelihood that a competitor can poach the skilled workers. With these changes in corporate structure, it's not only the provision of skills that has suffered; it's coordination between employers and providers of skills—once overlapping, now fragmented and separate—that now is lacking. How to provide these public goods once private actors are no longer able or willing to carry them as internal costs emerges as the central question for policy.

Is there a skill shortage? The PIE findings

The claim that a major part of today's unemployment reflects a problem of missing skills in candidates for production jobs is one heard across the

American political spectrum from Republican senator Marco Rubio to Chicago mayor Rahm Emanuel, who told *New York Times* columnist Thomas Friedman that he finds himself "staring right into the whites of the eyes of the skills shortage."[9] Trade associations, too, name the skill shortage as one of the key problems in the American economy. The National Association of Manufacturers in 2011 cited a survey that found 74 percent of firms reporting deficiencies in the skills of candidates for jobs that hindered expansion and productivity gains.[10] Economists find these claims hard to understand in an economy with high unemployment of recently employed workers. Could skill requirements have escalated so rapidly from 2008 to 2012? More generally, economists expect that when a factor needed for production is scarce, its price will rise. Yet even with an increase in overall manufacturing employment from October 2010 to October 2012, manufacturing wages rose only moderately (6.9 percent in average hourly wages in manufacturing from 2008 to 2011, compared with 6.7 percent for average hourly wages across all private sector jobs.)[11] Even the wage hikes of more highly skilled occupational groups (like mechanical engineering technicians) within the manufacturing workforce over the period 2008–2011 were too modest to suggest strong demand and short supply.[12]

The PIE researchers heard claims about skill shortages in some of our interviews in the United States, but found no consistent pattern in the skills the managers found lacking. Often when we heard the charge, it was difficult to determine whether the problem was actually the absence of qualified candidates, or else the weak and erratic supply of qualified candidates at the wage the employer was offering. How should we evaluate the complaint of an employer in the greater Boston labor market who says the problem is that high school grads he hires for $9 an hour have "poor work attitudes" because they are willing to quit and "go down the road" to another job for $10 an hour? In a realm in which anecdotes flourish and accusing fingers point in all directions (poor STEM education in public education; a young generation with bad values and drug habits; employers who don't invest in training; unions that are inflexible and divisive; a bad rap for manufacturing jobs as dirty, dull, and dangerous), it seemed valuable to carry out a survey that would try to establish objectively for a large and representative sample of manufacturing establishments whether skills are lacking for positions they wish to fill and which ones they are.

The principal aim of the PIE survey was to collect concrete data on the skill needs of employers and on observable patterns of job vacancies and hiring. In October 2012 a questionnaire was sent to 2,700 manufacturing establishments randomly selected from the Dun & Bradstreet database.[13] The sample was representative of the different sizes of manufacturing establishments by employment level, as reported for 2010 by the U.S. Bureau of the Census County Business Patterns survey. As in the sample we used for the "Main Street manufacturers" interviews discussed in chapter 4, baking, printing, and publishing establishments were excluded. A Kinko's copy store was not what we considered manufacturing, even if the U.S. census still does. The PIE respondents were usually plant managers or human resource staff. By the close of the survey in January 2013, 34.5 percent of the plants had sent back forms, and 874 questionnaires were available for analysis. The distribution of respondents generally corresponded to the distribution of firms by size, except for large firms with more than 500 employees, which were under-represented in the questionnaires that were returned. This was corrected for in the weighting scheme used in analyzing the data.

In order to determine whether firms were actually experiencing difficulties in hiring, the managers were asked about filling positions for "core" production workers. The question of how long it takes to hire workers with the right skills has also been front and center in recent research on vacancies across the U.S. labor market. In a newly released study Davis, Faberman, and Haltiwanger report that the average time required to fill vacancies sharply increased, from 15 business days in 2009 to 23 business days in 2012.[14] Not finding the right skills in candidates might be one interpretation of the shift. But another explanation would be that employers are still nervous about the strength of the economic recovery and therefore hesitant about signing on new workers. In order to understand the persistent high level of unemployment in the United States and to get priorities right, it's important to try to adjudicate between these perspectives. Indeed, each of these plausible explanations points in a different direction for policies to address the problem: the former toward education and training; the latter toward macroeconomic measures.

The PIE survey aimed to establish the number of job openings for manufacturing establishments, the duration of the vacancies, and managers' views about why they were not finding the right candidates. Although

41 percent of managers said that core production workers had become more difficult to recruit over the past two years (2010–2012), the PIE survey reveals that most employers do not experience extended vacancies—defined as vacancies that last for three months or more—for these positions. The median time required to fill a vacancy was four weeks. At the same time, however, the survey did identify 24 percent of firms in which some positions remained unfilled for three or more months. Sixteen percent report such vacancies were equal to or greater than 5 percent of their core production workforce. Many of the managers in firms that have long-term vacancies see this problem as a "major obstacle to increasing financial success." While in the whole sample only 16.1 percent of the managers thought "lack of access to skilled workers is a major obstacle to increasing financial success," in those establishments with 5 percent or more long-term vacancies, 41 percent of the managers expressed this degree of alarm. So even if long-term vacancies are not an issue for most firms, they are a big problem for some companies.

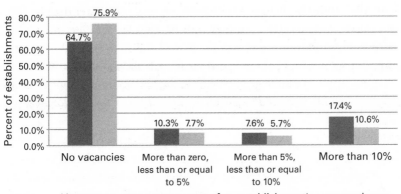

FIGURE 7.1
Vacancies
Source: PIE manufacturing skills survey.

What characterizes those firms with job openings they have trouble filling? To pose a question with some precision about skill levels, the PIE researchers identified for respondents some basic reading, mathematics, computer, and interpersonal skills. Basic reading was defined as the ability to read a short manual; basic writing as the ability to write a short note; math, the ability to add, subtract, divide, multiply, and do fractions; and basic computer skills as once-a-week use. As figure 7.1 suggests, even for these simple skills, not all employers require all capabilities. The survey then asked about combinations of more advanced skills. All of these are quite readily accessible with community college–level instruction or even quality high-school vocational education. For example, for computer skills, the question was whether the job required computer-aided design or computer-aided manufacturing skills; for math, whether the candidate needed particular skills such as probability, statistics, geometry, or calculus. Table 7.2 shows the percent of establishments requiring at least one advanced skill and the percentage requiring two or more advanced skills. As for the interpersonal skills involved in working with others and team work, more than two-thirds of the companies found them to be important. About three-quarters of the managers wanted workers to be able to do quality checks on their output. Rather surprisingly, fewer than half the employers felt they needed workers with the capacity for independent initiative—as formulated in questions about "ability to initiate new tasks without guidance," or "ability to critically evaluate options."

Overall, the findings suggest that the skills most manufacturing firms require are within reach of high-school graduates.[15] The more advanced

TABLE 7.1
Basic skill demands

Percent of establishments requiring basic reading for core jobs	76
Percent of establishments requiring basic writing for core jobs	61
Percent of establishments requiring basic math for core jobs	74
Percent of establishments requiring basic reading, writing, and math skills for core jobs.	52
Percent of establishments reporting that usage of computers at least several times a week is part of the core job	63

Source: PIE Manufacturing Survey.

TABLE 7.2
Percent of establishments requiring advanced skills by number of additional skills required

	At least one additional skill	Two or more additional skills
Advanced reading	53%	25%
Advanced writing	22%	4%
Advanced math	38%	12%
Advanced computer	42%	23%

Source: PIE Manufacturing Survey.

combinations of skills are ones readily available in most community colleges. In the American manufacturing workforce by 2009–2010, all but 13.1 percent of workers had at least graduated from high school and 54.3 percent had schooling and degrees beyond high school.[16] So there is little evidence of across-the-board skill demands that go beyond the capabilities and credentials of the population. Nor—despite claims about the educational levels needed in the new economy—does the demand for advanced skills seem to be rising rapidly. When the researchers asked for the opinion of respondents about whether skill requirements had increased a lot over the past five years, only 7.1 percent agreed; 34.4 percent felt they had increased somewhat; and 48.2 percent saw no change, or a decline in requirements (10.1 percent).

Still, even though most firms seem to be finding workers with the requisite skills without much difficulty, there is a significant fraction of firms (almost a quarter of them) that do have some job openings that go begging for more than three months. Understanding these firms and their needs is important, because they may be the proverbial canaries in the mine providing early warning of a more general disaster about to unfold. First, there's a negative finding that is important to note. Given the amount of media attention paid to the "character defects" of the young generation of workers, it is striking that such factors as failing the drug test or exhibiting signs of poor work ethic play so small a role in explaining recruitment difficulties (see table 7.3). Second, in turning to significant factors, when the respondents were asked why they could not fill the positions, the overwhelming reason was difficulty in finding candidates

TABLE 7.3

Firms' most important explanation for long-term vacancies

	Percent	
Candidates lack general skills	7.1	Note overwhelming importance of skills and much weaker role for character issues
Candidates lack job specific skills	42.7	
Candidates fail drug test	2.2	
Poor attitude/character	2.2	
Poor interpersonal skills	2.3	
Insufficient resources for recruiting	7.9	
Wages not attractive	14.0	
Working conditions difficult	0.5	
Too few candidates apply	6.8	

with specific job skills. The firms that explained their hiring problems in this way tended to be firms that were seeking more advanced math and reading competence. Smaller firms also reported more recruiting difficulties than larger ones. They tended to be companies with weak or no connection to community colleges and other training institutions. Most strikingly, they were firms that were bringing more new products to market each year than the average firm. If it's the more innovative companies that are having more hiring problems, then there is real reason for concern for the future, when more firms will start adopting advanced manufacturing technologies requiring higher levels of math and reading competence in the workforce. There is another factor at work here, too, in accounting for hiring difficulties. A significant predictor of increased levels of vacancies was paying wages that are below those of other area employers of similar core production workers. Thus the firms that experience difficulty in recruiting workers include both high-road firms that are pushing the envelope in terms of skill demands and low-road firms that reluctant to pay market prices.

A third important reason to focus attention on the hiring problems of those firms that are reporting long-term vacancies today is that they suggest a huge problem in years to come when the aging of the current workforce leads to a massive wave of retirements. In the 2009–2010 manufacturing workforce, 17.2 percent of the workers were over 55 years old.[17] Bureau of Labor Statistics projections suggest that even when likely drops in aggregate manufacturing employment are taken into account, there will be large replacement issues when the current generation of production workers retires.

How will we train the new manufacturing workforce?

Filling today's skill gaps, recruiting and educating a new generation of manufacturing workers to replace those exiting the labor force, training for jobs that demand new combinations of book learning, hands-on experience, proficiency with digital technology, and ability to manage relationships face to face and with distant collaborators—these are the labor market challenges we face today in the United States. Meeting these challenges will require very different institutions than those that trained the workforce even in the recent past, for those arrangements have, for the most part, been scaled down or eliminated as the result of changes in corporate organizations. The profound transformation of corporate structures described in chapter 2 along with the expansion of American multinational production facilities outside the United States over the past two decades have led to very different ways of providing training from those that educated the workforce thirty years ago.

At Timken, a global industrial company that engineers mechanical components and high-performance steel, we could trace the impact of shifts in corporate structure. The Ohio-based company was founded in 1899 and today has $5 billion in sales and 20,000 workers in 63 plants in Ohio and around the world. We heard from Timken CEO James Griffith and Board Chairman Ward J. "Tim" Timken, Jr., and from their senior managers as they talked about changes in company strategy over the past twenty years and changes in careers, from which we could trace the impact of shifts in corporate structure.[18] Through most of the company's history, Timken specialized in tapered roller bearings. As one manager put it, "We were the 800 pound gorilla in only one niche." From the 1980s on, global competition heated up. The fortunes of U.S. automakers, then among Timken's largest customers, declined. Technological advances lengthened the life of bearings by a multiple of ten, so replacement orders declined. Timken's products risked becoming commodities that could be turned out in "good enough" quality by hungry competitors around the world. A new leadership team decided on deep changes to chart a new course. The new strategy aimed at becoming more profitable and diversified, growth based upon its ability to improve the reliability and efficiency of machinery. That meant a stronger focus on core Timken engineering knowledge in metallurgy, friction management, and mechanical power transmission. The company extended its product lines and introduced more services associated with those products; transformed a highly vertically integrated organization into one that retained core strengths and differentiating capabilities in-house, while outsourcing more standard elements of production; and expanded its manufacturing footprint in Asia and Eastern Europe to be closer to customers in new markets. Each of these strategic shifts has had profound consequences on corporate structure and on the workforce. These shifts also aimed at improving the company's performance across economic cycles.

A deep understanding of customers' applications grows from shared knowledge across its businesses' related metallurgy, tribology, lubrication, and load/stress analysis. In fact, 60 percent of Timken steel goes into applications that contain other Timken products. On that basis, the company created new alloy steels and extended from tapered roller bearings to cylindrical and spherical bearings, mechanical systems, and even full gearboxes. "It wasn't just a matter of asking the tech guys to come up with something," as one manager put it. Timken's Tech Center in Canton, with its 420 engineers and technicians, played a key role, but Timken also needed to acquire and integrate other companies. Buying existing companies was a critical mechanism for obtaining market spaces and customer channels as well as technologies that could broaden Timken's reach and capabilities. Some of the companies they bought were service providers, since Timken had come to recognize how bundling its products together with services could increase the profitability of the whole business. Indeed in some of the businesses, such as autos, in which Timken sells components to original equipment makers (OEMs), it's the substantial profits earned on aftermarket parts and services that constitute the basic rationale for hanging on to an original parts production business with very thin margins. As part of the strategic shift to bring manufacturing closer to customers, Timken purchased or opened plants in new markets, such as Asia and Eastern Europe, while continuing to serve developed markets from its traditional base in the United States and Western Europe. In 2000 Timken did $2.5 billion in sales with a workforce of 21,000; in 2012, $5 billion in sales with 20,000 employees. In 1998, 75 percent of Timken's sales were in the United States; today it's 62 percent—but with major variation across product lines: 55 percent of the bearings sales are now abroad, but 90 percent of Timken's very high performance steel is sold in the U.S. Steel is heavy and expensive to ship, but some Timken customers are willing to pay that premium to move it to their markets in Asia. The same is true for the largest Timken bearings—an ultralarge bearing used on wind towers weighs about four tons: it's just too costly to make it in Ohio and ship it to China. These large bearings now are made in the United States, China, and Romania, offering a more local-for-local solution. Although it is unlikely that the largest bearings will ever be shipped around the world, among the innovations in the works at Timken are projects aimed at reducing logistics costs. We saw the beginnings of collaboration with a supplier (Industrial Origami) whose fold-up and reusable metal crates are an alternative in some cases to the one and a half tons of wood that Timken now has to assemble into shipping crates for its bearings.

As the old vertically integrated structures at Timken have been reworked into new businesses, there have been great changes in how Timken acquires the skills it needs in its workforce. Several of the managers we met had started as apprentices at Timken and worked their way up. Stephen Johnson, the director for process technology, had joined the company in an apprenticeship program at British Timken. Randy Kiko, the manager for prototype operations, came to Timken in April 1979 in the machinist apprenticeship program based in Canton—just eight months after finishing high school. In Kiko's early years at Timken there were 60 to 100 apprentices. But as Timken started expanding its operations abroad, the apprenticeship program shrank. When most hiring was taking place far from Canton, training was hard to manage from the center across dispersed locations. The Training Department, as it had existed for decades, dissolved. As of the mid 1990s, Timken moved away from on-site training instructors at facilities. The company's main Technology Center in Ohio began outreach to third parties to maintain a flow of skilled workers. The center works with high schools and technical programs to support machining and engineering skills. Kiko, who supervises the high school program in Canton, Ohio, told us that local parents and kids are eager for jobs at Timken. Timken brings in a few students for summer jobs after their junior year in high school, and eventually takes two or three to spend half their senior year in the prototype shop at the Tech Center, rotating through several functions. Promising candidates are hired after graduation, paid $9 an hour, and sent to training programs at Stark State or other community colleges or even four-year colleges. Timken pays for two-thirds of the cost of an associate degree and also pays a salary to the student while in school. The company has similar programs at other facilities around the world.

Timken's recent efforts to fill its skills needs are collaborations with local educational institutions. Two examples near its Ohio headquarters are with Stark State Community College and with the University of Akron. These collaborations not only create new curricula and degree programs; they are actually locating base knowledge and research centers at the colleges so that students can get hands-on experience with the latest equipment and technologies. One of the problems a company like Timken faces when it outsources part of its production is giving employees in the company the kind of hands-on experience they need both to design new products and to monitor suppliers. The new collaborations with the University of Akron and with Stark State address the issue of providing job-specific skills on Timken equipment along with basic engineering classes—and they do it with resources that now include public funds.

At Stark State Community College in North Canton, Ohio, Timken is building a technology and test center in which students can get experience operating and maintaining equipment for ultralarge bearings, some of which are used in wind turbines. Stark State has 15,500 students, two-thirds of whom are part-time. For Timken, the joint facility serves to test and validate products as well as to train students, some of whom may eventually work for Timken. Timken had also considered locating the test plant close to one of its large-bore bearing production plants but the advantages of having it at Stark State so close to headquarters and visiting customers opened up opportunities for greater collaboration with Timken technologists and customer training. It also made it possible to obtain the public funds that will support about half the cost of the new facility. In the past, one Timken manager observed, such a test center would have been within Timken's own four walls. Locating this virtual extension of Timken's workforce within Stark State, however, lowers Timken's costs significantly. Stark State's first trial of such collaboration was in 2005, when it convinced Rolls-Royce to locate a fuel cell R&D center on campus. Stark State leased Rolls a facility as a sole-use property and started a fuel-cells engineering certificate program. The community college also offered to be a partner in going after state money (Ohio Third Frontier grants) and federal NSF money and raised $18 million from these sources for Rolls. The facility grew, and about 60 jobs are associated with it.[19]

At the University of Akron, Timken has entered into a new collaboration for a research center on engineered surfaces, building from coatings research equipment and staff who have been transferred out of Timken and into the university.[20] The new center at the University of Akron is located next to a corrosion laboratory created with $24 million in funding from the Department of Defense. Coatings were a "stranded technology" in a company focused on bearings and special steels. While necessary for the company's products, coatings were not going to be developed as a new business line by Timken, and so the high potential of Timken's coatings' innovation was not going to be fully exploited. Now relocated at the University of Akron in an industrial consortium that other companies are starting to join, the coatings research is ripe to give rise to start-ups that Timken, the University of Akron, and other industrial partners will create. As part of the collaboration, the university is creating a new bachelor of science program in corrosion engineering, the first in the country. Some of its graduates may be recruited by Timken, but others will undoubtedly find their ways into the many metalworking companies of northeast Ohio. Timken has in a novel way built a stream of skilled workers and developed R&D and test facilities in arrangements that transfer some of the costs onto public budgets. Here a company has acted as a convener for industry and education by putting resources of its own on the table and offering to allow others to use them on condition that they, too, contribute to the pot. Timken's new programs with Stark State Community College and with the University of Akron show one pathway along which American industries and communities are adjusting to the profound changes in corporate structures and the global economy of the past three decades. How resilient this pathway can be to financial market pressures may be tested if the activist investors seeking to break up Timken succeed.

PIE researchers studied another case, which, like Timken's, starts with the disappearance of traditional apprenticeships. Rochester, New

York, is the center of one of the world's leading optics clusters. Kodak, Bausch and Lomb, and Xerox started in Rochester and, along with optics/photonics companies like Corning, were large local employers. In its heyday in the 1980s, Kodak employed over 60,000 workers in Rochester. In the early 1960s, Kodak worked with Monroe Community College to create a two-year associate program for optics technicians. The program prepared students for jobs in operating sophisticated lens grinding and polishing equipment. Kodak filled the classes with Kodak apprentices. When Kodak's business started going downhill, its workforce shrank. Today Kodak has only about 5,000 workers in Rochester. As Kodak declined, it reduced its commitment to apprenticeships and to the Monroe Community College program. In recent years, the program had only a handful of students, and its survival seemed unlikely.

Although Kodak was no longer doing well, smaller firms in the optics cluster had grown up over the years and were flourishing. These include companies that make lenses for 3D movies, components for semiconductor lithography, and sophisticated glass grinding and polishing equipment. These firms need skilled optics technicians. But they are too small to run full-scale apprenticeship programs and were too dispersed to be able to initiate together an industry-run program. Moreover each one needed rather specific skill sets. Coordination failures rather than lack of market demand were on the verge of killing the skills input into Rochester's optics industry. The solution that emerged was the work of a determined individual in the Rochester Regional Photonics Cluster (RRPC) industry association, along with a dynamic leader of one of the local optics firms. The RRPC and this executive persuaded Monroe Community College to continue the optics program. It established an advisory board of executives of small and medium-sized optics firms to advise on curriculum. The RRPC started working with high schools and high school guidance counselors, who over the years had lost contact with the optics industry, as the locus had shifted from large and visible corporate giants like Kodak to small specialty firms like Optimax and OptiPro. Corning made a major contribution to the program for new facilities and equipment, and one of the new small firms, Sydor Optics also contributed. In this example, it was an intermediary (RRPC) that overcame a coordination failure and provided a new pathway for training the workforce.

In another region the PIE researchers studied, coordination came from a public intermediary. In western Massachusetts, the Hampden County Regional Employment Board (REB) is mandated by federal job training legislation to work with firms, localities, and educational institutions in the operation of the Workforce Investment Act. When the local machining association faced a shortage of skilled workers as the result of the closing of several large companies in the Springfield area that had previously trained apprentices, the association approached the REB. The employment board brought firms together with five vocational high schools and two community colleges. The connections between the schools and the companies had been thin and intermittent. With active intervention from the REB, the parties started to work on curriculum development and on training programs for supervisors and for unemployed workers; they also organized career fairs and company visits to encourage high school students to consider machining jobs. The gaps began to close.

Educating workers for employment in biotechnology and pharmaceutical companies is in some ways a different challenge than providing skills for firms in established industrial sectors, since connections between firms in the new industries and schools need to be built virtually from scratch. In both situations today, however, success depends on linking schools and training programs that can produce the diversity of skills the new firms need to employers of very different sizes. One case PIE examined was training for the biotech industry in North Carolina, where, since the end of the 1980s, private and public sectors have invested heavily in facilities and in human capital. In a state that has lost hundreds of thousands of jobs in its traditional textile, furniture, and tobacco industries, training and retraining the workforce has been critical to employment as well as to the establishment of a dynamic new sector that today has over 500 companies. They range from multinationals like GlaxoKlineSmith, Merck, Novartis, and Biogen Idec to start-ups. A variety of labor market intermediaries have coordinated the development of new curricula in the state's universities and community colleges to provide workers with various capabilities for these diverse firms. These intermediaries themselves meet in NCBioImpact, a group that convenes stakeholders ranging from foundations, the Durham Chamber of Commerce, the North Carolina Biotech Center, and companies. A firm like Biogen Idec, which has close to 300 production workers at its Research Triangle Park Pharmaceutical Operations and Technology facility, seeks four-year-degree graduates for these positions and works closely with the Biomanufacturing Training and Education Center (BTEC) at North Carolina State University to which Biogen has contributed equipment on which students can be trained. The Biomanufacturing Research Institute and Technology Enterprise (BRITE) program at North Carolina Central University also has four-year-degree programs to educate students with classes and internships for biotech jobs. There are 58 community colleges in North Carolina, and BioNetwork creates shared biotech workforce training services that enable these colleges to deliver credentials for their students that are recognized by employers. In 2011 BioNetwork trained over 4,300 students in short courses. More than 80 percent were workers being retrained.

Toward a new American system of skill production

PIE research on jobs and skills suggests that failures of coordination and lack of public goods provision are at the origin of the "holes in the ecosystem" that chapter 4 described as the problem for Main Street manufacturers. Training used to be carried out by a few large companies both in-house and by the support the big companies provided to local vocational institutions; the spillovers flowed into small and medium-sized firms in the regional economy. In the new global economy production has fragmented and is now carried out in smaller enterprises, each one of which has only very limited internal resources for training, and each one has rather different needs and strategies. In some cases the PIE research studied, like the BioNetwork in Research Triangle Park, North Carolina, Timken in Ohio, and the Rochester optics cluster, a new system is emerging that brings together the objectives and resources of multiple actors—firms and community colleges and high schools and governments—in order to educate the workforce. But there are steep barriers to generalizing such examples. The market does not solve the problem of aligning the needs of multiple, dispersed actors for skills. And there's a great danger of underinvestment in skills. Since workers are free to change jobs, no employers today can count on fully capturing the benefits of their own internal investment in training. In today's environment, the firm that does invest in training constantly risks poaching by its competitors.

The most promising approaches identified in the PIE research to solving these dilemmas about skill provision—both where opportunities for linking training to employment are lacking or weak and in regions in which modules of a new system are emerging—involved organizations that act as intermediaries to knit together demand from fragmented sources and tie it into training programs. While the PIE research did find examples like BioImpact, BioNetwork, BRITE, and BTEC in North Carolina, individual private companies like Timken, or community colleges and universities, or industry associations like RRPC, or employment boards like those in Springfield, Massachusetts, and Cincinnati, Ohio, behaving as intermediaries, the appearance of these convenors and coordinators is fortuitous, uneven, and scattered. The challenge is to strengthen these institutions and establish them more broadly across the country.

8

Building New Pathways from Innovation to the Market

In the many reports on manufacturing of the past four years, there are dozens of policy recommendations for strengthening production in America. They range from changing tax codes, financial markets, and trade rules, to reforming education, immigration controls, and intellectual property regimes. They also include, among many other proposals, the Information Technology & Innovation Foundation's "fifty ways to leave your competitiveness woes behind you" by creating engineering and manufacturing institutes for applied R&D, increasing funding for the Commerce Department's Manufacturing Extension Partnership, making R&D tax credits permanent, transforming Fannie Mae into an industrial bank.[1] Some of us in the PIE taskforce would support some or even most of these recommendations. The individually authored research papers that are being published in *Production in the Innovation Economy*, a companion volume to this one, take up and consider specific recommendations in some detail. As a group, however, we think that the most urgent task is to identify a basis for establishing priorities among targets for public and private action. Our priority is bringing innovation into life in the economy. We see a vigorous flow from ideas into the market as critical to growth and to the well-being and dynamism of society. Production plays a vital role in the translation of innovation into goods and services, and learning by making feeds back into new innovation. These connections between innovation and production have been the focus of PIE research in start-ups, Main Street companies, and U.S.-based multinationals and abroad in leading competitors and partners.

The PIE project started by acknowledging the great strength of innovation in the United States. We realize, though, that neither at MIT nor in the country at large can this strength be taken for granted as if it were a natural endowment of the territory. It may seem as if innovation is just in Americans' genes. But analysis of the rise and fall of different organizations that have generated critical innovations in the United States in various periods tells a different story. Extraordinary public and private investments and policy reforms were needed to recreate the infrastructure of innovation when wars ended, when corporate structures changed, or when transformative waves of new technology swept through society. Where is Bell Labs today? Sustaining the kinds of innovative capabilities that Bell Labs nurtured fifty years ago did not mean keeping Bell Labs on life support. But it did and does take reinventing and investing long term in other institutions capable of generating innovations of a kind and scale to transform industries. For keeping the stream of early-stage R&D full and rich with new possibilities, federal government investment is essential.

While we recognize the importance of strengthening innovation at the source, PIE's main focus has been on the next issues in sequence involving innovation and the economy: the translation of new ideas—once generated—into the market, creating new profits, new industries, and new jobs. Equally important, PIE has examined learning that takes place in the process of developing and producing these new goods and services and businesses. Initial failures are overcome, novel solutions are puzzled out, and unforeseen opportunities feed back into challenges for future innovation. The research presented in this book suggests many reasons to be concerned about the health of these activities in the American economy. In this final chapter we return to practices and institutions we have found in the course of the research that show potential for accelerating the rate of innovations moving into the market and consider how these models could be generalized. The approaches that the PIE taskforce sees as most promising in the United States are ones that would build an open infrastructure of capabilities that many firms could draw on and combine with their own internal resources to bring more new ideas to life in the world. This infrastructure we call an *industrial ecosystem*, for it expresses the concept of vital capabilities—skills, funding, precompetitive R&D, suppliers, facilities, knowledge—that firms need but cannot create wholly by themselves with their own means. In looking at the various efforts across the United States to build common capabilities, we have found quite different arrangements emerging, for example, as between the governance rules of SEMATECH and those in the Timken–University of Akron agreement or those in the Philadelphia-based Energy Efficient Building Hub, but there are some common principles. The question about how individuals and groups can cooperate in the use of common resources was one that underlay the research agenda of Elinor Ostrom, the Nobel laureate, whose work focused on the very different governance institutions that have emerged in communities around the world to manage common-pool resources, like forests, water systems, and policing.[2] From her theoretical work and field observations, Ostrom concluded that there was no single best governance system for regulating any of these systems involving multiple actors and complex interests. Rather, she and her collaborators identified a set of "design principles" that might be implemented in different ways under varying circumstances. The takeaway insight is that we should be looking for common principles rather than a single best pathway for rebuilding capabilities.

Home alone

Over the three years of the PIE research, we have observed a number of shifts in the domestic and international economy that are favorable for American manufacturing. Since the end of the recession, there has been a certain rebound of industries like motor vehicles, which had been on the rocks, and is now experiencing a comeback. Half a million manufacturing jobs have been created. A decline in energy prices with the increase in domestic natural gas production because of hydraulic fracturing ("fracking") is good for American industry, though exactly how much of that impact will translate into American jobs is uncertain and debatable.[3] Wages are rising rapidly in China, and for that reason, there have been very optimistic predictions about a "reshoring" of work to the United States, with, for example, Boston Consulting Group's estimate of 2.5 to 5 million new jobs to be created by 2020 as a result of American exports and reshoring.[4] While there have indeed been some much-heralded returns, as in the General Electric Louisville appliance factory, the overall numbers are still rather small.[5] Production moved to China to use low-wage labor, but today the density and capabilities of the supplier networks, like those of Foxconn, that have built up around what were earlier just low-wage, low-skill factories, anchor these plants far more securely than simple wage rates could. The PIE interviews in the Chinese renewable energy companies, for example, found Chinese capabilities for scaling up these advanced products and processes that are considerable. In the energy technology and production sector, moreover, location decisions are driven by demand, market growth, and manufacturers' capabilities, and so higher wages in China, are not likely to lead to return of these activities to the United States with long-entrenched players and only modest rates of growth.[6]

Overall, PIE researchers emerged from the project with rather modest expectations about work returning to the United States from abroad. We have focused, rather, on changes already visible in the economy—even when still small and local—that might make companies more likely to keep, increase, and locate new activities and new employment in this country. One way of facilitating such outcomes is to accelerate the development of the advanced manufacturing technologies and a more decentralized production system described in chapter 6. If we can build institutions to introduce these technologies broadly and rapidly through the industrial base, this would support more domestic production. But even if macroeconomic winds (revival of demand, energy prices, wage rates) continue blowing in a favorable direction, even with advanced manufacturing technologies, for the American economy to capture momentum from these forces, deep changes in industrial ecosystems are needed throughout the country.

As we thought about the hundreds of interviews we conducted and the work of the individual PIE research modules, a compelling picture emerged. It is of a country with great potential for innovation and for enabling innovation—in university, industry, and public laboratories and R&D centers and in firms of diverse sizes and specializations. These innovative capabilities are reflected not only in the sheer numbers of valuable patents filed in the United States, but in the performance of firms that "repurpose" innovation from one use to another and in the skills of firms like metalworking shops that work with start-ups as they develop prototypes. We see particular promise in firms bundling new valuable services together with hardware. One striking example of the potential of such a paradigm comes from a Taiwanese company, MediaTek, which in 2011 started bundling its chipsets with a "turnkey solution" including instructions for making a smartphone, software to run it, and production help, and within 18 months had captured half of the Chinese smartphone chip market.[7] These chips bundled with services allowed domestic Chinese phone makers to reduce costs and time to market. We have seen models like this in our interviews. These types of firms and others are the diverse producers of innovation that we have found across the country. The picture that emerges from our research, however, is one in which too much of this innovation does not translate into profits and jobs in this country, although it may abroad.

How much is too much? This question is impossible to answer in general, for there are many reasons why an apparently promising idea may not make it to market. It might be less good than it first seemed; too complex or too expensive to commercialize; bungled by managers; beaten out to the finish line by competitors. In some sectors, like renewable energy, the entrenchment of established players and the lack of strong, consistent demand may best explain why new firms do not take off here but do in the rapid-growth markets of Asia. But very often we have seen yet another scenario at work. However difficult to measure exactly, the finding from the various projects of the PIE research is that when managers of American companies try to put together the critical inputs for development and commercialization of innovation, there are missing elements that cannot be readily substituted for by their own internal resources or with the finance available for development and commercialization projects in this country. These issues are least pressing today in the vibrant regional clusters on the two coasts and in a few other locales like Raleigh-Durham and Austin, for these clusters have deep labor markets of skilled workers and rich concentrations of venture capitalists. But even in those regions, the PIE research on scale-up presented in chapter 3 identified missing links to commercialization in the "inflection band" stages of development in the course of which production shifts from pilot stage to large scale and for which tens of millions of dollars of additional funding may be needed. Toward the end of the PIE project, we started hearing new doubts voiced about whether the venture capital industry would continue to invest as heavily as it has in the past in even the earlier stages of development. If this proves to be the case, the findings of the scale-up research reported in chapter 3 that found generous venture capital support for a large fraction of the MIT-originated start-ups over 5 to 7 years may offer too optimistic a prospect. There may be new challenges about access to capital on the near horizon. For these issues involving access to capital for start-ups moving into commercialization, on a terrain with rapidly changing dynamics and players, we recognize the need for additional research before formulating policy recommendations.

In the United States in between the Silicon Valleys, Seattles, and Cambridges—that is, through most of the country—serious basic weaknesses in the industrial ecosystem are already far more prevalent. In some companies we interviewed (for example, in a large defense contractor, in an aerosol can top maker, in a rubber parts maker) these weaknesses took the form of managers' worrying about having to bring parts of production back in-house because they feared for the survival of their suppliers. The cost of substituting for missing suppliers would divert resources from the development of new lines of business. In other Main Street companies we saw, the problems showed up in the length of development cycles, as the companies slowly dripped in resources out of their previous year's profits—without access to much or any outside funding. Elsewhere—and in a significant fraction of the firms surveyed on jobs and skills in the nationally representative sample of manufacturing establishments—companies found their expansion slowed by difficulties in locating and recruiting people with the right skills. The manifestations of holes in the ecosystem were diverse, but they seemed to point to the weaknesses of a disaggregated industrial system with few external resources commonly available to actors.

It may always have been the case that firms needed some inputs not of their own making, for example, when recruiting workers who had been trained in a local big company's apprenticeships. Companies may in the past, too, have relied on some external institutions for coordination, perhaps provided by local bankers, in addition to integration within the company or market signals. But today, in an economy in which production is fragmented across global value chains and in which average firm size is smaller than before, coordination and resources to complement those of individual actors have become ever more important. In an evolution that we have traced out in chapter 2 in an account of changes in the economy over the past thirty years, commonly available resources like training, local banking, and multiple supplier sources have disappeared, thus opening great holes in the industrial ecosystem. When there are resources available outside the company, they are often scattered, difficult to access, and hard to bring together. These holes in the ecosystem are in effect market failures, that is, valuable goods, services, and coordination, the benefits of which cannot be appropriated by any single actor and that therefore are likely to be undersupplied in the economy. Underprovision of these goods, services, and coordination lengthens the time it takes for innovations to move into the market and reduces the volume of those that make it. Among other factors, the weaknesses of the ecosystem also weigh in determining the location of the production facilities and jobs that are associated with bringing these innovations into the market. If the goal is sustainable economic growth of good jobs and companies across the United States, we will need to rebuild these resources and make them available as public or semipublic goods in regional industrial ecosystems. Firms with a wide range of potential contributions to innovation could then draw more amply on capabilities complementary to their own. In most cases, firms would have to contribute to the production of these capabilities as a condition of using them, but a firm would be neither sole provider nor sole beneficiary.

Rebuild but not resurrect. We feel no nostalgia for the American production system of the four postwar decades. Today, innovations and entrepreneurs are coming out of an ever greater multiplicity and diversity of domestic and foreign sites. New businesses can draw on manufacturing capabilities owned and operated by others—both at home and abroad. Innovators, big and small, from advanced industrial societies or from developing economies, no longer need to create a full set of production facilities within their own four walls before they can bring their products to market. The advent over the past thirty years of a more open global economy with powerful new partners and competitors around the world has thus created great opportunities for innovation. But the changes in American corporate structures and then the globalization of the economy have also weakened and destroyed resources that firms used to draw on in combination with assets they generated in-house to develop and commercialize their ideas. The weaknesses and gaps of a more disaggregated industrial system pose problems for firms of all kinds: startups that need suppliers nearby to develop their prototypes and first production runs; small and medium manufacturers unable to access foreign capabilities as part of their operations; even multinationals, we discovered, suffer the lack of local skills, suppliers, and partners. Too many American firms today are "home alone": constrained by having available only those resources that they generate themselves in-house to use when they go to scale up their new ideas.

Models for a new American industrial ecosystem

In a more fragmented industrial world, how can we substitute for the coordination, knowledge diffusion, scale-up resources, and leadership that once were available in an economy in which large vertically integrated firms played a dominant role? How today can we create complementary capabilities—skills, expertise, finance, services, and technologies—that firms could access and combine with their own as they try to bring new ideas into the market? In Germany we have observed an economy that is rich in such capabilities and that retains a strong manufacturing sector. But too many parts of the German scene—like family-owned manufacturers (Mittelstand), each with several thousand employees and strong export markets, local bankers, a resilient apprenticeship system—are missing in the United States for us to believe that we could replicate the German model, even if we multiplied Fraunhofer Institutes across the country—desirable as that might be. A PIE interview and facilities tour at the Fraunhofer Center for Manufacturing Innovation associated with Boston University and follow-up interviews with some of the firms that use them found ample evidence of the value it provides via access to expertise, testing, and expensive equipment for companies trying to scale up ideas to commercialization.[8] A manager from a Fortune 500 company that uses the Boston Fraunhofer CMI told us: "Once U.S. companies had their own internal development groups staffed with manufacturing and product development engineers, but these have been cut to the point that very few companies are doing their own internal innovation now. We do product development, but the manufacturing innovation part has been severely cut back. So we work hand in hand with an organization like Fraunhofer and view them as part of our team." While this arrangement allows the company to gain some of the advantages of economies of scale through contracting with Fraunhofer, it does not build connections to suppliers or other actors in the system. In Germany, in contrast, the Fraunhofer Institutes are not stand-alone organizations, but one among multiple nodes in dense networks of R&D institutions with multiple sources of funding including from the federal government for small and medium-sized companies that partner with others and cooperate with research institutions like Fraunhofer or an industry research institute. In these networks, industry associations help firms find "matching" partners for projects.

It's not only what's missing in the United States that would make replication of the German model impossible; it's what's strong in American innovation that requires different institutions to flourish. In the wake of the profound transformation of corporate structures in the United States, institutions linking innovation to new company and new job creation did indeed emerge in some regions in the United States. As companies like AT&T restructured and the research institutions they supported, like Bell Labs, disappeared, regions like those around Cambridge, Seattle, and Silicon Valley have evolved novel governance structures and cooperative patterns to channel innovation growing out of university and public laboratories and out of start-up firms into the economy. These regions have become so prosperous that many other localities in the United States and abroad have tried to imitate them and to create "clusters" in new industries, like software, biotech, or electronics. A few of these deliberate efforts have been very successful, as in clusters around San Diego, California, or the Hsinchu Science Park in Taiwan. But many other attempts have fizzled, and as one state economic development official in Ohio expressed it frankly, a kind of "cluster fatigue" has set in.

There has been less experience with and less reflection on designing measures to generate common resources for an industrial environment with many firms in diverse sectors. Yet this is the approach that may work best across much of the United States. As Delgado, Porter, and Stern concluded from their research on clusters and regional economies: "Regional policies that harness complementaries across related economic activity are likely to be much more effective than those that prioritize high-wage or high-tech clusters where there is little pre-existing strength within the region."[9] The policies required to identify and consolidate such complementaries will vary, depending on the mix of firms, capabilities, and institutions in a given region. Although the term "policy" usually implies government action, the "first movers" identified in the PIE research have often been private firms, trade associations, local community colleges, dynamic individuals, as well as public authorities. The set of cases we have examined encompasses a portfolio of private and public initiatives that include incentivizing efforts to bring together existing but isolated actors; connecting schools that are educating future workers with the employers who hire them; pooling and reducing the risks associated with developing new technologies; getting the benefits of economies of scale by sharing facilities too expensive for any but the largest firm to have in-house; and creating and diffusing technology before there's a clear path to commercializing it or a firm willing to commit to developing it. However diverse the cases and circumstances, we see at work the same common underlying functions being performed: convening, coordinating, and reducing risk by pooling risk.

All through this book we have presented examples of emergent forms of coordination in industrial America. Perhaps the best-known example of industry collaboration in which companies pool risk and share facilities is SEMATECH.[10] SEMATECH is a consortium of semiconductor and semiconductor equipment makers founded with funding from both the Department of Defense and from companies in 1987, at a time when foreign, mainly Japanese, integrated-device makers were rapidly expanding their technological capabilities and market share, and the American industry was in perilous straits and seemed to be heading for the rocks. SEMATECH is widely regarded as a success story, for today the U.S. semiconductor industry remains the world's technology leader and a strong source of innovation and employment in the United States. It is the leading U.S. export sector. The spill overs from its innovation and dynamism pour into many other high tech sectors in the United States, like medical devices and software. It employs about 200,000 people across the country. In the 1980s, this was an industry built around a few large "integrated-device manufacturers" like IBM, Hewlett Packard, and Texas Instruments that tightly integrated within their own four walls the critical functions of design, chip making, packaging and assembly, and tool making. By the mid-1990s, technological advances were fragmenting the industry into a modular one, in which separate companies each performed distinct functions and linked up their designs, processes, and products through supply chains. Across the trajectory of technological advance, the fundamental challenges the industry faces for making each new generation of wafers are the extraordinarily heavy investments required in R&D and new production facilities and the coordination of multiple dependencies between companies located at critical nodes along the supply chain for the complementary investments and R&D needed to execute the shift from one generation of wafers to the next, for example, the transition from 200 mm wafers to 300 mm wafers and now to 450mm. The innovation cycle for these transitions is about 15 years, and during this period, companies need to make huge investments in tools, to test these tools in an integrated environment with those produced by others, and to test them performing at scale. There are critical development gaps in the technology for producing the new generation involving unknowns so complex and expensive to resolve that no single company is likely to make the necessary investment in R&D.

SEMATECH provides convening, coordinating, and risk-pooling functions that have thus far enabled a fragmented industry with enormous innovative capacity and market potential to overcome its inherent vulnerability to market failures. It reduces the risks of individual companies by bringing them together for road mapping, benchmarking, agreeing on standards, and investing in some common R&D and testing facilities. The common technology development that SEMATECH sponsors takes place at those precompetitive points in the process where there's a critical gap, but no single company willing to assume the risk of investing in the R&D and equipment to span the gap. SEMATECH thus addresses market failures arising from failures of coordination and from undersupply of capital at critical development junctures. SEMATECH evolved from an association jointly funded by government and only American companies, to one funded by industry with foreign as well as American companies. SEMATECH evolved again as it relocated from Texas to Upstate New York near the State University of New York-Albany College of Nanoscale and Engineering, near GLOBALFOUNDRIES, a major chipmaker, and an hour and a half away from IBM's East Fishkill semiconductor facility. The relocations to Upstate New York of both SEMATECH and GLOBALFOUNDRIES were strongly supported by state funding. The state's tax and cash commitments to GLOBALFOUNDRIES have been estimated at about $1.4 billion. The state has also contributed about one-third of SEMATECH's annual budget as well as building labs, clean rooms, and degree programs at the neighboring

SUNY-College of Nanoscale and Engineering. Today SEMATECH has five core members, IBM, Intel, Samsung, TSMC, and GLOBAL-FOUNDRIES, members from semiconductor equipment makers (like Applied Materials, LAM, Novellus), and noncore members that provide materials and services in semiconductor supply chains.

SEMATECH in many ways seems a special case. The industry globally is dominated by a few very large players, and the lion's share of cutting edge innovation and advance along the trajectory traced out by Moore's law takes place in American companies. The technology is modular; and differentiation takes place in processes. So the big chipmakers need to have equipment and material manufacturers on board for making the same new tools for each new wafer generation. The capital equipment costs involved in retooling and new plant facilities for new generations of wafers are colossal, and so roadmapping plays a critical role in reducing the risks for all participants. SEMATECH is also special because it benefits from specific legislative protection against antitrust proceedings.[11] But even though the industry has exceptional features, SEMATECH fundamentally has to deal with the same generic issue that we have identified in the rest of the economy: market failures that emerge when integrated production evolves into disaggregated modular production carried out by a multiplicity of firms. As a convener, SEMATECH also confronts many of the same challenges we saw for institutions elsewhere in the economy that are seeking to coordinate and intermediate: how to assemble and sustain a rich enough set of incentives to induce collaboration; how to resolve tensions arising out of the heterogeneous interests of participants; and, especially important in the SEMATECH case, how to provide services significant enough that even the big players find it worthwhile to stay in the game and not swoop out their marbles for solo plays.

SEMATECH has a long and successful experience in sharing risks and creating capabilities that benefit multiple firms in the semiconductor industry. PIE also examined a number of experiments in convening and coordinating of more recent origin. Some of the most interesting grow out of private initiatives. In Ohio, as described in chapters 1 and 7, we found Timken, a manufacturer of tapered bearings and specialty steel, acting as a "convener" when it transferred its coating laboratories and researchers to the University of Akron, collaborated in creating new degree programs, and opened these resources to other companies and to the university and the region—on condition that they also contribute. In the course of an interview with a Mentor, Ohio, high-precision machining firm that had come up in the sample of Main Street manufacturers, its family owners told about getting together with competitors to jointly work out curricula for a machining program in a local community college. Twenty years ago, the owners said, they would not even have talked to competitors for fear of letting slip information about their capabilities or their customers. It's still risky, they said, but worth it. PIE researchers in Rochester, New York, saw a case of near collapse of skills provision for the optics industry, when Kodak, the region's largest employer, declined, and its support for in-house training and for an optics program at a local community college disappeared. There still were many good jobs in the optics industry to be had—but located in a scattering of young small high-tech companies, no one of which could support the community college program or even pay for much in-house training. The solution that emerged was the work of a determined individual in the Rochester Regional Photonics Cluster (RRPC) industry association along with a dynamic leader of one of the local optics firms. They saw the connections that could be made between all the small firms and the community college and worked together to persuade Monroe Community College to continue the optics program.

These examples of regenerating the industrial ecosystem and others that are documented in chapters on advanced manufacturing, jobs, and skills, Main Street manufacturers, and scale-up in this book and in its companion volume, *Production in the Innovation Economy,* are promising, but they are also fortuitous. When we looked in detail at their origins, we found special individuals and companies who were willing to go far beyond their ordinary job descriptions and ways of doing business. The United States abounds in entrepreneurial people but without institutional bases their efforts often remain isolated and hard to sustain. These positive but chancy interventions are unlikely to produce complementary capabilities on the scale needed to transform regional ecosystems across the United States.

We wondered how public initiatives and funding could be used more systematically to initiate and thicken connections among actors in industrial ecosystems. Could we identify common principles of public action to build resources of use to multiple private and public actors to combine with their own capabilities—without privileging or protecting one or another firm? Would it be possible to use public resources to catalyze large private-sector participation—not to substitute for it? Three publicly initiated programs we learned about seemed interesting cases in which to examine such mechanisms at work.[12] Each of them is still in its early stages, so they ought to be thought of as experiments, not yet as successes (or failures). Close to home, we visited the Massachusetts Clean Energy Center. A quasi-public entity created by the legislature in 2008 to catalyze growth of a clean energy economy in Massachusetts, the MassCEC is funded by deposits into a Renewable Energy Trust on the order of $23 million to $24 million a year. These sums come from customers of all Massachusetts investor-owned utilities and five municipal light departments that pay voluntarily. The agency plays a key role as a convener and coordinator in the region's renewable energy sector; and James Bowen, the MassCEC director of business development, described a suite of MassCEC programs designed to pool and reduce risks and fill gaps that individual startups and firms in the renewable energy sector cannot manage on their own: demonstration projects, pilot projects, bringing in international partners.[13] To facilitate stronger bonds in the regional ecosystem, many of MassCEC's programs require that any companies they support come in with partners. One demonstration project helped fund the first in-ocean test of a tidal energy turbine in the region, while forging new connections between an academic center at the University of Massachusetts at Dartmouth, a tidal turbine maker, FreeFlow Power, an ultracapacitor energy storage device maker, FastCap, seeking new markets for its product, and the Massachusetts Maritime Academy, which provided the barge test platform and found an opportunity to train its cadets in the offshore energy industry. None of these diverse actors had ever worked together before.[14]

In another high-profile case, the MassCEC invested $18.2 million in state funding to secure an additional $26.7 million in federal Department of Energy funds to build a world-class wind-blade testing facility that has created new shared regional capabilities and attracted new industry and government partners to the region. Massachusetts is not among the states that hand out the largest tax incentives to induce individual companies to locate within their borders. In fact, Bowen argued, it is better for an agency like MassCEC to invest $18 million in a wind-blade test facility that acts as a common resource for the regional ecosystem and can attract wind blade makers from companies around the world to use it than to give a similar-sized tax break to a single wind-blade company that could go out of business or move out of state—leaving nothing behind. Open since May 2011, the National Wind Technology Testing Center has already tested 11 blades including five extensive fatigue tests meant to simulate 20 years of real-world wear and tear and the effects of great wind gusts.[15] Wind-blade testing is extremely expensive and for an ultralong blade could take as long as a year. Having access to an independent testing lab allows multiple competitors to share costly equipment and expertise and to get impartial verification of their results. The facility has attracted a diverse set of individual firms, including California-based Clipper Windpower, Blade Dynamics of New Orleans, Lousiana, and Denmark's LM Wind Power.[16] Access to the facility's unique capabilities was cited as a key reason blade maker TPI Composites of Scottsdale, Arizona, opened a new blade R&D and prototyping facility in nearby Fall River, Massachusetts.[17] And the test facility has strengthened the region's involvement with the National Renewable Energy Laboratory, headquartered in Golden, Colorado, and with federal partners at the Department of Energy.[18]

PIE also studied the Energy Efficient Buildings Hub (EEB Hub) in Philadelphia, Pennsylvania. This program is funded both by the Department of Energy ($123 million over 5 years) and as a "Regional Innovation Cluster" (RIC) by grants from DOE, the Department of Commerce, the Small Business Administration and the state of Pennsylvania. A Pennsylvania State University initiative brought together research universities, six industry partners, and a number of regional economic development agencies in the 2011 winning proposal for the EEB Hub. Its facilities are now located at the Navy Yard, a 1,200-acre former Navy base that has been redeveloped over the last several years by the Philadelphia Industrial Development Corporation into an office and industrial park. From experience in organizing the project and now serving as its director, Paul Hallacher of Pennsylvania State University emphasized two critical preconditions for such an institution. First, government needed to put significant funding on the table in order to incentivize companies to put their own resources into the project. The funds promised by the federal government to the EEB Hub were far greater than even the largest university research centers can offer. This commitment concretizes the convening role of government, for the conditional promise of funding makes it desirable for others to pledge their own human and material capital in order to benefit from the new resources on offer. Secondly, Hallacher underscored the importance of building trust and real partnership through thousands of hours spent during the phase of team building in discussing technical and geographic focus and membership with potential participants and through openness and transparency during those discussions.[19] These are approaches that members of the winning team for the National Additive Manufacturing Innovation Institute now located in Youngstown, Ohio, also stressed. In building ecosystem institutions, they told us, top-down methods and claims to authority based on technical expertise just do not work. Wary potential partners want to be sure that they will have a real voice in the direction of the new institution, and the only way they can test this is by seeing how their own interests and ideas are taken into account by others during the initial phases of project design.

The dual missions of the EEB Hub are, first, to bring together a wide variety of industry, public, and university actors to develop and deploy technologies and business models to reduce energy use in existing buildings, and secondly and concurrently, to create an energy-based regional innovation cluster. Pennsylvania has a large supplier population of small and medium-sized manufacturing companies but relatively fewer large OEMs (original equipment manufacturers: the brand-name companies). The idea is to build "open innovation supply chains" to link these small and medium-sized suppliers to the large global companies and to research and innovative start-up firms flowing out of universities. The stretch goal for the regional innovation cluster, Hallacher said, is to make SMEs in the greater Philadelphia region into the preferred suppliers for big companies in the sector of the building industry focused on energy efficiency.

In recruiting big companies for the EEB Hub, it was not possible to get direct competitors to join, in contrast to the SEMATECH model of core membership by the largest semiconductor makers. Rather, the EEB Hub had to bring in companies located at different points along the supply chain for making and deploying energy-efficient technologies in buildings. Six became full members: Balfour Beatty, a construction services company; Bayer, a materials company; IBM; Lutron, a lighting and lighting controls company; and PPG Industries, formerly Pittsburgh Plate Glass Company and now maker of a wide range of coatings and specialty products; and United Technologies. The firms told us that bringing suppliers and customers together was the key attraction. As one manager put it: "If I were king for a day, I'd require any project using public funds for research to engage potential users of the research because otherwise there's not much chance of getting anything that impacts society." Another emphasized that the EEB Hub is about getting market development and engagement in a very fragmented industrial sector, one in which value chains are complex with heterogeneous actors from designers to manufacturers and small suppliers to construction companies and real estate brokers. The objective of organizing a market for energy-efficient building materials, designs, and business models coexists alongside the objective of technology development—another interest of the industry participants. One manager regretted that there was not a greater focus on technology a bit further out and too risky for his own company to want to fund itself. But the same man also said: "Our interest is first to get people to use our products.

In this fascinating experiment in building a new industrial ecosystem, one other type of participant needs special mention. Regional economic development agencies have played important parts in bringing the EEB Hub into existence. The Ben Franklin Technology Partners, the country's oldest technology-based economic development agency, was involved from the start in the roadmapping that identified potential partners and assets for the EEB Hub. The Ben Franklin Technology Partners provides seed capital for start-ups, supports the commercialization stage of these firms, and has raised about $1.2 billion for follow-on investment in 475 companies over the past 10 years. The Ben Franklin Technology Partners also scouts for emergent technologies in university research and tries to match them up with existing capabilities in the industrial base of the region. They are carrying out a roadmapping similar to the one they did for energy-efficient buildings for innovative water and wastewater products and technologies and forming a "Delaware Valley Water Alliance" to try to accelerate the commercialization of new products in this domain by assisting innovators to validate the performance of their products. Roadmapping in these cases is not about mapping the evolution of a specific technology, as in familiar cases of technology roadmapping. Instead, this kind of regional or industrial roadmapping focuses on identifying research capabilities, trendline analysis of business and policy environments, looking for policy or economic or technology barriers, and studying markets and established companies in the market. From this analysis, Ben Franklin develops a plan for convening and aligning regional stakeholders, identifying and reducing key barriers to the growth of the industrial sector, and connecting the needs and capabilities of these parties. With the EEB Hub in its third year, the Ben Franklin Technology Partners will help launch and manage an incubator and commercialization center. The regional Manufacturing Extension Partnership (MEP) program (called Delaware Valley Industrial Research Center) and the Philadelphia Industrial Development Corporation are also involved in the EEB Hub. At this early stage, however, the main result for these organizations is a hope that connections made with small and medium-sized suppliers and big companies in the EEB Hub might lead to new contracts. There are not yet many concrete results on this front. One of the staff in these programs commented: "Small and medium-sized companies are the last ones to the social network table. Perhaps because of their limited resources or focus or mentality or just being busy. They don't see the value added. It's a tough threshold to get them to see that a bit of time invested now that may not yield immediately is worth it. It was a virtually impossible sell twenty years ago. Now they're starting to go on plant tours, to go to networking meetings. It's opening up." The Hub is clearly work under construction.

The third case of a publicly initiated ecosystem we considered is the less-than-a-year-old National Additive Manufacturing Innovation Institute.[20] It is too soon to evaluate any of its efforts, but there are lessons to be drawn from the kinds of response that were elicited by the government's call for team proposals to establish the institution. NAMII is the first of fifteen manufacturing innovation institutes that the Obama administration has announced it will create across the country. Additive manufacturing, sometimes called 3D printing, is a process of fabrication by deposition of successive layers of materials like powdered metals and polymers to form an object to the exact specification of a digital design. In contrast, traditional machining forms objects by drilling or cutting away and hollowing out materials. Additive manufacturing offers the alluring prospect of making it inexpensive to fabricate unique or customized objects for commercial and military purposes, of radically accelerating time from design to product, of reducing materials and energy use, and, most optimistically, of democratizing production. "Print me a Stradivarius," read the cover story of the *Economist* (February 10, 2011) about "how a new manufacturing technology will change the world." Aside from unleashing creativity in a new industrial world, there are the gains to be realized in an old world that has constantly to be replacing its worn out parts—from hips and teeth to parts of fifty-year-old coal-fired power plants. The Department of Defense has to buy hundreds of Stradivari worth of components every year to replace aging components of older defense systems. If these components could be made on an individual as-needed basis instead of DOD's having to support whole production lines and suppliers and warehousing of spare parts, there would be enormous cost savings. These potential uses made the Department of Defense a natural funder for NAMII.

The eventual customers and suppliers of these technologies cut across multiple industrial sectors—aerospace, medical devices, new materials, renewable energy, automotives, construction, and more. But the willingness of any of the major players in these industries to make significant investment in additive technologies has been checked by skepticism about whether 3D printing will ever work to turn out anything much beyond prototypes and plastic objects. Additive technologies have in fact been around for several decades, but thus far their applications have been quite limited because of issues about quality, conformance, and durability with the materials currently used and because these printing machines take too long to produce single objects. Many companies might benefit were these technologies to be advanced to a point where they could be incorporated in equipment capable of rapidly producing components with the quality possible with today's precision machining—but what it would take to arrive at that point is highly uncertain and hence risky. These are the starting points for NAMII—technologies with potential for applications across multiple sectors, the need to coordinate a diverse set of players across the industrial terrain to bring these technologies into the market, risks still too high for any one company to accept, and benefits too diffuse for any one company to appropriate.

Given these hurdles to developing additive manufacturing technologies and diffusing them through industry, the process of formation of NAMII offers important insights into how government convening and funding can catalyze coalition among diverse private sector interests. The $30 million of initial funding proposed by the government generated multiple proposals from competing alliances of universities, industrial research groups, companies, and state economic development agencies. Eventually, the $30 million on offer from the federal government was matched by $40 million from the private sector.[21] What seems distinctive about the consortium with the winning proposal is not so much clear technological superiority to the competing teams, but stronger commitment to an institutional design mobilizing multinational and small and medium-sized companies along with community colleges and universities around an objective of transforming regional manufacturing. The winning alliance listed as supporters 86 companies, 10 research universities, 9 workforce development members (including community colleges) and 18 nonprofits (including regional development agencies like Ben Franklin Technology Partners, MAGNET, and NorTech). TechBelt Initiative, a regional collaboration, two universities, Carnegie-Mellon and Case Western, and Timken, a large Ohio-headquartered company, played critical roles in forming this coalition. This was a major new kind of involvement for the research universities, although as one of the faculty leaders observed: "We realized that we were already doing a lot that was translational and manufacturing-oriented, even if we hadn't labeled or marketed it in that way." These key actors saw the process of proposal development and institution building as a lever to transform the region by linking supplier manufacturing in Northeast Ohio and Southwest Pennsylvania to advanced manufacturing technology. They saw that this objective required building as wide a coalition as possible, and they brought in regional development groups like MAGNET and NorTech, community colleges, and state universities, and these groups brought in many companies they worked with. Because much of the federal funding comes from the Department of Defense, the team chose to run the projects through the National Center for Defense Manufacturing and Machining, an organization with long experience in defense contracting.

NAMII has been launched—but many fundamental questions about its mission, modes of operation, and membership are still to be resolved. It is worth signaling them, since they are likely to arise in future institutions that attempt to bring together partners with such diverse structures and interests. They seem inherent in the structure and scope of such organizations. There are some basic questions about membership: Should the members all be organizations with strong physical presence in the same region? If funds are coming from federal agencies like the Department of Defense, should companies and universities from elsewhere in the country be allowed to participate? Or does the objective of building strong regional supply networks in close proximity to innovators and OEMs justify limiting participation to those located in the region? Can foreign companies belong? Would they need to have production facilities in the region? Or in the United States? As in the case of SEMATECH, NAMII needs to determine on an ongoing basis which levels of membership should provide access to which set of organizational resources.

Then there are questions about who reaps the commercial value of the capabilities created in an open innovation system. What is the roadmap for profitability in an open innovation system? There are no start-up companies yet in the NAMII membership, but there are small companies who have niche proprietary technologies in the additive domain. These companies face unique risks—on one side, of seeing larger firms appropriate innovation and run with it faster; on the other side, of seeing their proprietary intellectual property become obsolete. The need exists to figure out what's enough protection for these companies' intellectual property to induce them to participate but not so much as to stifle new developments. The universities involved in more basic research on these technologies may also need to reconsider their habitual policies for dealing with intellectual property when work is carried out with industry partners. How are traditional practices about publication affected? If NAMII aims to facilitate the commercialization of technology, how does membership in NAMII affect the tax-exempt status of universities?

In addition, how do the interests of the federal government funders—or of any of the sponsors—shape the new institutions? A federal funding agency, like the Department of Defense, may be fundamentally concerned with issues of procurement and national security, while regional stakeholders' main objective might be rebuilding the regional economy. The revenues of some of the member companies may depend on contracting with the federal agencies, and they may need domestic suppliers for those contracts. Other private sector companies may be focused on selling in global markets and able to switch between regional supply chains and contract manufacturers anywhere in the world. Some federal funding agencies, such as the Department of Commerce, have institutional capacity and responsibility for issues involving workforce training. Regional community colleges and employment agencies may have different perspectives and experience in these areas. The governance structures that can accommodate such diverse interests and provide a significant enough voice in roadmapping technologies and investment in common facilities and programs to keep them all in the same institution will, it seems to us, vary in different places and circumstances.

The cases we have described should then be thought of as experiments in rebuilding the American industrial ecosystem. What seems most valuable to extract from their diversity are some common principles. As a start, we think it useful to distinguish between the primary and essential role that government plays in supporting basic and early-stage research and the role of government in translational activities. In these latter activities, the goal is to move innovation toward the market, so joining the objectives, interests, and strategies of private sector actors to the public interest is critical to cooperation. Public policy in support of the industrial ecosystem requires government to act as a convener, but private sector and regional groups need to be in the driver's seat over the long haul. Even when government contributes significant resources, private groups still need to be fully involved in defining the rules of engagement, the boundaries of membership, the criteria of evaluation, the modes of operation, and the tasks to be accomplished jointly.

Second, building trust among the partners is an essential phase in reconstituting the industrial ecosystem, so the lengthy discussions and insistence on transparency and debates over technical objectives and membership criteria and geographic scope that all those we interviewed described in the ramping up of these institutions are valuable processes. When the "convener"—whether public or private—offers to put resources on the table, conditional on others adding to the pot, there's a more or less explicit deadline. The tension between the time constraint of the deadline and the lengthy processes of building trust and consensus seems to us ultimately a desirable one. It's in managing this tension to advance cooperation that leaders play a vital and creative role.

Third, a key principle in building new institutions for the ecosystem should be to incentivize contributions on some scale from a wide but defined set of participants who can hope to gain benefits. No single public or private entity should be the sole provider of funds; no single firm or group should be the sole beneficiary of resources. While this principle of requiring "skin in the game" is simple to articulate, in practice it is difficult to operationalize. Too much skin—whether the government's or a private convener's—and the desired forms of coordination and cooperation are unlikely to emerge. Too little skin, and free-riding is likely to subvert the project. In a fundamental sense, flourishing industrial ecosystems do create public goods like skilled workers, easy access to banking services, and an abundance of technologically sophisticated suppliers. It is not possible to imagine exactly matching defined contributions to defined benefits or cutting off the noncontributors from access to public goods. The challenge for public policy is to create incentives for deep private involvement in building networks from which, inevitably and desirably, there will be public spillovers.

Fourth, the resources committed by public and private actors to the industrial ecosystem should be invested in institutions that can withstand the withdrawal of any single participant. There is no infallible blueprint for institutional resilience, but a principle of providing resources only to firms applying in consortia with others could improve the likelihood that even if one member of an industrial ecosystem project pulls out, that the institution would survive and that other participants would still find it valuable to support. In the creation of new institutions, we should seek to avoid the common situation today of public resources being channeled to individual companies in a wild competition for plant locations and employment, only to end up a few years later with the closing or relocation of the plant and little or nothing left in the community. A *New York Times* report on the fate of the more than $80 billion of benefits in the form of cash grants, loans, tax breaks, and property tax abatements that states and towns hand out every year to induce companies to locate or stay within their communities shows that when such companies close plants or move out, little of value remains for the community.[22] Courts have ruled that companies cannot be held to assurances about creating jobs. And communities can end up worse off, having diverted their tax revenues from spending on education and infrastructure into subsidies for the companies.

For situations created by today's scramble to attract industrial location with tax credits, PIE has no remedy. But we think we need to identify other design principles for new institutions to accelerate the flow of innovation into the market. Many innovations will fail, and it would be a waste of the community's resources to prop them up. The objective, rather, should be to create organizations capable of sustaining multiple streams of innovation and of restating objectives and recomposing teams and resources as one or another project falls by the wayside and others show promise. Industrial ecosystems need to nourish technological capabilities and human skills that can be deployed and redeployed across multiple streams of innovation—some of which will fail, some of which may succeed. We have observed that some factors favorable to producing these outcomes are requiring partnerships as a condition for funding, developing mixed portfolios of innovation with shorter- and longer-term trajectories, and anchoring these industrial ecosystem institutions in relationships with research universities with long experience in sustaining innovative teams through cycles of success and failure. The organizations we have studied are experiments under construction: we need to be sure we invest in the efforts needed to learn from their experience.

As the MIT researchers in the Production in the Innovation Economy teams have fanned out to follow the trajectories of innovation in small high-tech start-ups, in Main Street manufacturers, in the research centers of the world's largest multinationals, and abroad in some of our main commercial partners and competitors, our own understanding of when and how innovation can come to life in the economy has been transformed. We have watched great inventions in search of machine shops and suppliers capable of making prototypes and pilot projects; great start-ups in search of funds first here, then abroad, to commercialize products on a large scale; and plain good ideas about improving products and processes remain unrealized. Our own initial lofty conceptions of innovation as the discovery of new general purpose technologies that burst into the world and create whole new industries have been brought down to American earth by recognizing the need to tie them to the challenges of sustaining the human talents and material capabilities required to build these new industries. As researchers, we still have our dreams; after the PIE project, we realize we need partners to bring them into the world.

Notes

Chapter 1

1. Michael L. Dertouzos et al., *Made in America: Regaining the Productive Edge* (Cambridge, MA: MIT Press, 1989).

2. Among the early and most systematic attempts to lay out the range of dangers for the United States resulting from weaknesses in manufacturing was Gregory Tassey, "Rationales and Mechanisms for Revitalizing U.S. Manufacturing R&D Strategies," *Journal of Technology Transfer* 35, no. 3 (2010).

3. National Science Board, *Science and Engineering Indicators 2012* (Arlington, VA: National Science Foundation, 2012), pp. 6–21, 22.

4. Dertouzos et al., *Made in America;* Susan Helper, Timothy Krueger, and Howard Wial, *Locating American Manufacturing: Trends in the Geography of Production* (Washington, DC: Brookings Institution, 2012); Susan Houseman et al., *Offshoring and the State of American Manufacturing* (Kalamazoo, MI: W.E. Upjohn Institute, 2010); Erica Fuchs and Randolph Kirchain, "Design for Location? The Impact of Manufacturing Offshore on Technology Competitiveness in the Optoelectronics Industry," *Management Science* 56, no. 12 (2010); Charles W. Wessner and Alan W. Wolff, eds., *Rising to the Challenge: US Innovation Policy for the Global Economy* (Washington, DC: National Academies Press, 2012).

5. National Science Board, "Science and Engineering Indicators 2012."

6. Booz & Company, "The Global Innovation 1000: How the Top Innovators Keep Winning," *strategy+business*, no. 61, Winter 2010, http://www.booz.com/media/file/sb61_preprint_Global-Innov1000-10408.pdf; interview with Senior Vice President Barry Jaruzelski, May 25, 2011.

7. There were 29 software firms and an additional 10 firms for which researchers could not find any recent records, leaving 150 production-oriented start-ups.

8. The data were acquired from the Corporate Research Board, LLC, and are described in Spencer L. Tracy, Jr., "Accelerating Job Creation: The Promise of High-Impact Companies," Corporate Research Board, LLC for SBA Contract Number SBAHQ-10-M-44. www/sba.gov/sites/default/files/HighImpactReport.pdf/

9. OECD, *Proposed Standard Practice for Surveys of Research and Experimental Development—Frascati Manual* (Paris: OECD, 2002).

10. http://www.masstank.com/files/mass_tank_goldwind_press_release22112.pdf/

11. For the reuse of legacy capabilities in industrial change, see Suzanne Berger and MIT Industrial Performance Center, *How We Compete: What Companies around the World Are Doing to Make It in Today's Global Economy* (New York: Currency Doubleday, 2005).

12. Raymond Vernon, "International Investment and International Trade in the Product Cycle," *Quarterly Journal of Economics* 80 (1966).

13. Because of Apple's spectacular success, we frequently refer to this model in our work. Apple did not agree to be interviewed for this project, and we have had no access to Apple other than to publicly available information about the company.

14. See a fuller account of these changes in Berger et al., *How We Compete*.

15. Gerald F. Davis, *Managed by the Markets: How Finance Re-Shaped America* (Oxford: Oxford University Press, 2009).

16. Mercedes Delgado, Michael E. Porter, and Scott Stern, "Clusters, Convergence, and Economic Performance" (National Bureau of Economic Research, 2012), Working Paper 18250.

Chapter 2

1. Colin Clark, *The Conditions of Economic Progress* (New York: Macmillan, 1957 [1940]).

2. For an approach that emphasizes the tradables sector, see Michael Spence, "The Impact of Globalization on Income and Employment: The Downside of Integrating Markets," *Foreign Affairs* 90, no. 4 (2011): 28–41.

3. Clark, *The Conditions of Economic Progress*.

4. U.S. Department of Labor, Bureau of Labor Statistics, "International Comparisons of Annual Labor Force Statistics, Adjusted to U.S. Concepts, 1970–2011," table 7, http://www.bls.gov/fls/flscomparelf.htm/

5. "United Nations National Accounts Main Aggregates Database," http://unstats.un.org/unsd/snaama/selbasicFast.asp/

6. U.S. share of world manufacturing output in 2010 was reported by IHS Global Insight. China was slightly ahead for the first time with 19.8 percent. U.S. Department of Labor, Bureau of Labor Statistics. "Extended Mass Layoffs Associated with Domestic and Overseas Relocations, First Quarter 2004," http://www.bls.gov/news.release/reloc.nr0.htm/

7. Gary Becker, The Becker-Posner Blog, 2012, "Concern About the Decline in Manufacturing in the United States?," http://www.becker-posner-blog.com/2012/04/concern-about-the-decline-in-manufacturing-in-the-united-states-becker.html/, April 22, 2012.

8. Richard Posner, The Becker-Posner Blog, 2012, "Decline of U.S. Manufacturing—Posner," http://www.becker-posner-blog.com/2012/04/decline-of-us-manufacturingposner.html/, April 22, 2012.

9. Chinese statistics being somewhat less than clear on some of the points, another commentator making the same point claims 16 million lost Chinese manufacturing jobs in more or less the same period. Tim Worstall, "That Giant Sucking Sound of Manufacturing Jobs Going to China," *Forbes*, February 3, 2012; Robert D. Atkinson et al., "Worse

Than the Great Depression: What Experts Are Missing About American Manufacturing Decline" (Washington, DC: Information Technology & Innovation Foundation, 2012).

10. U.S. Department of Commerce, U.S. Census Bureau, and U.S. Bureau of Economic Analysis, *U.S. International Trade in Goods and Services* (Washington, DC, 2012), http://www.bea.gov/newsreleases/international/trade/2012/trad0412.html/.

11. Susan Houseman et al., "Offshoring and the State of American Manufacturing" (Kalamazoo, MI: W.E. Upjohn Institute, 2010); Susan N. Houseman and Kenneth F. Ryder, "Measurement Issues Arising from the Growth of Globalization: Conference Summary" (Kalamazoo, MI: W.E. Upjohn Institute, 2010).

12. Ibid., 11.

13. Susan Helper, Timothy Krueger, and Howard Wial, "Locating American Manufacturing: Trends in the Geography of Production" (Washington, DC: Brookings Institution, 2012).

14. Houseman et al., "Offshoring and the State of American Manufacturing."

15. Helper, Krueger, and Wial, "Locating American Manufacturing: Trends in the Geography of Production."

16. U.S. Department of Labor, Bureau of Labor Statistics. "International Comparisons of Annual Labor Force Statistics, Adjusted to U.S. Concepts, 1970–2011," table 7, 2012 http://www.bls.gov/fls/flscomparelf.htm/

17. U.S. Department of Labor, Bureau of Labor Statistics (2011). "Hourly Compensation in Manufacturing, in U.S. Dollars, 2010," http://www.bls.gov/news.release/ichcc.t01.htm/

18. The definition of globalization used here and the discussion that follows draws heavily on Berger et al., *How We Compete*. A broader view of globalization might include culture, language, ways of thinking, national identity, and security.

19. The best general introduction to globalization and presentation of evidence is Martin Wolf, *Why Globalization Works* (2004). The "Globalization Study" conducted at the MIT Industrial Performance Center, 1999–2005, carried out more than 500 interviews in the United States, Asia, and Europe and analyzed firm-level evidence on convergence and diversity. Berger et al., *How We Compete*.

20. Carliss Baldwin and Kim Clark, *Design Rules: The Power of Modularity* (Cambridge, MA: MIT Press, 2000); Timothy Sturgeon, "Modular Production Networks: A New American Model of Industrial Organization," *Industrial and Corporate Change* 11, no. 3 (2002).

21. Maurice Obstfeld and Alan M. Taylor, "Globalization and Capital Markets," in *Globalization in Historical Perspective*, ed. Michael D. Bordo, Alan M. Taylor, and Jeffrey G. Williamson (Chicago: University of Chicago Press, 2003).

22. Pew Research Center, "Americans Are of Two Minds on Trade" (Washington, DC: Pew Research Center Working Paper 1795, 2010).

23. Some economists always doubted. They acquired a very distinguished voice when Paul Samuelson joined their ranks and worried about outcomes in which one large economy like China's could win across the board. Paul Samuelson, "Where Ricardo and Mill Rebut and Confirm Arguments of Mainstream Economists Supporting Globalization," *Journal of Economic Perspectives* 18, no. 3 (2004): 35–146.

24. Robert Z. Lawrence, *Is Trade to Blame for Rising U.S. Income Inequality?* (Washington, DC: Petersen Institute for International Economics, 2008); David Autor, David Dorn, and Gordon H. Hanson, "The China Syndrome: Local Labor Market Effects of Import Competition in the United States" (Cambridge, MA: National Bureau of Economic Research, NBER Working Paper No. 18054, 2012).

25. Some economists, like Dani Rodrik (Dani Rodrik, *Has Globalization Gone Too Far?* [Washington, DC: Institute for International Economy, 1997]), did argue that even expanding "intra-industry" trade among countries with similar wage levels would increase the elasticity of labor supply and hence have negative effects on wages and job security.

26. For an early effort to consider the impact of fragmentation of tasks and outsourcing on manufacturing employment, see Robert C. Feenstra and Gordon H. Hanson, "The Impact of Outsourcing and High-Technology Capital on Wages: Estimates for the U.S. 1979–1990," *Quarterly Journal of Economics* 114, no. 3 (1999); U.S. Department of Labor, Bureau of Labor Statistics, "Extended Mass Layoffs Associated with Domestic and Overseas Relocations, First Quarter 2004," http://www.bls.gov/news.release/reloc.nr0.htm

27. "US Bureau of Labor Statistics, Current Employment Statistics," http://www.bls.gov

28. On Sweden, Finland, and Norway, see Karolina Ekholm and Katarina Hakkala, "International Production Networks in the Nordic/Baltic Region" (Paris: Organization for Economic Co-operation and Development, OECD Trade Policy Working Paper no. 61, 2008).

29. Lawrence F. Katz and David Autor, "Changes in the Wage Structure and Earnings Inequality," in *Quarterly Journal of Economics*, ed. Orley Ashenfelter and David Card (Amsterdam: Elsevier Science, 1999); David Autor, Frank Levy, and Richard J. Murnane, "The Skill Content of Recent Technological Change: An Empirical Exploration" (Cambridge, MA: National Bureau of Economic Research, NBER Working Paper No. 8337, 2001); Daron Acemoglu and David Autor, "Skills, Tasks and Technologies: Implications for Employment and Earnings" (Cambridge, MA: National Bureau of Economic Research, NBER Working Paper 16082, 2010).

30. Mohammad Abdul Munim Joarder, A.K.M. Nurul Hossain, and Md. Mahbubul Hakim, "Post MFA Performance of Bangladesh Apparel Sector," *International Review of Business Research Papers* 6, no. 4 (2010).

31. Autor, Dorn, and Hanson, "The China Syndrome."

32. Andrew B. Bernard, Bradford J. Jensen, and Peter K. Schott, "Survival of the Best Fit: Exposure to Low-Wage Countries and the Uneven Growth of U.S. Manufacturing Plants," *Journal of International Economics* 68, no. 1 (2006).

33. Autor, Dorn, and Hanson, "The China Syndrome," p. 23.

34. Ibid., p. 29.

35. Ibid., p. 27.

36. Ibid., p. 12.

37. Ibid., p. 19.

38. Thomas J. Holmes, "The Case of the Disappearing Large Employer Manufacturing Plants: Not Much of a Mystery after All" (Minneapolis, MN: Federal Reserve Bank of Minneapolis, 2011).

39. Autor, Dorn, and Hanson, "The China Syndrome," p. 14.

40. Nicholas Bloom, Mirko Draca, and John Van Reenen, "Trade-Induced Technical Change? The Impact of Chinese Imports on Innovation, It, and Productivity" (Cambridge, MA: National Bureau of Economic Research, 2011).

41. Gary Fields, *Territories of Profit: Communications, Capitalist Development, and the Innovative Enterprises of G. F. Swift and Dell Computer* (Stanford: Stanford University Press, 2004); Alfred D. Chandler, Jr., *The Visible Hand: The Managerial Revolution in American Business* (Cambridge, MA: Belknap/Harvard University Press, 1977).

42. Peter F. Drucker, "The New Society," *Harper's Magazine* 199, no. 1192 (1949).

43. *Encyclopaedia Britannica*, volume 9 (Chicago: University of Chicago Press, 1949), pp. 493–494.

44. Cited in Alison Grant, "Timken Shareholders Vote to Split Company in Two, Separating Steel and Bearings Businesses," *The Plain Dealer*, May 7, 2013; and Timken, "Timken: Metal Testing," *Financial Times*, May 10, 2013.

45. Gerald F. Davis, *Managed by the Markets: How Finance Re-Shaped America* (Oxford: Oxford University Press, 2009).

46. Ibid., p. 93.

47. Interview, March 3, 2011.

48. David A. Hounshell and John Kenly Smith, Jr., *Science and Corporate Strategy: DuPont R&D, 1902–1980* (New York: Cambridge University Press, 1989 [1988]).

49. Ibid., p. 223.

50. Ibid., p. 287.

51. Ibid., p. 597.

52. A. Thackray, J. L. Sturchio, P.T. Carroll, and R. F. Bud, *Chemistry in America, 1876–1976, Historical Indicators* (Boston: Kluwer Academic Publishers, 1985), cited in Chris Tucker and Bhaven Sampar, "Laboratory-Based Innovation in the American Innovation System," in Michael Crow and Barry Bozeman, *Limited by Design: R&D Laboratories in the U.S. National Innovation System* (New York: Columbia University Press, 1998).

53. Jon Gertner, *The Idea Factory: Bell Labs and the Great Age of American Innovation* (New York: Penguin, 2012).

54. William H. Whyte, Jr., *The Organization Man* (New York: Simon and Schuster, 1956), p. 209).

55. Hounshell and Smith, *Science and Corporate Strategy*, pp. 388, 406.

56. Ibid., p. 431.

57. http://holmdel-hazlet.patch.com/articles/alcatel-lucent-redevelopment-plan-ok-d-by-holmdel-township-committee/ (accessed August 6, 2012).

58. For a recent effort to measure the returns to large firms from acquisition in lieu of in-house R&D, see Gordon M. Phillips and Alexei Zhdanov, "R&D and the Incentives from Merger and Acquisition Activity," *Review of Financial Studies* 26, no. 1 (2013).

59. Barry Jaruzelski and Kevin Dehoof, "Beyond Borders: The Global Innovation 100," *strategy+business*, no. 53, Winter 2008, http://www.strategy+business.com/article/08405?gko=87043/

60. Robert E. Hall and Susan E. Woodward, "The Burden of the Non-Diversifiable Rise of Entrepreneurship," *American Economic Review*, June 2010.

61. "How Innovative is China? Valuing Patents" *The Economist*, January 5, 2013, p. 52.

62. Presentation to the PIE Commission, May 16, 2012.

63. Interview June 13, 2011.

64. In January 20, 2011, testimony before the House Ways and Means Committee, American Enterprise Institute economist Kevin A. Haslett showed the effective average corporate tax on U.S. firms in 1996 as 29.7 percent and in 2010 as 29 percent; in non-U.S. OECD countries over the same period it fell from 29.7 percent to 20.5 percent.

65. Interview with Alexander Cutler, January 20, 2012.

66. Presentation of John G. Cox to the PIE Commission, March 21, 2012. PIE researchers also carried out on-site interviews at Biogen Idec in Research Triangle Park, North Carolina, January 9, 2012.

Chapter 3

1. This chapter draws on the research paper of Elisabeth B. Reynolds, Hiram Samel, and Joyce Lawrence, "Learning by Building: Complementary Assets and the Migration of Capabilities in U.S. Innovation Firms" in *Production in the Innovation Economy*, ed. R. Locke and R. Wellhausen (Cambridge, MA: MIT Press, 2013), and contributions from the PIE faculty working on "scale up": Richard K. Lester, Charles Sodini, Fiona Murray, and Olivier de Weck.

2. Naomi R. Lamoreaux and Kenneth L. Sokoloff, eds., *Financing Innovation in the United States, 1870 to the Present* (Cambridge, MA: MIT Press, 2007).

3. Dertouzos et al., *Made in America*.

4. Example drawn from Ralph Gomory in Nathan Rosenberg, Ralph Landau, and David Mowrey, eds., *Technology and the Wealth of Nations* (Stanford: Stanford University Press, 1992), p. 389.

5. Fred Block and Matthew R. Keller, "Where Do Innovations Come From? Transformations in the U.S. Economy, 1970–2006," *Socioeconomic Review* 7 (2009).

6. See Josh Lerner, *The Architecture of Innovation* (Boston: Harvard Business Review Press, 2012).

7. Josh Lerner, "The Narrowing Ambitions of Venture Capital," *MIT Technology Review* 115, no. 6 (2012).

8. Presentation by Thomas Connelly, executive vice president and chief innovation officer, DuPont, at MIT, April 30, 2012.

9. http://www.photonicsonline.com/doc.mvc/DuPont-Broadens-OLED-Base-With-Uniax-Buy-0001/

10. http://gigaom.com/cleantech/dupont-buys-solar-ink-maker-innovalight/ (accessed November 4, 2012).

11. MIT PIE interviews in China, 2011, 2012.

12. Yochai Benkler, "Coase's Penguin: Linux and the Nature of the Firm," *Yale Law Journal* 112 (2002): 369. Henry Chesborough, *Open Innovation: The New Imperative for Creating and Profiting from Technology* (Boston: Harvard Business School Press, 2005).

13. Raymond M. Wolfe, "Business R & D Performed in the United States Cost $291 Billion in 2008 and $282 Billion in 2009," in *InfoBrief* (National Science Foundation, National Center for Science and Engineering Statistics).

14. See Lamoreaux and Sokoloff, *Financing Innovation in the United States, 1870 to the Present.*

15. Greg Linden, Kenneth L. Kraemer, and Jason Dedrick, "Who Captures Value in the Apple iPad?," Syracuse University's Information Space, http://infospace.ischool.syr.edu/2011/06/29/who-captures-value-from-the-ipad/; Jason Dedrick, Kenneth L. Kraemer, and Greg Linden, "Who Profits from Innovation in Global Value Chains? A Study of the iPod and Notebook PCs," *Industrial and Corporate Change* 19, no. 1 (2009).

16. In all but a few cases, the company was created based on technology developed at MIT. In a few cases, companies licensed MIT technology after a company was formed.

17. There were 29 software firms and an additional ten firms for which the researchers could not find any recent records, leaving 150 production-oriented start-ups.

18. Edward B. Roberts and Charles E. Eesley, "The Entrepreneurial Impact: The Role of M.I.T: An Updated Report," *Foundations and Trends in Entrepreneurship* 7, no. 1–2 (2011).

19. Enrico Moretti, *The New Geography of Jobs* (Boston: Houghton Mifflin Harcourt), p .86; Milken Institute reference, Information Technology and Innovation Foundation (ITIF) ranking.

20. Robert E. Hall and Susan E. Woodward, "The Burden of the Nondiversifiable Risk of Entrepreneurship," *American Economic Review* 100, no. 3 (2010). The authors find that out of 22,004 venture backed companies founded between 1987 and 2008, 40 percent were still active, 26 percent were acquired and 34 percent were either closed or effectively worth zero.

21. SBIR/STTR (Small Business Innovation Research/Technology Transfer) grants are early-stage translational funds coordinated through the Small Business Administration and awarded by different branches of the federal government. The median grant for the MIT TLO firms receiving awards was $1.3 million. In total, the MIT TLO firms received $108 million. Venture capital reporting is voluntary. It may be possible that firms received venture funds, but they or the venture firms did not report it. In this case, the event would not be recorded here.

22. By definition, these firms were all founded between 1997 and 2003 and have remained independent. Of the 82 firms for which we have data, 11 closed and 19 merged with or were sold to another firm, leaving 52 independent firms. Revenue for merged firms is not included, as separate sales figures for the acquired firms (technology) are not reported.

23. Mick Mountz, presentation to the PIE Commission, October 12, 2011.

24. Interview—CEO, advanced materials firm, April 14, 2012.

25. Interview—CEO, integrated surgical device manufacturer, April 25, 2012.

26. Erica Fuchs and Randolph Kirchain, "Design for Location? The Impact of Manufacturing Offshore on Technology Competitiveness in the Optoelectronics Industry," *Management Science* 56, no. 12; Chia-Hsuan Yang, Rebecca Nugent, and Erica R. H. Fuchs, "Gains from Others' Losses: Technology Trajectories and the Global Division of Firms" (Carnegie-Mellon University). Presentation to PIE Commission, April 4, 2012.

27. G. P. Pisano and W. C. Shih, *Producing Prosperity: Why America Needs a Manufacturing Renaissance* (Cambridge, MA: Harvard Business School Press, 2012).

Chapter 4

1. Enrico Moretti, *The New Geography of Jobs* (Boston: Houghton Mifflin Harcourt, 2012).

2. Ibid., p. 83.

3. Ibid., pp. 74–81.

4. National Science Board, *Science and Engineering Indicators 2012* (Arlington, VA: National Science Foundation 2012), p. 6-6.

5. Ibid, p. 6-14.

6. On the contributions to value added of high- and low-tech manufacturing in OECD countries, see Nick Von Tunzelmann and Virginia Acha, "Innovation in 'Low-Tech' Industries," in *The Oxford Handbook of Innovation*, ed. Jan Fagerberg, David C. Mowery, and Richard R. Nelson (Oxford: Oxford University Press, 2005).

7. National Science Board 2012, pp. 6-21–6-22.

8. Ibid., p. 6-28.

9. Sylvia Pagan Westphal, "Boston Scientific Settles Spat," *Wall Street Journal*, September 22, 2005; Stephen Heuser, "Boston Scientific, Medinol Settle Row. Natick Firm Will Pay $750m in Battle over Stent Design, Contract," *Boston Globe*, September 22, 2005.

10. OECD, *Proposed Standard Practice for Surveys of Research and Experimental Development—Frascati Manual* (Paris: OECD, 2002).

11. Interview with Daniel E. Berry, president and CEO, MAGNET (Manufacturing and Growth Network), Cleveland, Ohio, April 6, 2012.

12. Advanced Manufacturing Partnership (AMP) Steering Committee, "Report to the President on Capturing Domestic Competitive Advantage in Advanced Manufacturing" (Washington, DC, July, 2012).

13. Interview with Michael Bernas, head of project office, global production, Festo, May 9, 2011.

14. L. Frederico Signorini, ed., *Lo Sviluppo Locale. Un'indagine della Banca d'Italia sui distretti industriali* (Rome: Donzelli, 2000).

15. Mercedes Delgado, Michael E. Porter, and Scott Stern, "Clusters, Convergence, and Economic Performance" (National Bureau of Economic Research, 2012), working paper 18250.

16. Ibid, p. 11.

17. Spencer L. Tracy, Jr., "Accelerating Job Creation: The Promise of High-Impact Companies," Corporate Research Board, LLC for SBA Contract Number SBAHQ-10-M-0144, www.sba.gov/sites/default/files/HighImpactReport.pdf

18. Ibid.

19. Calculation by Spencer L. Tracy, Jr., to authors.

20. Interview, October 13, 2011.

21. http://spectrum.ieee.org/consumer-electronics/audiovideo/quantum-dots-are-behind-new-displays/

22. Interview, April 25, 2012.

23. Interview, January 26, 2012.

24. Interview, January 19, 2012.

25. Interview, January 17, 2012.

26. Interview, September 30, 2011.

27. Interview, January 17, 2012.

28. Interview, April 25, 2012.

29. Interview with Donald Sadoway, September 6, 2012, and with Phil Giudice, October 11, 2012.

30. Asked why they did not start training these skills for young engineering graduate recruits, the response was it took too long, and everyone was just too busy. The company was booming. Interview, August 20, 2011.

Chapter 5

1. Atlas Venture partner and Advanced Electron Beams board member, Jeff Fagnan, cited in *Boston Business Journal*, May 18, 2012, http://www.bizjournals.com/boston/blog/startups/2012/05/advanced-electron-beams-to-shut-down.html/ (accessed November 28, 2012).

2. http://data.worldbank.org/indicator/NV.IND.MANF.ZS/ (accessed December 19, 2012). Value added in manufacturing is calculated as the output of industries considered as manufacturing in the International Standard Industrial Classification code (ISIC). The employment statistics are from the U.S. Bureau of Labor Statistics.

3. McKinsey Global Institute, "Manufacturing the Future: The Next Era of Global Growth and Innovation" (2012), p. 23; Swedish Agency for Growth Policy Analysis, "The Performance and Challenges of the Swedish National Innovation System: A Background Report to the OECD" (2011).

4. McKinsey Global Institute, "Manufacturing the Future," p. 25.

39. Autor, Dorn, and Hanson, "The China Syndrome," p. 14.

40. Nicholas Bloom, Mirko Draca, and John Van Reenen, "Trade-Induced Technical Change? The Impact of Chinese Imports on Innovation, It, and Productivity" (Cambridge, MA: National Bureau of Economic Research, 2011).

41. Gary Fields, *Territories of Profit: Communications, Capitalist Development, and the Innovative Enterprises of G. F. Swift and Dell Computer* (Stanford: Stanford University Press, 2004); Alfred D. Chandler, Jr., *The Visible Hand: The Managerial Revolution in American Business* (Cambridge, MA: Belknap/Harvard University Press, 1977).

42. Peter F. Drucker, "The New Society," *Harper's Magazine* 199, no. 1192 (1949).

43. *Encyclopaedia Britannica*, volume 9 (Chicago: University of Chicago Press, 1949), pp. 493–494.

44. Cited in Alison Grant, "Timken Shareholders Vote to Split Company in Two, Separating Steel and Bearings Businesses," *The Plain Dealer*, May 7, 2013; and Timken, "Timken: Metal Testing," *Financial Times,* May 10, 2013.

45. Gerald F. Davis, *Managed by the Markets: How Finance Re-Shaped America* (Oxford: Oxford University Press, 2009).

46. Ibid., p. 93.

47. Interview, March 3, 2011.

48. David A. Hounshell and John Kenly Smith, Jr., *Science and Corporate Strategy: DuPont R&D, 1902–1980* (New York: Cambridge University Press, 1989 [1988]).

49. Ibid., p. 223.

50. Ibid., p. 287.

51. Ibid., p. 597.

52. A. Thackray, J. L. Sturchio, P.T. Carroll, and R. F. Bud, *Chemistry in America, 1876–1976, Historical Indicators* (Boston: Kluwer Academic Publishers, 1985), cited in Chris Tucker and Bhaven Sampar, "Laboratory-Based Innovation in the American Innovation System," in Michael Crow and Barry Bozeman, *Limited by Design: R&D Laboratories in the U.S. National Innovation System* (New York: Columbia University Press, 1998).

53. Jon Gertner, *The Idea Factory: Bell Labs and the Great Age of American Innovation* (New York: Penguin, 2012).

54. William H. Whyte, Jr., *The Organization Man* (New York: Simon and Schuster, 1956), p. 209.

55. Hounshell and Smith, *Science and Corporate Strategy*, pp. 388, 406.

56. Ibid., p. 431.

57. http://holmdel-hazlet.patch.com/articles/alcatel-lucent-redevelopment-plan-ok-d-by-holmdel-township-committee/ (accessed August 6, 2012).

58. For a recent effort to measure the returns to large firms from acquisition in lieu of in-house R&D, see Gordon M. Phillips and Alexei Zhdanov, "R&D and the Incentives from Merger and Acquisition Activity," *Review of Financial Studies* 26, no. 1 (2013).

27. The account that follows is based largely on research by PIE researchers Edward Steinfeld, Jonas Nahm, and Florian Metzler in China and also on a concurrent two-year research project on new energy firms by this team. In all they conducted more than 100 interviews. The findings were reported in a PIE working paper, Jonas Nahm and Edward S. Steinfeld, "Scale-Up Nation: Chinese Specialization in Innovative Manufacturing," March 12, 2012; and presented to the PIE Commission by Edward S. Steinfeld on May 2, 2012.

28. Interview, August 10, 2011.

29. Dan Breznitz and Michael Murphree, *Run of the Red Queen*. New Haven: Yale University Press, 2011.

30. Charles Duhigg and Keith Bradsher, "How the U.S. Lost Out on iPhone Work," http://www.nytimes.com/2012/01/22/business/apple-america-and-a-squeezed-middle-class.html?pagewanted=all&_r=0/

31. Kevin Bullis, "Why Boston Power Went to China," *MIT Technology Review*, December 6, 2011.

32. Erin Ailworth, "Massachusetts firm in $1.25b deal in China," *Boston Globe*, May 21, 2012.

33. The following sections draw on Nahm and Steinfeld, "Scale-Up Nation."

34. Interview, January 10, 2011.

35. Raymond Vernon, "International Investment and International Trade in the Product Cycle," *Quarterly Journal of Economics* 80, no. 2 (May 1966): 190–207; Pisano and Shih, *Producing Prosperity*.

36. Interview, June 8, 2011.

37. Interview with Theodor Peters, Vensys, in "Das Vensys Konzept," *Wind-Kraft Journal*, no. 6 (2009), p. 18.

38. www.vensys.de/energy-en/index.php/

39. "Das Vensys Konzept," p. 22.

40. Interview, July 29, 2011.

41. Suzanne Berger and Richard K. Lester, eds., *Made by Hong Kong* (New York: Oxford University Press, 1997); Edward S. Steinfeld, "China's Shallow Integration: Networked Production and the New Challenges for Late Industrialization," *World Development* 32, no. 11 (2004); Edward S. Steinfeld, "Cross-Straits Integration and Industrial Catch-Up," in S. Berger and R. K. Lester, *Global Taiwan* (Armonk, NY: M.E. Sharpe, 2005), pp. 228–279.

42. Jason Dedrick, Kenneth L. Kraemer, and Greg Linden, "Who Profits from Innovation in Global Value Chains? A Study of the iPod and Notebook PCs," *Industrial and Corporate Change* 19, no. 1 (2009); Greg Linden, Kenneth L. Kraemer, and Jason Dedrick, "Who Captures Value in the Apple iPad?," Syracuse University's Information Space, http://info-space.ischool.syr.edu/2011/06/29/who-captures-value-from-the-ipad/

43. David Barboza, "Supply Chain for iPhone Highlights Costs in China," *New York Times*, July 5, 2010.

Chapter 6

1. The first sections of this chapter draw on research by Professor Olivier de Weck, two MIT undergraduate research assistants, Jonté Craighead and Darci Reed; and Andrew Oswald, an MS student in Engineering Systems Division. Interviews with MIT faculty engaged in research relevant to manufacturing as well as respondents (29) to a survey sent to U.S. university programs in industrial and manufacturing engineering were used in the analysis.

2. Advanced Manufacturing Partnership (AMP) Steering Committee, "Report to the President on Capturing Domestic Competitive Advantage in Advanced Manufacturing" (Washington, DC, July, 2012), p. 1.

3. Stephanie S. Shipp et al., *Emerging Global Trends in Advanced Manufacturing* (Alexandria, VA: Institute for Defense Analyses, 2012), P-4603, p. 4.

4. These seven technology categories regroup twenty-four technologies listed in a variety of recent reports, in our colleagues' self-designated areas of research, and in a literature review of 500 papers on manufacturing published since 2008. These seven categories are illustrative of important possibilities. But there are additional processes and technologies to be explored.

5. The following section draws on text and work by Professor Sanjay Sarma with research assistance from Linda Yu Liu, an MIT undergraduate with a 2011 BS thesis, *A Case Study of the Manufacturing and Shipping Costs of Outsourcing* and from Radu Gogoana, a PIE student researcher, with a 2012 SM thesis, *Internal Resistance Variances in Lithium-Ion Batteries and Implications in Manufacturing.*

6. Elizabeth Olson, "A Shift from Company Cars," *New York Times,* http://www.nytimes.com/2010/11/23/business/23share.html/

7. Jay Wright Forrester, *Industrial Dynamics* (Waltham, MA: Pegasus Communications, 1961).

8. J. D. C. Little, "Little's Law as Viewed on Its 50th Anniversary," *Operations Research* 59, no. 3 (2011).

9. Daniel Jones, Daniel Roos, and James P. Womack, *The Machine That Changed the World* (New York: Harper Perennial, 1990).

10. S. E. Sarma et al., "Rapid Product Realization from Detail Design," *Computer-Aided Design* 28 (1996).

11. Chris Anderson, "In the Next Industrial Revolution, Atoms Are the New Bits," *Wired* 18, no. 1 (January 25, 2010).

12. Michael Leitner, "Economies of Scale in Semiconductor Manufacturing," *Addison-Wesley Information Series* (2004); Radu Gogoana, "Internal Resistance Variances in Lithium-Ion Batteries and Implications in Manufacturing" (Massachusetts Institute of Technology, 2012).

13. Thomas E. Hendricks, "Purchasing Consortiums: Horizontal Alliances among Firms Buying Common Goods and Services: What? Who? Why? How?" (The Center for Advanced Purchasing Studies, 1996). The Crescent Purchasing Consortium is one example: http://www.thecpc.ac.uk/

14. Gogoana, "Internal Resistance Variances in Lithium-Ion Batteries and Implications in Manufacturing."

15. The research of Joe Foley, a former MIT PhD student now at the University of Reykjavik, demonstrates some of these advances.

16. "Marconi Fellow Paul Baran," http://www.marconisociety.org/fellows/bios/paul_baran.html/

17. Raff D'Andrea, "A Revolution in the Warehouse: A Retrospective on Kiva Systems and the Grand Challenges Ahead," *IEEE Transactions on Automation Science and Engineering* 9, no. 4 (2012).

18. Keith Wagstaff, "Amazon's $775 Million Acquisition of Kiva Systems Could Shift How Businesses See Robots," http://techland.time.com/2012/03/21/amazons-775-million-acquisition-of-kiva-systems-could-shift-how-businesses-see-robots/

19. Sanjay Sarma, David Brock, and Daniel Engels, "Radio Frequency Identification and the Electronic Product Code," *IEEE Micro* 21, no. 6 (2001).

20. Research and Innovation Technology Administration, U. S. Department of Transportation, www.rita.dot.gov/publications/bits/publications/

21. B. Starr McMullen, "Purchased Transportation and Ltl Motor Carrier Costs: Possible Implications for Market Structure," *Journal of the Transportation Research Forum* 31, no. HS-041 177.1991(1991).

22. Thomas M. Corsi et al., "Deregulation, Strategic Change, and Firm Performance among Ltl Motor Carriers," *Transportation Journal* 31, no. 1 (1991).

23. Hau L. Lee, V. Padmanabhan, and Seugjin Whang, "The Bullwhip Effect in Supply Chains," *Sloan Management Review* 38, no. 3 (Spring 1997).

Chapter 7

1. Paul Osterman and Andrew Weaver, "Skills and Skill Gaps in Manufacturing," in Locke and Wellhausen, *Production in the Innovation Economy,* and Andrew Weaver and Paul Osterman, "The New Skill Production System: Policy Challenges and Solutions in Manufacturing Labor Markets," in Locke and Wellhausen, *Production in the Innovation Economy.*

2. United States and National Commission on Technology Automation and Economic Progress, "Technology and the American Economy Report," in *Report of the National Commission on Technology, Automation, and Economic Progress* (Washington, U.S. Govt. Printing Office, February 1966), p. xii.

3. *Technology and Employment: Innovation and Growth in the U.S. Economy,* ed. Richard M. Cyert and David C. Mowery (Washington, DC: National Academy Press, 1987), p. 3.

4. Erik Brynjolfsson and Andrew McAfee, *Race against the Machine* (Lexington, MA: Digital Frontier Press, 2011), p. 37.

5. Rowena Gray, "Taking Technology to Task: The Skill Content of Technological Change in Early Twentieth Century United States" (European Historical Economics Society Working Papers in Economic History, no. 9, October 2011).

6. Claudia Goldin and Lawrence F. Katz, *The Race between Education and Technology* (Cambridge, MA: Belknap/Harvard University Press, 2008); Daron Acemoglu and David Autor, "Skills, Tasks, and Technologies," in *Handbook of Labor Economics*, ed. Orley Ashenfelter and David Card (North Holland: Elsevier, 2011). "What Does Human Capital Do? A Review of Goldin and Katz's the Race between Education and Technology," *Journal of Economic Literature* 50, no. 2 (2012): 426–463.

7. Carmen M. Reinhart and Kenneth S. Rogoff, *This Time Is Different* (Princeton: Princeton University Press, 2009).

8. Thomas J. Holmes, "The Case of the Disappearing Large Employer Manufacturing Plants: Not Much of a Mystery after All" (Minneapolis, MN: Federal Reserve Bank of Minneapolis, 2011), Policy Paper 11-4, 2011, pp. 1–26; Samuel E. Henly and Juan M. Sanchez, "The U. S. Establishment-Size Distribution: Secular Changes and Sectoral Decomposition," *Economic Quarterly* 95, no. 4 (2009): 419–454.

9. Marco Rubio, "Speech at the Kemp Foundation Leadership Award Ceremony," http://www.humanevents.com/2012/12/04/marco-rubio-paul-ryan-speaking-tonight-liveblogging-from-human-events/; John Croman, "Skills Gap Focus of Minnesota High Tech Employees," http://www.kare11.com/news/elections/politics/article/994247/222/Skills-gap-focus-of-Minnesota-high-tech-employers/; Thomas L. Friedman, "A Progressive in the Age of Austerity," *New York Times Sunday Review* (2011), http://www.nytimes.com/2011/10/16/opinion/sunday/friedman-a-progressive-in-the-age-of-austerity.html?_/

10. "Survey: Boiling Point? The Skills Gap in the U.S. Manufacturing" (Deloitte and The Manufacturing Institute, October 17, 2011).

11. Osterman and Weaver, "Skills and Skill Gaps in Manufacturing."

12. Ibid.

13. The survey instrument was designed by PIE researchers Paul Osterman and Andrew Weaver and administered by the University of Massachusetts Center for Survey Research. For details on survey design, administration, and analysis, see the two chapters by Osterman and Weaver in Locke and Wellhausen, *Production in the Innovation Economy*.

14. Steven J. Davis, R. Jason Faberman, and John C. Haltiwanger, "The Establishment-Level Behavior of Vacancies and Hiring," *Quarterly Journal of Economics* Advanced Access publication, January 31, 2013 (accessed March 6, 2013). See also the report on this research, Catherine Rampell, "With Positions to Fill, Employers Wait for Perfection," *New York Times*, http://www.nytimes.com/2013/03/07/business/economy/despite-job-vacancies-employers-shy-away-from-hiring.html?adxnnl=1&ref=catherinerampell.&adxnnlx=1366902030-MX6BAe0cU1OZpIPgXBV7p&_r=1&

15. This finding is consistent with that of other empirical studies of the same question. See Michael Handel, "A New Survey of Workplace Skills, Technology, and Management Practices" (Northeastern University, Working Paper, 2008).

16. These calculations were compiled from Current Population Surveys Outgoing Rotation Group raw data downloaded from http://www.nber.org/data/morg.html/. See Osterman and Weaver, "Skills and Skill Gaps in Manufacturing."

17. These calculations from Current Population Surveys Outgoing Rotation Group raw data, 2009 and 2010 combined, downloaded from http://www.nber.org/data/morg.html/. See ibid.

18. Interviews, January 23 and 24, 2012, and January 2013.

19. Interviews with Dr. Dorey Diab, Provost and Chief Academic Officer, Stark State Community College, January 24, 2012, and with Dr. John O'Donnell, former president of Stark State and currently president of MassBay Community College, November 15, 2012.

20. Interviews with Dr. Ajay Mahajan, Associate Dean for Research and Professor, Mechanical Engineering, University of Akron; Dr. George Haritos, Dean, College of Engineering, University of Akron, Dr. Gary L. Doll, Director, Timken Engineered Surfaces Laboratory, University of Akron; Thomas B. Stimson, Vice President Business Process Advancement, Timken, January 23, 2012.

Chapter 8

1. Stephen Ezell and Robert D. Atkinson, "Fifty Ways to Leave Your Competitiveness Woes Behind: A National Trade Sector Competitiveness Strategy," ITIF, September 20, 2012.

2. Elinor Ostrom's seminal work is *Governing the Commons* (Cambridge: Cambridge University Press, 1990).

3. Nelson D. Schwartz, "Rumors of a Cheap-Energy Jobs Boom Remain Just That," *New York Times*, April 1, 2013, http://www.nytimes.com/2013/04/02/business/economy/rumors-of-a-cheap-energy-jobs-boom-remain-just-that.html?pagewanted=all&_r=0/

4. http://www.bcg.com/media/pressreleasedetails.aspx?id=tcm:12-116389/

5. Antonio Regalado, "Made in America, Again," *MIT Technology Review*, January 11, 2013, http://www.technologyreview.com/news/509326/made-in-america-again/

6. On the challenges of scaling up new energy companies in the United States, see the analysis in Richard K. Lester, "Energy Innovation," in Locke and Wellhausen, eds., *Production in the Innovation,* and in Richard K. Lester and David M. Hart, *Unlocking Energy Innovation: How America Can Build a Low-Cost, Low-Carbon Energy System* (Cambridge: MIT Press, 2011), pp. 99–120.

7. Lin Yang, "MediaTek Chips Change China's Smartphone Market," *New York Times*, January 8, 2013, p. B4.

8. Interview with Professor Andre Sharon, Director, Fraunhofer Center for Manufacturing Innovation, Boston University, December 7, 2012.

9. Mercedes Delgado, Michael E. Porter, and Scott Stern, *Clusters, Convergence, and Economic Performance* (National Bureau of Economic Research, 2012), p. 6.

10. Presentation to PIE Commission by Dan Armbrust, president and CEO, SEMATECH, October 3, 2012.

11. Fears about antitrust continue to dog collaboration among even small and medium-size Main Street manufacturers. The founder of a new Ohio association of precision machining firms told us of warily hiring a lawyer to reassure participants that their collective action would not constitute grounds for an antitrust case.

12. See also the recent report issued by the Council on Competitiveness, American Energy and Manufacturing Competitiveness Partnership, *The Power of Partnerships*, April, 2013.

13. Interview, February 13, 2013.

14. Interview, February 13, 2013. See also "Muskeget Tidal Energy Project," New England Marine Renewable Energy Center, http://www.mrec.umassd.edu/resourcecenter/muskegettidalproject/

15. Peter Kelly-Detwiler, "The Wind Technology Testing Center: Pushing the Envelope on Wind Technology," *Forbes*, January 9, 2013, http://www.forbes.com/sites/peterdetwiler/2013/01/09/the-wind-technology-testing-center-pushing-the-envelope-on-wind-technology/

16. John Winkel, "WTTC opens upsized wind blade test facility," *Composites World.com*, December 1, 2012, http://www.compositesworld.com/articles/wttc-opens-upsized-wind-blade-test-facility/

17. Ibid.

18. Interview with James Bowen, February 13, 2013.

19. Interview, February 1, 2013.

20. For discussions that informed the account that follows, we are grateful to respondents in several PIE company interviews as well as observations by Professor Lisa Camp, associate dean, Strategic Initiatives, Case School of Engineering, Case Western Reserve University, and Professor Gary Fedder, Director of the Institute for Complex Engineered Systems, Carnegie Mellon University. The interpretation (and possible misinterpretation) are PIE's.

21. http://www.whitehouse.gov/the-press-office/2012/08/16/we-can-t-wait-obama-administration-announces-new-public-private-partners/

22. http://www.nytimes.com/2012/12/02/us/how-local-taxpayers-bankroll-corporations.html/

Index